The Gospel
Of
Barnabas

**Notes and Commentary
M. A. Yusseff**

INTRODUCTION:

The Authenticity of
The Gospel Of Barnabas

Deficiency In Early Scholarship

Early in the twentieth century, Lonsdale and Laura Ragg translated the Italian translation of the Gospel of Barnabas into English, and wrote an introduction in which they expressed the mistaken opinion that the Gospel account was not authentic. They had a number of serious handicaps which may account for their mistaken conclusion. The first is described in the preface to their own translation: "The translators have encountered many unforseen difficulties during the four years in which the work has been in their hands; much of the translation has been hewn out on pilgrimage, or in small hotel rooms, and *far from books of reference.*" Another handicap was that they did not have the benefit of the Dead Sea Scrolls with which to make certain comparisons, since the scrolls had not been discovered yet. And then there was what appears to have been their own unscientific bias against the Gospel, because it does not conform to the Graeco-Roman tradition that characterizes the Gentile New Testament.

The authenticity of the Gospel of Barnabas has already been demonstrated in a work entitled: *The Dead Sea Scrolls, The Gospel of Barnabas, and The New Testament.* Additional research under good research conditions, providing access to numerous reference sources, has provided even more evidence substantiating its authenticity too extensive to go into here. Let us consider however, an avoidable mistake made by the Raggs Concerning the "Hundred Year Jubilee," simply because of some of the deficiencies previously mentioned. And because some people still do not know that the Raggs are in error in their opinion on this matter, since this subject is not discussed in the above mentioned work demonstrating the authenticity of the Gospel.

Hundred Year Jubilee

According to the Books of Moses, during the seventh year all land had to be allowed to lie idle and debts were to be written off. This was to be the practice after the Israelites had settled in Canaan.

This law concerning the Jubilee, called for an Israelite to cultivate his land six years, but not the seventh, as it was held to be a sabbath for the Lord God, during which time one was not to sow nor reap for his own benefit, but rather, the whole community, as well as the domestic and wild beasts, were to be allowed to consume a share of the natural growth of the soil. Because the Sabbatical year came every seven years, and seven times seven sabbatical years equals forty-nine years, the fiftieth year is called the Jubilee, or year of the Jubilee, or Jubilee year. During the Jubilee the land regulations of a sabbatical year were in effect, along with the commandment to free all slaves of Israelite ancestry. So that the practice in theory was, to observe the Jubilee every fiftieth year. Now in the eighty-second chapter Jesus mentions observing the Jubilee every hundred years, and because under normal circumstances the Israelites were to observe the Jubilee every fiftieth year, the Raggs jumped to the wrong conclusion. It seems that the only hundredth year Jubilee that they were acquainted with, was one held by Boniface VIII in 1300 A.D., and even though the Church had officially stated, as the Raggs admit, that the hundredth year Jubilee was a custom of immemorial antiquity, the Raggs chose to ignore the Church and implied that the Church was being untruthful. What they failed to research, was that the Church was not talking about something that was characteristic of Christianity or Judaism, but rather it was referring to a dim memory of an ancient historical event that caused the Nazarenes to speak of the Jubilee as occurring every hundred years.

Going back into Israelite history we find that the first sabbatical year was observed twenty-one years after the arrival of the Israelites in Canaan, and that the first Jubilee was observed thirty-three years later, so that it was not observed in the fiftieth year, but the fifty-fourth. After that it was observed every fifty years until the tribes of Gad, Reuben and the half-tribe of Manasseh were exiled in 722 B.C., now according to some sources the prophet Jeremiah brought the tribes back, if so, it appears that the Jubilee was once again observed sometime in the fifth century B.C., until the final exile of the Jews by Nebuchadnezzer (r. 605-562 B.C.). Thus the evidence indicates that the Israelites were not necessarily consistent in observing the Jubilee every fifty years, particularly in adverse circumstances. So that the observance of the Jubilee every hundredth year as a standard practice amongst the Nazarenes prior to the birth of Jesus, because of what they considered adverse conditions is not far fetched, but rather it is quite possible. In fact, it is more than possible. For it is reported in ancient Israelite history that Simeon Macabee was murdered in the month of Shevat, in 135 B.C., and that John Hyrcanus (134-104 B.C.) his son, sought revenge for the murder of his father, and that in so doing he besieged the fortress of Dagon, in which Ptolemy the murderer had taken refuge. The siege dragged on, but as a result of famine due to the fact that it was a sabbatical year, John Hyrcanus was forced to raise the Siege.

"The sabbatical year nearest to that date," says the Encyclopedia Judica, "was in the year 3724 of the creation, i.e., 37 B.C.E., since Josephus tells us that in Herod's conquest of Jerusalem in the summer of that year, the besieged in the city suffered from a food shortage because of the sabbatical year." The same source goes on to state that: "*The 98 years between those two dates are equivalent to 14 shemittah [shemittah=Sabbatical years] without an intervening Jubilee year, and is confirmed from other references.*" And one or two years later the "*Hundredth Year Jubilee*" was evidently held in 36 or 35 B.C., therefore the Church was right and the Raggs were wrong. And Jesus' reference to the hundredth year Jubilee is supported by Israelite history.

He, the Lord God knows all things, and therefore He knew that this would come to light in conjunction with the other evidence concerning the authenticity of the Gospel of Barnabas.

M.A. Yusseff

The Gospel

Of

Barnabas

About Barnabas the Commandment is
If he comes unto you, receive him.''
(Epistle to the Colossians, 4:10)

True Gospel of Jesus, called Christ, a new Prophet sent by God to the world: according to the description of Barnabas his apostle.

Barnabas, apostle of Jesus the Nazarene, called Christ,[1] to all them that dwell upon the earth desireth peace and consolation.

Dearly beloved, the great and wonderful God hath during these past days visited us by his prophet Jesus Christ in great mercy of teaching and miracles, by reason whereof many, being deceived of Satan, under pretence of piety, are preaching most impious doctrine, calling Jesus son of God, Repudiating the circumcision ordained of God for ever, and permitting every unclean meat: among whom also Paul hath been deceived, whereof I speak not without grief: for which cause I am writing that truth which I have seen and heard, in the intercourse that I have had with Jesus, in order that ye may be saved, and not be deceived of Satan and perish in the judgement of God. Therefore beware of every one that preacheth unto you new doctrine contrary to that which I write, that ye may be saved eternally.

The great God be with you and guard you from Satan and from every evil. Amen.

1. In this first chapter is contained the annunciation of the angel Gabriel to the Virgin Mary concerning the birth of Jesus.

In these last years a virgin called Mary, of the lineage of David, of the tribe of Judah, was visited by the angel Gabriel from God. This virgin, living in all holiness without any offence, being blameless and abiding in prayer with fastings, being one day alone, there entered into her chamber the angel Gabriel, and he saluted her, saying: 'God be with thee, O Mary'.

The Annunciation

The virgin was affrighted at the appearance of the angel; but the angel comforted her saying: 'Fear not, Mary, for thou hast found favour with God, who hath chosen thee to be mother of a prophet, whom he will send to the people of Israel in order that they may walk in his laws with truth of heart'. The virgin answered: 'Now how shall

---

[1] *called Christ*. Christ, the translation of Messiah, signifies "the person anointed" (I Sam. 10:1; 16:13). When a prophet did the anointing, it signified "the Lord's anointed" (I Sam. 16:6). Not only kings, but priests were anointed before taking office (I Chr. 16:22; Ps. 105:15). But in no sense does it signify savior in the pagan sense adopted by the Gentile founders of Christianity.

I bring forth sons, seeing I know not a man?' The angel answered: 'O Mary, God who made man without a man is able to generate in thee man without a man, because with him nothing is impossible.' Mary answered: 'I know that God is almighty, therefore his will be done.' The angel answered: 'Now be conceived in thee the prophet, whom thou shalt name Jesus: and thou shalt keep him from wine and from strong drink and from every unclean meat, because the child is an holy one of God.' Mary bowed herself with humility, saying: 'Behold the handmaid of God, be it done according to thy word.' The angel departed, and the virgin glorified God, saying: Know, O my soul, the greatnes of God, and exult, my spirit, in God my Saviour; for he hath regarded the lowliness of his handmaiden, insomuch that I shall be called blessed by all the nations, for he that is mighty hath made me great, and blessed be his holy name. For his mercy extendeth from generation to generation of them that fear him. Mighty hath he made his hand, and he hath scattered the proud in the imagination of his heart. He hath put down the mighty from their seat, and hath exalted the humble. Him who hath been hungry hath he filled with good things, and the rich he hath sent empty away. For he keepeth in memory the promises made to Abraham and to his son for ever'.

2. The warning of the angel Gabriel given to Joseph concerning the conception of the Virgin Mary.

Mary having known the will of God, fearing the people, lest they should take offence at her being great with child, and should stone her as guilty of fornication,[2] chose a companion of her own lineage, a man by name called Joseph, of blameless life: for he as a righteous man[3] feared God and served him with fastings and prayers, living by the works of his hands, for he was a carpenter.

Such a man the virgin knowing, chose him for her companion and revealed to him the divine counsel.

Joseph being a righteous man, when he perceived that Mary was great with child, was minded to put her away because he feared God. Behold, whilst he slept, he was rebuked by the angel of God saying, 'O Joseph, why art thou minded to put away Mary thy wife? Know that whatsoever hath been wrought in her hath all been done by the will of God. The virgin shall bring forth a son, whom thou shall

---

[2] *guilty of fornication.* In accordance with the law (Deut. 22:13-21).

[3] *a righteous man.* What is said here of Joseph, is descriptive of those Essenes spoken of by Philo: Indeed, they are men utterly dedicated to the service of God; they do not offer animal sacrifice, judging it more fitting to render their minds truly holy.'' Which viewpoint corresponds with Jesus' toward sacrifice, chap. 32.

call by the name Jesus; whom thou shalt keep from wine and strong drink and from every unclean meat, because he is an holy one of God from his mother's womb. He is a prophet of God sent unto the people of Israel, in order that he may convert Judah to his heart, and that Israel may walk in the law of the Lord, as it is written in the law of Moses. He shall come with great power, which God shall give him, and shall work great miracles, whereby many shall be saved.'

Joseph, arising from sleep, gave thanks to God, and abode with Mary all his life, serving God with all sincerity.

3. Wonderful birth of Jesus and appearance of angels praising God.

There reigned at that time in Judaea Herod, by decree of Caesar Augustus, and Pilate was governor in the priesthood of Annas and Caiaphas. Wherefore, by decree of Augustus, all the world was enrolled; wherefore each one went to his own country, and they presented themselves by their own tribes to be enrolled. Joseph accordingly departed from Nazareth, a city of Galilee, with Mary his wife, great with child, to go to Bethlehem (for that it was his city, he being of the lineage of David), in order that he might be enrolled according to the decree of Caesar. Joseph having arrived at Bethlehem, for that the city was small, and great the multitude of them that were strangers there, he found no place, wherefore he took lodging outside the city in a lodging made for a shepherds' shelter. While Joseph abode there the days were fulfilled[4] for Mary to bring forth. The virgin was surrounded by a light exceeding bright, and brought forth her son without pain, whom she took in her arms, and wrapping him in swaddling-clothes, laid him in the manger, because there was no room in the inn. There came with gladness a great multitude of angels to the inn, blessing God and announcing peace

---

[4] *days were fulfilled.* Herod the Great, reigned in Judea from 37 to 4 B.C., three years prior to the end of his reign, Jesus was born. The Romans took a census of the Empire every 14 yrs. for revenue and military purposes, so that a census was taken in 7 B.C. during Herod's reign. A Roman inscription discovered at Antioch, indicates that Quirinus (Luke 2:2) was involved in taking the census in 7 B.C., just as he was in 6-7 A.D. The legate of Syria was responsible for supervising the governing of Judea, and although Pilate was not officially appointed governor of Judea until 25-26 A.D., he evidently functioned as an agent for the legate as early as 7 B.C. Annas was officially appointed high priest in 7 A.D., while Caiphas became high priest about 18 A.D., but the evidence here and in other sources indicate that these men were leaders before their official appointments. It also indicates that Jesus was born in 7 B.C.

to them that fear God. Mary and Joseph praised the Lord for the birth of Jesus, and with greatest joy nurtured him.

4. Angels announce to the shepherds the birth of Jesus, and they, after having found him, announce him.

At that time the shepherds were watching over their flock,[5] as is their custom. And, behold, they were surrounded by an exceeding bright light, out of which appeared to them an angel, who blessed God. The shepherds were filled with fear by reason of the sudden light and the appearance of the angel: 'Behold, I announce to you a great joy, for there is born in the city of David a child who is a prophet of the Lord; who bringeth great salvation to the house of Israel. The child ye shall find in the manger, with his mother, who blesseth God.' And when he had said this there came a great multitude of angels blessing God, announcing peace to them that have good will. When the angels were departed, the shepherds spake among themselves, saying: 'Let us go even unto Bethlehem, and see the word which God by his angel hath announced to us.' There came many shepherds to Bethlehem seeking the new-born babe, and they found outside the city the child that was born, according to the word of the angel, lying in the manger. They therefore made obeisance to him, and gave to the mother that which they had, announcing to her what they had heard and seen. Mary therefore kept all these things in her heart, and Joseph (likewise), giving thanks to God. The shepherds returned to their flocks, announcing to everyone how great a thing they had seen. And so the whole hill- country of Judaea was filled with fear, and every man laid up this word in his heart, saying: 'What, think we, shall this child be?'

5. Circumcision of Jesus.

When the eight days were fulfilled according to the law of the Lord, as it is written in the book of Moses, they took the child and carried him to the temple to circumcise him. And so they circumcised the child, and gave him the name Jesus, as the angel of the Lord had said before he was conceived in the womb. Mary and Joseph perceived

---

[5] *watching over their flock.* According to the Talmud, the flocks were put out to graze in March and brought in again the beginning of November, so that this event must have occurred at some point during this eight month period. Scientific investigation of weather in this area of the world, which has not changed significantly in 2000 years has demonstrated the wisdom of this practice. The December 25th, birth date derived from paganism, is fictional, and was not used until the fourth century onward.

that the child must needs be for the salvation and ruin of many. Wherefore they feared God, and kept the child with fear of God.

6. Three magi are led by a star in the east to Judaea, and, finding Jesus, make obeisance to him and gifts.

In the reign of Herod, king of Judaea, when Jesus was born, three magi[6] in the parts of the east were observing the stars of heaven. Whereupon appeared to them a star of great brightness,[7] wherefore having concluded among themselves, they came to Judaea, guided by the star, which went before them, and having arrived at Jerusalem they asked where was born the King of the Jews. And when Herod heard this he was affrighted, and all the city was troubled. Herod therefore called together the priests and the scribes, saying: 'Where should Christ be born?' They answered that he should be born in Bethlehem; for thus it is written by the prophet: 'And thou, Bethlehem, art not little among the princes of Judah: for out of thee shall come forth a leader, who shall lead my people Israel.'

Herod accordingly called together the magi and asked them concerning their coming: who answered that they had seen a star in the east, which had guided them thither, wherefore they wished with gifts to worship this new King manifested by his star.

Then said Herod: 'Go to Bethlehem and search out with all diligence concerning the child; and when ye have found him, come and tell it to me, because I also would fain come and worship him.' And this he spake deceitfully.

7. The visitation of Jesus by magi, and their return to their own country, with the warning of Jesus given to them in a dream.

The magi therefore departed out of Jerusalem, and lo, the star which appeared to them in the east went before them. Seeing the star[8] the magi were filled with gladness. And so having come to

---

[6] *magi*. This name originally applied to the priest caste among the Medes, it was later applied to other eastern men held to be wise. At this time astronomy and astrology were intertwined, and the chief interest of the magi.

[7] *a star of great brightness*. Residing east of Judea, to the magi the star would appear in the west. Evidence from the ancient observatory at Sippar in Babylonia, shows that on May 29, 7 B.C. in the morning sky, for at least two hours, the conjunction of Saturn and Jupiter in the constellation of Pisces occurred giving the appearance of a large brilliant star. Sippar was advanced enough to calculate the second conjunction on October 3, and the last one on December 4. The grazing practices of the shepherds in conjunction with the evidence from Sippar, indicates that Jesus was born shortly before October 3rd.

[8] *Seeing the star.* Babylonian astrologers considered Saturn to be the special star of Syria and Palestine (The Bible As History, p. 391). According to Werner Keller,

Bethlehem, outside the city, they saw the star standing still above the inn where Jesus was born. The magi therefore went thither, and entering the dwelling found the child with his mother, and bending down they did obeisance to him. And the magi presented unto him spices, with silver and gold, recounting to the virgin all that they had seen.

Whereupon, while sleeping, they were warned by the child not to go to Herod; so departing by another way they returned to their own home, announcing all that they had seen in Judaea.

8. Jesus is carried in flight to Egypt, and Herod massacres the innocent children.

Herod seeing that the magi did not return, believed himself mocked of them; whereupon he determined to put to death the child that was born.[9] But behold while Joseph was sleeping there appeared to him the angel of the Lord, saying: 'Arise up quickly, and take the child with his mother and go into Egypt, for Herod willeth to slay him.' Joseph arose with great fear, and took Mary with the child, and they went into Egypt, and there they abode until the death of Herod; who, believing himself derided of the magi, sent his soldiers to slay all the new-born children in Bethlehem. The soldiers therefore came and slew all the children that were there, as Herod had commanded them. Whereby were fulfilled the words of the prophet, saying: 'Lamentation and great weeping are there in Ramah; Rachel lamenteth for her sons, but consolation is not given her because they are not.'

9. Jesus, having returned to Judaea, holds a wondrous disputation with the doctors, having come to the age of twelve years.

When Herod was dead, behold the angel of the Lord appeared in a dream to Joseph, saying: 'Return into Judaea, for they are dead that willed the death of the child.' Joseph therefore took the child with Mary (he having come to the age of seven years), and came to

---

a rabbinic writer named Abarbanel (1437-1508), reported that Jewish astrologers had ascribed to the conjunction of Saturn and Jupiter in the constellation of Pisces, a sign of the advent of the Israelite Messiah (Ibid, 388).

[9] *he determined to put to death the child.* Herod's bloody career began with the extermination of all probable and possible rivals for the throne (Atlas of the Bible, p. 113. L.H. Grollenberg). The end of his reign involved the strangulation of two of his sons in 7 B.C., and another after that, along with many other poor souls. So that the charge against him, of having massacred the children in order to slay Jesus, is in character with this King.

Judaea; whence, hearing that Archelaus, son of Herod, was reigning in Judaea, he went into Galilee, fearing to remain in Judaea; and they went to dwell at Nazareth.

The child grew in grace and wisdom before God and before men.

Jesus, having come to the age of twelve years, went up with Mary and Joseph to Jerusalem to worship there according to the law of the Lord written in the book of Moses.[10] When their prayers were ended they departed, having lost Jesus, because they thought that he was returned home with their kinsfolk. Mary therefore returned with Joseph to Jerusalem, seeking Jesus among kinsfolk and neighbors. The third day they found the child in the temple, in the midst of the doctors, disputing with them[11] concerning the law. And every one was amazed at his questions and answers, saying: 'How can there be such doctrine in him, seeing he is so small and hath not learned to read?'

Mary reproved him, saying: 'Son, what hast thou done to us? Behold I and thy father have sought thee for three days sorrowing.' Jesus answered: 'Know ye not that the service of God ought to come before father and mother?' Jesus then went down with his mother and Joseph to Nazareth, and was subject to them with humility and reverence.

10. Jesus, at the age of thirty years, on Mount Olives, miraculously receiveth the gospel from the angel Gabriel.

Jesus having come to the age of thirty years, as he himself said unto me, went up to Mount Olives with his mother to gather olives. Then at midday as he was praying, when he came to these words: 'Lord, with mercy...,' he was surrounded by an exceeding bright light and by an infinite multitude of angels, who were saying: 'Blessed be God.' The angel Gabriel presented to him as it were a shining mirror, a book, which descended into the heart of

---

[10]*in the book of Moses.* Their journey to Jerusalem was in connection with Exodus 23:15.

[11]*disputing with them.* A child's education began at home, at the age of 5 or 6, he entered elementary school where he was instructed in the Law. From about 75 B.C. compulsory education at an elementary school had been in effect that was attached to a synagogue. Every sizeable village had one, so that at least a portion of the silent years was most likely typical of a young student, and thought to be not worth mentioning. At twelve young men were more directly responsible for their obedience to the Law; on their 13th birthday they put on the Phylacteries for the first time, which were worn at the recital of his daily prayers. Jesus' contention with the rabbis while twelve years old and their amazement with his understanding shows that he had far exceeded what was expected of one his age.

Jesus[12] in which he had knowledge of what God hath done and what hath said and what God willeth insomuch that everything was laid bare and open to him; as he said unto me: 'Believe, Barnabas, that I know every prophet with every prophecy, insomuch that whatever I say the whole hath come forth from that book.

Jesus, having received this vision, and knowing that he was a prophet sent to the house of Israel, revealed all to Mary his mother, telling her that he needs must suffer great persecution for the honour of God, and that he could not any longer abide with her to serve her. Whereupon, having heard this, Mary answered: 'Son, ere thou wast born all was announced to me; wherefore blessed be the holy name of God.' Jesus departed therefore that day from his mother to attend to his prophetic office.

11. Jesus miraculously healeth a leper, and goeth into Jerusalem.

Jesus descending from the mountain to come into Jerusalem, met a leper, who by divine inspiration knew Jesus to be a prophet. Therefore, with tears he prayed him, saying: 'Jesus, thou son of David, have mercy on me.' Jesus answered: 'What wilt thou, brother, that I should do unto thee?'

The leper answered: 'Lord, give me health.'

Jesus reproved him, saying: 'Thou art foolish; pray to God who created thee, and he will give thee health; for I am a man, as thou art.' The leper answered: 'I know that thou, Lord, art a man, but an holy one of the Lord. Wherefore pray thou to God and he will give me health.' Then Jesus, sighing, said: 'Lord God Almighty, for the love of thy holy prophets give health to this sick man.' Then, having said this, he said, touching the sick man with his hands in the name of God: 'O brother, receive thy health!' And when he had said this the leprosy was cleansed, insomuch that the flesh of the leper was left unto him like that of a child. Seeing which namely, that he was healed, the leper with a loud voice cried out: 'Come hither, Israel, to

---

[12]*which descended into the heart of Jesus.* The description here, of God's commissioning Jesus to prophethood, is definitely Essene. The following is descriptive of the rite of initiation into the Essene movement: "Then the priests are to invoke a blessing on all that have cast their lot with God, that walk blamelessly in all their ways; and they are to say: MAY HE BLESS THEE with all good and KEEP THEE from all evil, and *ILLUMINE thy heart with insight into the things of life, and GRACE THEE with knowledge of things eternal,* and LIFT UP HIS gracious COUNTENANCE TOWARDS THEE to grant thee peace everlasting" (The Dead Sea Scripture, p. 46.)

receive the prophet whom God sendeth unto thee.' Jesus prayed him, saying: 'Brother, hold thy peace and say nothing,' but the more he prayed him the more he cried out, saying: 'Behold the prophet! behold the holy one of God!' At which words many that were going out of Jerusalem ran back, and entered with Jesus into Jerusalem, recounting that which God through Jesus had done unto the leper.

12. First sermon of Jesus delivered to the people: wonderful in doctrine concerning the name of God.

The whole city of Jerusalem was moved by these words, wherefore they all ran together to the temple to see Jesus, who had entered therein to pray, so that they could scarce be contained there. Therefore the priests besought Jesus, saying: 'This people desireth to see thee and hear thee; therefore ascend to the pinnacle, and if God give thee a word speak it in the name of the Lord.'

Then ascended Jesus to the place whence the scribes were wont to speak. And having beckoned with the hand for silence, he opened his mouth, saying: 'Blessed be the holy name of God, who of his goodness and mercy willed to create his creatures that they might glorify him. Blessed be the holy name of God, who created the splendour[13] of all the saints and prophets before all things[14] to send him for the salvation of the world, as he spake by his servant David, saying: "Before Lucifer in the brightness of the saints I created thee." Blessed be the holy name of God, who created the angels that they might serve him. And blessed be God, who punished and reprobated Satan and his followers, who would not reverence him whom God willeth to be reverenced. Blessed be the holy name of God, who created man out of the clay of the earth, and set him over his works. Blessed be the holy name of God, who drove man out of paradise for having transgressed his holy precept. Blessed be the holy name of God, who with mercy looked upon the tears of Adam and Eve, first parents of the human race. Blessed be the holy name

[13] *the splendor*. The significance here, appears to be "the great light" of all the saints and prophets, signifying the propagator of the accumulation of the essential truths, and therefore the greater truth preached by all the prophets preceding the splendor himself.

[14]*before all things*. Here we have clear evidence that Jesus subscribed to that school of Israelite thought - in this matter - that held the belief that the Messiah was created by God before Creation, and appointed by God as such at the time of Creation. In this, he makes a further distinction between himself as the Israelite Messiah, and the last Messiah as the universal Messiah.

of God, who justly punished Cain the fratricide, sent the deluge upon the earth, burned up three wicked cities, scourged Egypt, overwhelmed Pharaoh in the Red Sea, scattered the enemies of his people, chastised the unbelievers, and punished the impenitent. Blessed be the holy name of God, who with mercy looked upon his creatures, and therefore sent them his holy prophets, that they might walk in truth and righteousness before him: who delivered his servants from every evil, and gave them this land, as he promised to our father Abraham and to his son for ever. Then by his servant Moses he gave us his holy law, that Satan should not deceive us; and he exalted us above all other peoples.

'But, brethren, what do we, to-day, that we be not punished for our sins?'

And then Jesus with greatest vehemence rebuked the people for that they had forgotten the word of God, and gave themselves only to vanity: he rebuked the priests for their negligence in God's service and for their worldly greed; he rebuked the scribes because they preached vain doctrine, and forsook the law of God; he rebuked the doctors because they made the law of God of none effect through their traditions. And in such wise did Jesus speak to the people, that all wept, from the least to the greatest, crying mercy, and beseeching Jesus that he would pray for them; save only their priests and leaders, who on that day conceived hatred against Jesus for having thus spoken against the priests, scribes, and doctors. And they meditated upon his death, but for fear of the people, who had received him as a prophet of God, they spake no word.

Jesus raised his hands to the Lord God and prayed, and the people weeping said: 'So be it, O Lord, so be it.' The prayer being ended Jesus descended from the temple; and that day he departed from Jerusalem, with many that followed him.

And the priests spoke evil of Jesus among themselves.

13. The remarkable fear of Jesus and his prayer, and the wonderful comfort of the angel Gabriel.

Some days having passed, Jesus having in spirit perceived the desire of the priests, ascended the Mount of Olives to pray. And having passed the whole night in prayer, in the morning Jesus praying said: 'O Lord, I know that the scribes hate me, and the priests are minded to kill me, thy servant; therefore, Lord God almighty and merciful, in mercy hear the prayers of thy servant, and save me from their snares, for thou art my salvation. Thou knowest, Lord, that I thy servant seek thee alone, O Lord, and speak thy word; for thy word is truth, which endureth for ever.'

When Jesus had spoken these words, behold there came to him the angel Gabriel, saying: 'Fear not, O Jesus, for a thousand thousand who dwell above the heaven guard thy garments, and thou shalt not die till everything be fulfilled, and the world shall be near its end.[15]

Jesus fell with his face to the ground, saying: 'O great Lord God, how great is thy mercy upon me, and what shall I give thee, Lord, for all that thou hast granted me?'

The angel Gabriel answered: 'Arise, Jesus, and remember Abraham, who being willing to make sacrifice to God of his only-begotten son[16] Ishmael, to fulfill the word of God, and the knife not being able to cut his son, at my word offered in sacrifice a sheep. Even so therefore shalt thou do, O Jesus, servant of God.

Jesus answered: 'Willingly, but where shall I find the lamb, seeing I have no money, and it is not lawful to steal it?'

Thereupon the angel Gabriel showed unto him a sheep, which Jesus offered in sacrifice, praising and blessing God, who is glorious for ever.

---

[15] *near its end.* The meaning is clear, Jesus did not die on the cross. Those who sought to slay this holy prophet were made to believe that he had been slain. Thus evil was not permitted to triumph over good. And the God of Abraham being the true God, accepts no bloody sacrifices in exchange for man's salvation (I Sam. 15:19-22; Ps. 51:16-17; Isa. 1:10-17; Prov. 21:3).

[16]*only-begotten son.* The identification of Ishmael as Abraham's only begotten son before the birth of Isaac is supported by Biblical evidence. Not only does the Bible openly say that Ishmael was born before Isaac, but it also says that his mother, Hagar, was the full fledged wife of Abraham, and not his concubine. For as pointed out by the Soncino Chumash, a book of the Jews, in its commentary to the book of Genesis, according to Hebrew law when a woman had been childless for ten years, *her husband had to marry another.* In this case it was Hagar. This is why we are told that she was *to be his wife.* (Gen. 16:1-3.) The Soncino Chumash emphatically states in accordance with the Bible, that Hagar was "*to be his wife. Not his concubine.*" (p. 76.) It is also explained in both Smith's and Peloubet's Bible Dictionaries, that the names of concubines and their children as supplementary family members appear in the patriarchal genealogies, (Gen. 22:24; I Chron. 1:32), and that their position and provision would depend on the father's will. (Gen. 25:6). If one will take the time to read I Chron. 1:1-34; it will be seen that the names of wives do not appear in the genealogies, because they are part of the family rather than supplementary. Thus the names of Abraham's wives, Sarah and Hagar, do not appear, but rather the names of their sons because they were the inheritors of their father's legacy. Keturah, on the other hand, having been his concubine appears in the list along with the names of her children, as supplementary family members (I Chron. 1:32). And indeed she is referred to as a concubine (I Chron. 1:32; Gen. 25: 6) and never as his wife since she did not enjoy the full distinction of that position as Sarah and Hagar.

14. After the fast of forty days, Jesus chooseth twelve apostles.

Jesus descended from the mount, and passed alone by night to the farther side of Jordan, and fasted forty days and forty nights, not eating anything day nor night, making continual supplication to the Lord for the salvation of his people to whom God had sent him. And when the forty days were passed he was an hungered. Then appeared Satan unto him, and tempted him in many words, but Jesus drove him away by the power of words of God. Satan having departed the angels came and ministered unto Jesus that whereof he had need.

Jesus, having returned to the region of Jerusalem, was found again of the people with exceeding great joy, and they prayed him that he would abide with them; for his words were not as those of the scribes, but were with power, for they touched the heart.

Jesus, seeing that great was the multitude of them that returned to their heart for to walk in the law of God, went up into the mountain, and abode all night in prayer, and when day was come he descended from the mountain, and chose twelve, whom he called apostles, among whom is Judas, who was slain upon the cross. Their names are:[17] Andrew and Peter his brother, fisherman; Barnabas, who wrote this, with Matthew the publican, who sat at the receipt of custom; John and James, sons of Zebedee; Thaddaeus and Judas; Bartholomew and Philip; James, and Judas Iscariot the traitor. To these he always revealed the divine secrets; but the Iscariot Judas he made his dispenser of that which was given in alms, but he stole the tenth part of everything.

15. Miracle wrought by Jesus at the marriage, turning the water into wine.

When the feast of tabernacles was nigh, a certain rich man invited Jesus with his disciples and his mother to a marriage.[18] Jesus

Therefore, when reference is made to Abraham's "only son" in Genesis 22:2, the reference is to Ishmael, who was the only son until his brother Isaac was born. When he was born, Ishmael was no longer the only son, for now there were two sons. Therefore, what has happened, is that the impious amongst Isaac's offspring have removed their uncle Ishmael's name from the twenty-second chapter of Genesis, and replaced it with their father's name, Isaac.

[17] *Their names are.* Because the authenticity of the Gospel of Barnabas has been demonstrated in: *The Dead Sea Scrolls, The Gospel of Barnabas, and The New Testament,* and further demonstrated in this work with additional data, we have here the correct list of the apostles, whereas the N.T. lists are contradictory.

[18] *to a marriage.* According to John 2:1, this event took place at Cana, however the account here does not mention Cana, and in light of the previous chapter, it may well have occurred in Jerusalem.

therefore went, and as they were feasting the wine ran short. His mother accosted Jesus, saying: 'They have no wine.' Jesus answered; 'What is that to me, mother mine?' His mother commanded the servants that whatever Jesus should command them they should obey. There were there six vessels for water according to the custom of Israel to purify themselves for prayer. Jesus said; 'Fill these vessels with water.' The servants did so. Jesus said unto them: 'In the name of God, give to drink unto them that are feasting.' The servants thereupon bare unto the master of the ceremonies, who rebuked the attendants saying: 'O worthless servants, why have ye kept the better wine till now?' For he knew nothing of all that Jesus had done.

The servants answered: 'O sir, there is here a holy man of God, for he hath made of water, wine.' The master of the ceremonies thought that the servants were drunken; but they that were sitting near to Jesus, having seen the whole matter, rose from the table and paid him reverence, saying: 'Verily thou art an holy one of God,[19] a true prophet sent to us from God!'

Then his disciples believed on him, and many returned to their heart, saying: 'Praised be God, who hath mercy upon Israel, and visited the house of Judah with love, and blessed be his holy name.

16. Wonderful teaching given by Jesus to his apostles concerning conversion from the evil life.

One day Jesus called together his disciples and went up on to the mountain, and when he had sat down there his disciples came near unto him; and he opened his mouth and taught them, saying; 'Great are the benefits which God hath bestowed on us, wherefore it is necessary that we should serve him with truth of heart. And forasmuch as new wine is put into new vessels, even so ought ye to become new men, if ye will contain the new doctrine that shall come out of my mouth. Verily I say unto you, that even as a man cannot see with his eyes the heaven and the earth at one and the same time, so it is impossible to love God and the world.[20]

---

[19] *an holy one of God.* This is one of the titles by which the Essenes identified themselves, and were evidently so identified by others. (See the work mentioned in the previous note.)

[20] *it is impossible to love God and the world.* "For instance, a man has two eyes, but he cannot look at the heavens and the earth at one and the same time, so it is not possible to combine the love of God with the love of the world at one and the same time" (Unknown).

'No man can in any wise serve two masters[21] that are at enmity one with the other; for if the one shall love you, the other will hate you. Even so I tell you in truth that ye cannot serve God and the world, for the world lieth in falsehood, covetousness, and malignity. Ye cannot therefore find rest in the world, but rather persecution and loss. Wherefore serve God and despise the world, for from me ye shall find rest for your souls, Hear my words, for I speak unto you in truth.

'Verily, blessed are they that mourn this earthly life, for they shall be comforted.

'Blessed are the poor who truly hate the delights of the world, for they shall abound in the delights of the kingdom of God.

'Verily, blessed are they that eat at the table of God, for the angles shall minister unto them.

'Ye are journeying as pilgrims. Doth the pilgrim encumber himself with palaces and fields and other earthly matters upon the way? Assuredly not; but he beareth things light and prized for their usefulness and convenience upon the road. This now should be an example unto you; and if ye desire another ensample I will give it you, in order that ye may do all that I tell you.

'Weigh not down your hearts with earthly desires, saying: "Who shall clothe us?" or "Who shall give us to eat?" But behold the flowers and the trees, with the birds, which God our Lord clotheth and nourisheth with greater glory than all the glory of Solomon. And he is able to nourish you, even God who created you and called you to his service; who for forty years caused the manna to fall from heaven for his people Israel in the wilderness, and did not suffer their clothing to wax old or perish, they being six hundred and forty thousand men, besides women and children. Verily I say unto you, that heaven and earth shall fail, yet shall not fail his mercy unto them that fear him. But the rich of the world in their prosperity are hungry and perish. There was a rich man whose incomings increased, and he said, "What shall I do, O my soul? I will pull down my barns because they are small, and I will build new and greater ones; therefore thou shalt triumph my soul!" Oh, wretched man! for that night he died. He ought to have been mindful of the poor, and to have made himself friends with the alms of unrighteous riches of this world: for they bring treasures in the kingdom of heaven.

'Tell me, I pray you, if ye should give your money into the bank to a publican, and he should give unto you tenfold and twentyfold,

---

21 *No man can in any wise serve two masters.* "It is not possible that a [servant] can serve two masters who are enemies one to another, therefore it is not possible for a servant [of God] to serve the world and God" (Unknown).

would ye not give to such a man everything that ye had? But I say unto you, verily, that whatsoever ye shall forgive and shall forsake for love of God, ye receive it back an hundredfold, and life everlasting. See then how much ye ought to be content to serve God.

17. In this chapter is clearly perceived the unbelief of Christians, and the true faith of Mumin.

When Jesus had said this, Philip answered: 'We are content to serve God, but we desire, however, to know God. For Isaiah the prophet said: "Verily thou art a hidden God," and God said to Moses his servant: "I am that which I am."[22]

Jesus answered: 'Philip, God is a good without which there is naught good: God is a being without which there is naught that is; God is a life without which there is naught that liveth; so great that he filleth all and is everywhere. He alone hath no equal. He hath had no beginning, nor will he ever have an end, but to everything hath he given a beginning and to everything shall he give an end. He hath no father nor mother;[23] he hath no sons, nor brethren, nor companions. And because God hath no body, therefore he eateth not, sleepeth not, dieth not, walketh not, moveth not, but abideth eternally without human similitude, for that he is incorporeal, uncompounded, immaterial, of the most simple substance. He is so good that he loveth goodness only; he is so just that when he punisheth or pardoneth it cannot be gainsaid. In short, I say unto thee, Philip, that here on earth thou canst not see him nor know him perfectly; but in his kingdom thou shalt see him for ever: wherein consisteth all our happiness and glory.'

Philip answered: 'Master, what sayest thou? It is surely written in Isaiah that God is our father; how, then, hath he no sons?'

Jesus answered: 'There are written in the prophets many parables, wherefore thou oughtest not to attend to the letter, but to the sense. For all the prophets, that are one hundred and forty-four thousand, whom God hath sent into the world, have spoken darkly.

---

[22] *"I am that which I am."* In Exodus 3:14, Yahweh asher yihweh (also yihyeh), I am that which I am, signifies: "He causes to be what comes into existence," in other words, God is saying, I am the Creator, the false gods having created nothing.

[23] *He hath no father nor mother.* Modern research by Professor Albright further demonstrates the authenticity of this Gospel, for he points out, another characteristic which distinguishes the God worshipped by the children of Abraham [both Ishmaelite and Israelite] is that He stands alone without any family connections, for he has no sons, daughters, or wives. Indeed, those who attribute such things to the God of Abraham are in error.

But after me shall come the Splendor[24] of all the prophets and holy ones, and shall shed light upon the darkness of all that the prophets have said, because he is the messenger of God.' And having said this, Jesus sighed and said: 'Have mercy on Israel, O Lord God and look with pity upon Abraham and upon his seed, in order that they may serve thee with truth of heart.

His disciples answered: 'So be it, O Lord our God!''

Jesus said: 'Verily I say unto you, the scribes and doctors have made void the law of God with their false prophecies, contrary to the prophecies of the true prophets of God: Wherefore God is wroth with the house of Israel and with this faithless generation.' His disciples wept at these words, and said: 'Have mercy, O God, have mercy upon the temple and upon the holy city, and give it not into contempt of the nations that they despise not thy holy covenant.' Jesus answered: 'So be it, Lord God of our fathers.'

18. Here is shown forth the persecution of the servants of God by the world, and God's protection saving them.

Having said this, Jesus said: 'Ye have not chosen me, but I have chosen you, that ye may be my disciples. If then the world shall hate you, ye shall be truly my disciples; for the world hath been ever an enemy of servants of God. Remember the holy prophets that have been slain by the world, even as in the time of Elijah ten thousand prophets were slain by Jezebel, insomuch that scarcely did poor Elijah escape, and seven thousand sons of prophets who were hidden by the captain of Ahab's host. Oh, unrighteous world, that knowest not God! Fear not therefore ye, for the hairs of your head are numbered so that they shall not perish. Behold the sparrows and other birds, whereof falleth not one feather without the will of God. Shall God, then, have more care of the birds than of man, for whose sake he hath created everything. Is there any man, perchance, who careth more for his shoes than for his own son? Assuredly not. Now how much less ought ye to think that God would abandon you, while taking care of the birds! And why speak I of the birds? A leaf of a tree falleth not without the will of God.

'Believe me, because I tell you the truth, that the world will greatly fear you if ye shall observe my words. For if it feared not to have its wickedness revealed it would not hate you, but it feareth to be revealed, therefore it will hate you and persecute you. If ye shall

---

[24] *But after me shall come the Splendor.* The term Splendor, corresponds to the term Illustrious, as a reference for the universal Messiah. The prophet who was yet to come.

see your words scorned by the world lay it not to heart, but consider how that God is greater than you: who is in such wise scorned by the world that his wisdom is counted madness. If God endureth the world with patience, wherefore will ye lay it to heart, O dust and clay of the earth? In your patience ye shall possess your soul. Therefore if one shall give you a blow on one side of the face, offer him the other that he may smite it. Render not evil for evil, for so do all the worst animals; but render good for evil, and pray God for them that hate you.[25] Fire is not extinguished with fire, but rather with water: even so I say unto you that ye shall not overcome evil with evil, but rather with good. Behold God, who causeth the sun to come upon the good and evil, and likewise the rain. So ought ye to do good to all; for it is written in the law: "Be ye holy, for I your God am holy; be ye pure, for I am pure: and be ye perfect, for I am perfect." Verily I say unto you that the servant studieth to please his master, and so he putteth not on any garment that is displeasing to his master. Your garments are your will and your love. Beware, then, not to will or to love a thing that is displeasing to God, our Lord. Be ye sure that God hateth the pomps and lusts of the world, and therefore hate ye the world.'

19. Jesus foretelleth his betrayal, and, descending from the mountain, healeth ten lepers.

When Jesus had said this, Peter answered: 'O teacher, behold we have left all to follow thee, what shall become of us?'

Jesus answered: 'Verily ye in the day of judgment shall sit beside me, giving testimony against the twelve tribes of Israel.'

And having said this Jesus sighed, saying: 'O Lord, what thing is this? for I have chosen twelve, and one of them is a devil.'

The disciples were sore grieved at this word; whereupon he who writeth secretly questioned Jesus with tears, saying: 'O master, will Satan deceive me, and shall I then become reprobate?'

Jesus answered: 'Be not sore grieved, Barnabas; for those whom God hath chosen before the creation of the world shall not perish. Rejoice, for thy name is written in the book of life.[26]

---

[25] *pray God for them that hate you.* Jesus was specifically sent to the Israelites, for they had gone astray (chap. 21), therefore what he says here of social interaction amongst them demonstrates the reaction he expected, as well as the sad state within the Israelite nation that they would act in such a way.

[26] *thy name is written in the book of life.* The significance here, is that all men are not chosen in this manner, only the prophets and sages of God, for such men trust and dearly love God, and choose to serve Him more so than the average person. Their responsibilities are great and often dangerous because of the opposition, but their inner strength and faith is such that it enables them to endure. Though they show

Jesus comforted his disciples, saying: "Fear not, for he who shall hate me is not grieved at my saying, because in him is not the divine feeling."

At his words the chosen were comforted. Jesus made his prayers, and his disciples said: 'Amen, so be it, Lord God almighty and merciful.'

Having finished his devotions, Jesus came down from the mountain with his disciples and met ten lepers, who from afar off cried out: 'Jesus, son of David, have mercy on us!"

Jesus called them near to him, and said unto them: 'What will ye of me, O brethren?"

They all cried out: 'Give us health!'

Jesus answered: 'Ah, wretched that ye are, have ye so lost your reason for that ye say: "Give us health!" See ye not me to be a man like yourselves. Call unto our God that hath created you and he that is almighty and merciful will heal you.

With tears the lepers answered: 'We know that thou art man like us, but yet an holy one of God[27] and a prophet of the Lord: wherefore pray thou to God, and he will heal us.

Thereupon the disciples prayed Jesus, saying: 'Lord, have mercy upon them.' Then groaned Jesus and prayed to God, saying: 'Lord God almighty and merciful, have mercy and hearken to the words of thy servant: and for love of Abraham our father and for thy holy covenant have mercy on the request of these men, and grant them health.' Whereupon Jesus, having said this, turned himself to the lepers and said: 'Go and show yourselves to the priests according to the law of God.'

The lepers departed, and on the way were cleansed. Whereupon one of them, seeing that he was healed, returned to find Jesus, and he was an Ishmaelite. And having found Jesus he bowed himself, doing reverence unto him, and saying: 'Verily thou art an holy one of God,' and with thanks he prayed him that he would receive him for servant. Jesus answered: 'Ten have been cleansed; where are the nine?' And he said to him that was cleansed: 'I am not come to be served, but to serve; wherefore go to thine home, and recount how much God hath done in thee, in order that they may know that the promises made to Abraham and his son, with the kingdom of God, are drawing nigh.' The cleansed leper departed, and having arrived

concern for their welfare in the next life, their ultimate blessing is assured by virtue of their obedience to God.

[27] *an holy one of God.* Here too, Jesus is identified by this Essene title.

in his own neighborhood recounted how much God through Jesus had wrought in him.

20. Miracle on the sea wrought by Jesus, and Jesus declares where the prophet is received.

Jesus went to the sea of Galilee, and having embarked in a ship sailed to his city[28] of Nazareth; whereupon there was a great tempest in the sea, insomuch that the ship was nigh unto sinking. And Jesus was sleeping upon the prow of the ship. Then drew near to him his disciples, and awoke him, saying: 'O master, save thyself, for we perish!' They were encompassed with very great fear, by reason of the great wind that was contrary and the roaring of the sea. Jesus arose, and raising his eyes to heaven, said: 'O Elohim Sabaoth, have mercy upon thy servants.' Then, when Jesus had said this, suddenly the wind ceased, and the sea became calm. Wherefore the seamen feared, saying: 'And who is this, that the sea and the wind obey him?'

Having arrived at the city of Nazareth the seamen spread through the city all that Jesus had wrought, whereupon the house where Jesus was, was surrounded by as many as dwelt in the city. And the scribes and doctors having presented themselves unto him, said: 'We have heard how much thou hast wrought in the sea and Judea: give us therefore some sign here in thine own country.'

Jesus answered: 'This faithless generation seek a sign, but it shall not be given them, because no prophet is received in his own country. In the time of Elijah there were many widows in Judea but he was not sent to be nourished save unto a widow of Sidon. Many were the lepers in the time of Elisha in Judea, nevertheless only Naaman the Syrian was cleansed.'

Then were the citizens enraged and seized him and carried him on to the top of a precipice to cast him down. But Jesus walking through the midst of them, departed from them.

---

[28] *sailed to his city.* The name by which the true followers of Jesus were known is Nazoreans (Nazarenes), in contrast to the followers of Paul, who are known as Christians, and Jesus himself was known as the Nazorean (Nazarene). It is now known that the term is sectarian, of which the Hebrew is Notsrim, and is not directly connected with the city of Nazareth. In the play on words current during this time, these exoteric associations were made; but esoterically the name relates to a community whose members regarded themselves as the true 'maintainers' or 'preservers' of the faith in its pristine form. Thus the Nazareth spoken of here is not the city that still bears that name, but rather a community within another community near a body of navigable water. Or a temporary or permanent Nazorean settlement near such a body of water.

21. Jesus healeth a demoniac, and the swine are cast into the sea. Afterwards he healeth the daughter of the Canaanites.

Jesus went up to Capernaum, and as he drew near to the city behold there came out of the tombs one that was possessed of a devil, and in such wise that no chain could hold him, and he did great harm to the man.

The demons cried out through his mouth, saying: 'O holy one of God, why art thou come before the time to trouble us.?' And they prayed him that he would not cast them forth.

Jesus asked them how many they were. They answered "Six thousand six hundred and sixty-six.[29] When the disciples heard this they were affrighted, and prayed Jesus that he would depart. Then said Jesus: 'Where is your faith: It is necessary that the demon should depart, and not I.' The demons therefore cried: 'We will come out, but permit us to enter into those swine.' There were feeding there near to the sea, about ten thousand swine belonging to the Canaanites. Thereupon Jesus said: 'Depart, and enter into the swine.' With a roar the demons entered into the swine, and cast them headlong into the sea. Then fled into the city they that fed the swine, and recounted all that had been brought to pass by Jesus.

Accordingly the men of the city came forth and found Jesus and the man that was healed. The men were filled with fear and prayed Jesus that he would depart out of their borders. Jesus accordingly departed from them and went up into the parts of Tyre and Sidon.

And lo! a woman of Canaan with her two sons, who had come forth out of her own country to find Jesus. Having therefore seen him come with his disciples, she cried out: 'Jesus, son of David, have mercy on my daughter, who is tormented of the devil!

Jesus did not answer even a single word, because they were of the uncircumcised people. The disciples were moved to pity, and said: 'O master, have pity on them! Behold how much they cry out and weep!'

Jesus answered: 'I am not sent but unto the people of Israel.' Then the woman, with her sons, went before Jesus, weeping and saying: 'O son of David, have mercy on me!' Jesus answered: 'It is not good to take the bread from the children's hands and give it to

---

[29] *Six thousand six hundred and sixty-six.* In the early development of alphabets and numbers, alphabets were given numerical values, so that the name of an object would have a numerical value as well. And it was often the practice of ancient pagans to give their gods names with the numerical value of 666. So that 666 appears to be an esoteric reference to idolatry (Worship of the Dead, p. 220.) The significance here appears to be that the man's insanity is the result of his idolatry.

the dogs.' And this said Jesus by reason of their uncleanness, because they were of the uncircumcised people.

The woman answered: 'O Lord, the dogs eat the crumbs that fall from their masters' table.' Then was Jesus seized with admiration at the words of the woman, and said: 'O woman, great is thy faith.' And having raised his hands to heaven he prayed to God, and then he said: 'O woman, thy daughter is freed, go thy way in peace.' The woman departed, and returning to her home found her daughter, who was blessing God.' Wherefore the woman said: 'Verily there is none other God than the God of Israel.' Whereupon all her kinsfolk joined themselves unto the law of [God], according to the law written in the book of Moses.

22. Miserable condition of the uncircumcised in that a dog is better than they.

The disciples questioned Jesus on that day, saying: 'O master, why didst thou make such answer to the woman, saying that they were dogs?'

Jesus answered: 'Verily I say unto you that a dog is better than an uncircumcised man.' Then were the disciples sorrowful, saying: 'Hard are these words, and who shall be able to receive them?'

Jesus answered: 'If ye consider, O foolish ones, what the dog doth, that hath no reason, for the service of his master, ye will find my saying to be true. Tell me, doth the dog guard the house of his master, and expose his life against the robber? Yea, assuredly. But what receiveth he? Many blows and injuries with little bread, and he always showeth to his master a joyful countenance. Is this true?'

'True it is, O master,' answered the disciples.

Then said Jesus: 'Consider now how much God hath given to man, and ye shall see how unrighteous he is in not observing the covenant of God made with Abraham his servant. Remember that which David said to Saul king of Israel, against Goliath the Philistine: "My lord," said David, "while thy servant was keeping thy servant's flock there came the wolf,[30] the bear, and the lion and seized thy servant's sheep: whereupon thy servant went and slew them, rescuing the sheep. And what is this uncircumcised one but like unto them? Therefore will thy servant go in the name of the Lord God of Israel, and will slay this unclean one that blasphemeth the holy people of God."

---

[30] *the wolf.* I Samuel 17:34-36, the writer failed to mention the wolf, or mention of the wolf dropped out of the text.

Then said the disciples: 'Tell us, O master, for what reason man must needs be circumcised?''

Jesus answered: 'Let it suffice you that God hath commanded it to Abraham, saying: "Abraham, circumcise thy foreskin and that of all thy house, for this is a covenant between me and thee for ever."'

23. Origin of circumcision, and covenant of God with Abraham, and damnation of the uncircumcised.

And having said this, Jesus sat nigh unto the mountain which they looked upon. And his disciples came to his side to listen to his words. Then said Jesus: 'Adam the first man having eaten, by fraud of Satan, the food forbidden of God in paradise, his flesh rebelled against the spirit; whereupon he swore, saying: "By God, I will cut thee!" And having broken a piece of rock, he seized his flesh to cut it with the sharp edge of the stone; whereupon he was rebuked by the angel Gabriel. And he answered: "I have sworn by God to cut it; I will never be a liar!"

'Then the angel showed him the superfluity of his flesh, and that he cut off. And hence, just as every man taketh flesh for the flesh of Adam, so is he bound to observe in his sons, and from generation to generation came down the obligation of circumcision. But in the time of Abraham there were but few circumcised upon the earth, because that idolatry was multiplied upon the earth. Whereupon God told to Abraham the fact concerning circumcision, and made this covenant, saying: "The soul that shall not have his flesh circumcised,[31] I will scatter him from among my people for ever."'

The disciples trembled with fear at these words of Jesus, for with vehemence of spirit he spake. Then said Jesus: 'Leave fear to him that hath not circumcised his foreskin, for he is deprived of paradise.' And having said this, Jesus spake again, saying: 'The spirit in many is ready in the service of God, but the flesh is weak. The man therefore that feareth God ought to consider what the flesh is, and where it had its origin, and whereto it shall be reduced. Of the clay of the earth created God flesh, and into it he breathed the breath of life, with an inbreathing therein. And therefore when the flesh shall hinder the service of God it ought to be spurned like clay and trampled on, forasmuch as he that hateth his soul in this world shall keep it in life eternal.

'What the flesh is at this present its desires make manifest - that it is a harsh enemy of all good: for it alone desireth sin.

---

[31] *not have his flesh circumcised.* Gen. 17:14.

'Ought then man for the sake of satisfying one of his enemies to leave off pleasing God, his creator? Consider ye this: All the saints and prophets have been enemies of their flesh for service of God: wherefore readily and with gladness they went to their death, so as not to offend against the law of God given by Moses his servant, and go and serve the false and lying gods.

'Remember Elijah,[32] who fled through desert places of the mountains, eating only grass, clad in goats' skin. Ah, how many days he supped not! Ah, how much cold he endured! Ah, how many showers drenched him and [that] for the space of seven years, wherein endured that fierce persecution of the unclean Jezebel!

'Remember Elisha,[33] who ate barley-bread, and wore the coarsest raiment. Verily I say unto you that they, not fearing to spurn the flesh, were feared with great terror by the king and princes. This should suffice for the spurning of the flesh, O men. But if ye will gaze at the sepulchres, ye shall know what flesh is.'

24. Notable example how one ought to flee from banqueting and feasting.

Having said this, Jesus wept, saying: 'Woe to those who are servants to their flesh, for they are sure not to have any good in the other life, but only torments for their sins. I tell you that there was a rich glutton who paid no heed to aught but gluttony, and so every day held a splendid feast. There stood at his gate a poor man by name Lazarus, who was full of wounds, and was fain to have those crumbs that fell from the glutton's table. But no one gave them to him: nay, all mocked him. Only the dogs had pity on him, for they licked his wounds. It came to pass that the poor man died, and the angels carried him to the arms of Abraham our father. The rich man also died, and the devils carried him to the arms of Satan; whereupon, undergoing the greatest torment, he lifted up his eyes and from afar saw Lazarus in the arms of Abraham. Then cried the rich man: "O father Abraham, have mercy on me, and send Lazarus, who upon his fingers may bring me a drop of water to cool my tongue, which is tormented in this flame."

'Abraham answered: "Son, remember that thou receivedst thy

---

[32] *Elijah.* See I Kings:19, where the account of Elijah's flight is greatly abbreviated. Jesus and the Essenes in general, accuse the Jews of having corrupted the Scriptures (The Dead Sea Scrolls, The Gospel of Barnabas, and The New Testament, pp. 12-13).

[33] *Elisha.* II Kings, 4:42.

good in the other life and Lazarus his evil: wherefore now thou shalt be in torment, and Lazarus in consolation."

'The rich man cried out again, saying: "O father Abraham, in my house there are three brethren of mine. Therefore send Lazarus to announce to them how much I am suffering, in order that they may repent and not come hither."

'Abraham answered: "They have Moses and the prophets, let them hear them."

'The rich man answered: "Nay, father Abraham; but if one dead shall arise they will believe."

'Abraham answered: "Whoso believeth not Moses and the prophets will not believe even the dead if they should arise."

'See then whether the poor are blessed,' said Jesus, 'who have patience, and only desire that which is necessary, hating the flesh. O wretched they, who bear others to the burial, to give their flesh for food of worms, and do not learn the truth.[34] So far from it that they live here like immortals, for they build great houses and purchase great revenues and live in pride."

25. How one ought to despise the flesh, and how one ought to live in the world.

Then said he who writeth: 'O master, true are thy words and therefore have we forsaken all to follow thee. Tell us then, how we ought to hate our flesh: for to kill oneself is not lawful, and living we needs must give it its livelihood.

Jesus answered: 'Keep thy flesh like a horse, and thou shalt live securely. For unto a horse food is given by measure and labour without measure, and the bridle is put on him that he may walk at thy will, he is tied up that he may not annoy any one, he is kept in a poor place, and beaten when he is not obedient: so do thou, then, O Barnabas, and thou shalt live always with God.

'And be not offended at my words, for David the prophet did the same thing, as he confesseth, saying: "I am as an horse before thee: and am always by thee."[35]

'Now tell me, whether is poorer he who is content with little, or he who desireth much? Verily I say unto you, that if the world had

---

[34] *do not learn the truth.* Since rich men and beggars were common at this time, this account would be most impressive upon the minds of the listeners in emphasizing three important points: 1) the temporary and uncertain nature of material blessings, 2) the responsibility of the rich toward the poor, and 3) the supremacy of God's law as a guide to salvation.

[35] *am always by thee.* In this discourse, Jesus is providing the interpretation of Psalm 73.

but a sound mind no one would amass anything for himself, but all would be in common. But in this is known its madness, that the more it amasseth the more it desireth. And as much as it amasseth, for the fleshly repose of others doth it amass the same. Therefore let one single robe suffice for you, cast away your purse, carry no wallet, no sandals on your feet; and do not think, saying: "What shall happen to us?" but have thought to do the will of God, and he will provide for your need, insomuch that nothing shall be lacking unto you.

'Verily I say unto you, that the amassing much in this life giveth sure witness of not having anything to receive in the other. For he that hath Jerusalem for his native country buildeth not houses in Samaria, for that there is enmity between these cities. Understand ye?'

'Yea, answered the disciples.

26. How one ought to love God. And in this chapter is contained the wonderful contention of Abraham with his father.

Then said Jesus: 'There was a man on a journey who, as he was walking, discovered a treasure in a field that was to be sold for five pieces of money. Straightway the man, when he knew this, sold his cloak to buy that field. Is that credible?"

The disciples answered: 'He who would not believe this is mad.'

Thereupon Jesus said: 'Ye will be mad if ye give not your senses to God to buy your soul, wherein resideth the treasure of love; for love is a treasure incomparable. For he that loveth God hath God for his own; and whoso hath God hath everything.'

Peter answered? 'O master, how ought one to love God with true love? Tell thou us.'

Jesus replied: 'Verily I say unto you that he who shall not hate[36] his father and his mother, and his own life, and children and wife for love of God, that such an one is not worthy to be loved of God.'

Peter answered: 'O master, it is written in the law of God in the book of Moses: "Honor thy father, that thou mayest live long upon the earth."[37] And further he saith: "Cursed be the son that obeyeth not his father and his mother"; wherefore God commanded that such a disobedient son should be by the wrath of the people stoned before

---

[36] *he who shall not hate.* Love and hatred are used here to designate strong decided preference for God over all else, and not taken literally, though it is suggested that one should keep their distance from them if they are a hinderance to serving God.

[37] *live long upon the earth.* Ex.20:12; and Deut. 27:16.

the gate of the city.[38] And now how biddest thou us to hate father and mother?'

Jesus replied: 'Every word of mine is true, because it is not mine, but God's, who hath sent me to the house of Israel. Therefore I say unto you that all that which ye possess God hath bestowed it upon you: and so, whether is the more precious, the gift or the giver? When thy father and thy mother, with every other thing is a stumbling-block to thee in the service of God, abandon them as enemies. Did not God say to Abraham: "Go forth from the house of thy father and of thy kindred, and come to dwell in the land which I will give to thee and to thy seed?" And wherefore did God say this, save because the father of Abraham was an image-maker, who made and worshipped false gods? Whence there was enmity between them insomuch that the father wished to burn his son.'

Peter answered: 'True are thy words, wherefore I pray thee tell us how Abraham mocked his father.'

Jesus replied: 'Abraham was seven years old when he began to seek God. So one day he said to his father:[39] "Father, what made man?"

'The foolish father answered: "Man; for I made thee, and my father made me."

Abraham answered: "Father, it is not so; for I have heard an old man weeping and saying: 'O my God, wherefore hast thou not given me children.'"

'His father replied: "It is true, my son, that God helpeth man to make man, but he putteth not his hand thereto; it is only necessary that man come to pray to his God and to give him lambs and sheep, and his God will help him."

'Abraham answered; "How many gods are there, father?"

'The old man replied? "They are infinite in number, my son."

'Then said Abraham: "O father, what shall I do if I shall serve one god and another shall wish me evil because I serve him not? In any wise there will come discord between them, and so war will arise among the gods. But if perchance the god that willeth me evil shall

---

[38] *stoned before the gate of the city.* Deut.21:18-21.

[39] *he said to his father.* Terah and Athar are one and the same person as Eusebius points out. In the Qur'an (9:114), we are told how Abraham, being kind hearted, and having promised his father that he would pray for him, did so. And it is this prayer that is referred to in Quran (14:41), where Abraham includes the mention of his parents as distinct from himself and the believers, though in the same prayer for the believers. The request of his father substantiates the statement of the Rabbis, that though the father was wicked at this point in his life he did repent before his death (Soncino Chumash, p.55).

slay my own god, what shall I do? It is certain that he will slay me also."

'The old man, laughing, answered: "O son, have no fear, for no god maketh war upon another god; nay, in the great temple there are a thousand gods with the great god Baal; and I am now nigh seventy years old, and yet never have I seen that one god hath smitten another god. And assuredly all men do not serve one god, but one man one, and another another."

'Abraham answered: "So, then, they have peace among themselves?"

'Said his father : "They have."

'Then said Abraham: "O father, what be the gods like?"

'The old man answered: "Fool, every day I make a god, which I sell to others to buy bread, and thou knowest not what the gods are like!" And then at that moment he was making an idol. "This," said he, "is of palm wood, that one is of olive, that little one is of ivory: see how fine it is! Does it not seem as though it were alive? Assuredly, it lacks but breath!"

'Abraham answered: "And so, father, the gods are without breath? Then how do they give breath? And being without life, how give they life? It is certain, father, that these are not God."

'The old man was wroth at these words, saying: "If thou wert of age to understand, I would break thy head with this axe: But hold thy peace, because thou hast not understanding!"

'Abraham answered: "Father, if the gods help to make man, how can it be that man should make the gods? And if the gods are made of wood, it is a great sin to burn wood. But tell me, father, how is it that, when thou hast made so many gods, the gods have not helped thee to make so many other children that thou shouldest become the most powerful man in the world?"

'The father was beside himself, hearing his son speak so; the son went on: "Father, was the world for some time without men?"

'"Yes," answered the old man, "and why?"

'"Because," said Abraham, "I should like to know who made the first God."

'"Now go out of my house!" said the old man, "and leave me to make this god quickly, and speak no words to me; for, when thou art hungry thou desirest bread and not words."

'Said Abraham: "A fine god, truly, that thou cuttest him as thou wilt, and he defendeth not himself!"

'Then the old man was angry, and said: "All the world saith that it is a god, and thou, mad fellow, sayest that it is not. By my gods, if thou wert a man I could kill thee!'' And having said this, he gave blows and kicks to Abraham, and chased him from the house.'

27. In this chapter is clearly seen how improper is laughter in men: also the prudence of Abraham.

The disciples laughed over the madness of the old man, and stood amazed at the prudence of Abraham.[40] But Jesus reproved them, saying: 'Ye have forgotten the words of the prophet,[41] who saith: ''Present laughter is a herald of weeping to come,: and further, ''Thou shalt not go where is laughter, but sit where they weep, because this life passeth in miseries''' then said Jesus: 'In the time of Moses, know ye not that for laughing and mocking at others God turned into hideous beasts many men of Egypt: Beware that in anywise ye laugh not at any one, for ye shall surely weep for it.'

The disciples answered: 'We laughed over the madness of the old man.'

Then said Jesus: 'Verily I say unto you, every like loveth his like, and therein findeth pleasure. Therefore, if ye were not mad ye would not laugh at madness.'

They answered: 'May God have mercy on us.'

Said Jesus: 'So be it.'

Then said Philip: 'O master, how came it to pass that Abraham's father wished to burn his son?'

Jesus answered: 'One day, Abraham having come to the age of twelve years, his father said to him: 'To-morrow is the festival of all the gods; therefore we shall go to the great temple and bear a present to my god, great Baal. And thou shalt choose for thyself a god, for thou art of age to have a god.''

'Abraham answered with guile: ''Willingly, O my father.'' And so betimes in the morning they went before every one else to the temple. But Abraham bare beneath his tunic an axe hidden. Whereupon, having entered into the temple, as the crowd increased Abraham hid himself behind an idol in a dark part of the temple. His father, when he departed, believed that Abraham had gone home before him, wherefore he did not stay to seek him.

---

[40] *the prudence of Abraham.* Even at this early age, Abraham displayed the characteristic spoken of by Josephus, who says: ''He [Abraham] was a person of great sagacity, both for understanding all things and persuading his hearers, and not mistaken in his opinions; for which reason he began to have higher notions of virtue than others had, and he determined to renew and to change the opinion all men happened to have concerning God.''

[41] *the words of the prophet.* The prophet spoken of here, is Solomon. See Ecclesiastes 7:2-3.

28.

'When every one had departed from the temple, the priests closed the temple and went away. Then Abraham took the axe and cut off the feet of all the idols, except the great god Baal. At its feet he placed the axe, amid the ruins which the statues made, for they, through being old and composed of pieces, fell in pieces. Thereupon, Abraham, going forth from the temple, was seen by certain men, who suspected him of having gone to thieve something from the temple. So they laid hold on him, and having arrived at the temple, when they saw their gods so broken in pieces, they cried out with lamentation: "Come quickly, O men, and let us slay him who hath slain our gods!" There ran together there about ten thousand men, with the priests, and questioned Abraham of the reason why he had destroyed their gods.

'Abraham answered: "Ye are foolish! Shall then a man slay God?[42] It is the great God that hath slain them. See you not that axe which he hath near his feet? Certain it is that he desireth no fellows."

'Then arrived there the father of Abraham, who, mindful of the many discourses of Abraham against their gods, and recognizing the axe wherewith Abraham had broken in pieces the idols, cried out: "It hath been this traitor of a son of mine, who hath slain our gods! for this axe is mine." And he recounted to them all that had passed between him and his son.

'Accordingly the man collected a great quantity of wood, and having bound Abraham's hands and feet put him upon the wood, and put fire underneath.

'Lo! God, through his angel, commanded the fire that it should not burn Abraham his servant. The fire blazed up with great fury, and burned about two thousand men of those who had condemned Abraham to death. Abraham verily found himself free, being carried by the angel of God near to the house of his father, without seeing who carried him and thus Abraham escaped death.'

29.

Then said Philip: 'Great is the mercy of God upon whoso loveth him. Tell us, O master, how Abraham came to the knowledge of God.'

---

[42] *Shall then a man slay God?* (The Christians might well be asked the same question). Now according to Josephus, through the application of logic and reasoning, Abraham concluded: "That there was but one God, the Creator of the universe; and that as to other [things looked upon as gods] if they contributed anything to the happiness of men, that each of them afforded it only according to his appointment, and not by their own power. (Antiquities of the Jews, chap.7)

Jesus answered: 'Having arrived nigh unto the house of his father, Abraham feared to go into the house; so he removed some distance from the house and sat under a palm tree, where thus abiding by himself he said: "It needs must be that there is a God who hath life and power more than man, since he maketh man, and man without God could not make man." Thereupon, looking round upon the stars, the moon, and the sun, he thought that they had been God. But after considering their variableness[43] with their movements, he said: "It needs must be that God move not, and that clouds hide him not: otherwise men would be brought to naught." Whereupon, remaining thus in suspense, he heard himself called by name, "Abraham!" And so, turning round and not seeing anyone on any side, he said: "I have surely heard myself called by name, 'Abraham.'" Thereupon, two other times in like manner, he heard himself called by name, "Abraham!"

'He answered: "Who calleth me!"

'Then he heard it said: "I am the angel of God, Gabriel."

'Therefore was Abraham filled with fear; but the angel comforted him, saying: "Fear not, Abraham, for that thou art friend of God; wherefore, when thou didst break in pieces the gods of men, thou wert chosen of the God of the angels and prophets; insomuch that thou art written in the book of life."

'Then said Abraham: "What ought I to do, to serve the God of the angels and holy prophets?"

'The angel answered: "Go to that fount and wash thee, for God willeth to speak with thee."

'Abraham answered: "Now, how ought I to wash me?"

'Then the angel presented himself unto him as a beautiful youth, and washed himself in the fount, saying: "Do thou in turn likewise to thyself, O Abraham." When Abraham had washed himself, the angel said: "Go up that mountain, for God willeth to speak to thee there."

'He ascended the mountain as the angel said to Abraham, and

---

[43] *But after considering their variableness.* His growing conviction that there must be only one God, was derived, says Josephus, from his observation of the "irregular phenomena that were visible both at land and sea, as well as those that happen to the sun, and moon and all the heavenly bodies," to which he applied logic and reasoning, and concluded "If these bodies had power of their own, they would certainly take care of their own regular motions; but since they do not preserve such regularity, they make it plain, that in so far as they co-operate to our advantage, they do it not of their own abilities, but as they are subservient to Him that commands them, to whom alone we ought justly to offer our honor and thanksgiving." (Ibid).

having sat down upon his knees he said to himself: "When will the God of the angels speak to me?"

'He heard himself called with a gentle voice: "Abraham!"'

'Abraham answered Him: "Who calleth me?"'

'The voice answered: "I am thy God, O Abraham."'

'Abraham, filled with fear, bent his face to earth, saying: "How shall thy servant hearken unto thee, who is dust and ashes!"'

'Then said God: "Fear not, but rise up, for I have chosen thee for my servant, and I will to bless thee and make thee increase into a great people. Therefore go thou forth from the house of thy father and of thy kindred, and come to dwell in the land which I will give to thee and to thy seed."'

'Abraham answered: "All will I do, Lord; but guard me that none other god may do me hurt."'

'Then spake God, saying: "I am God alone, and there is none other God but me. I strike down, and make whole: I slay, and give life; I lead down to hell, and I bring out thereof, and none is able to deliver himself out of my hands." Then God gave him the covenant of circumcision; and so our father Abraham knew God.'

And having said this, Jesus lifted up his hands, saying 'To thee be honor and glory, O God. So be it!'

30.

Jesus went to Jerusalem, near unto the Senofegia (Tabernacles), a feast of our nation. The scribes and Pharisees having perceived this, took counsel to catch him in his talk.

Whereupon, there came to him a doctor, saying: 'Master, what must I do to have eternal life?'

Jesus answered: 'How is it written in the law?'"

The tempter answered, saying: 'Love the Lord thy God, and thy neighbor. Thou shalt love thy God above all things, with all thy heart and thy mind, and thy neighbor as thyself.'

Jesus answered: 'Thou hast answered well; therefore go and do thou so, I say, and thou shalt have eternal life.'

He said unto him: 'And who is my neighbor?'

Jesus answered, lifting up his eyes: 'A man was going down from Jerusalem to go unto Jericho, a city rebuilt under a curse.[44] This man on the road was seized by robbers, wounded and stripped; whereupon they departed, leaving him half dead. It chanced that a

---

[44] *a city rebuilt under a curse.* This refers to the warning uttered by Joshua (Joshua 6:26) which came to pass in the days of Hiel (I Kings 16:34).

priest passed by that place, and he, seeing the wounded man, passed on without greeting him. In like manner passed a Levite, without saying a word. It chanced that there passed [also] a Samaritan, who, seeing the wounded man, was moved to compassion, and alighted from his horse, and took the wounded man and washed his wounds with wine, and anointed them with ointment, and binding up his wounds for him and comforting him, he set him upon his own horse. Whereupon, having arrived in the evening at the inn, he gave him into the charge of the host. And when he had risen on the morrow, he said: "Take care of this man, and I will pay thee all." And having presented four gold pieces to the sick man for the host, he said: "Be of good cheer, for I will speedily return and conduct thee to my own home."'

'Tell me,' said Jesus, 'which of these was the neighbor?'

The doctor answered: 'He who showed mercy.'

Then said Jesus: 'Thou has answered rightly; therefore go and do thou likewise.'

The doctor departed in confusion.[45]

31.

Then drew near unto Jesus the priests, and said: 'Master, is it lawful to give tribute to Caesar?' Jesus turned round to Judas, and said: 'Hast thou any money?' And taking a penny in his hand, Jesus turned himself to the priests, and said to them: 'This penny hath an image: tell me, whose image is it?'

They answered: 'Caesar's.'

'Give therefore,' said Jesus, 'that which is Caesar's to Caesar, and that which is God's give it to God.'

Then they departed in confusion.[46]

And behold there drew nigh a centurion, saying: 'Lord, my son is sick; have mercy on my old age!'

Jesus answered: 'The Lord God of Israel have mercy on thee!'

---

[45] *The doctor departed in confusion.* The Samaritans were looked upon as Gentiles by the Jews, and therefore considered inferiors, a contributing factor to the doctor's (rabbi's) confusion. For to do as the good Samaritan would be to do good even to one who might hold you in disdain.

[46] *Then they departed in confusion.* "Caesar" was the title of the Roman emperors. Tiberious was emperor at this time, so that the coin bore his image in accordance with Roman practice. Jesus' answer to those who sought to confound him, was fully in accordance with an axiom of the Israelite teachers, that "where a ruler's coin is current, having some marking pertaining to his reign, his sovereignty is acknowledged." Thus those who sought to confound him, were confounded instead.

The man was departing; and Jesus said: 'Wait for me, for I will come to thine house, to make prayer over thy son.'

The centurion answered: 'Lord, I am not worthy that thou, a prophet of God, shouldest come unto my house, sufficient unto me is the word that thou hast spoken for the healing of my son; for thy God hath made thee lord over every sickness, even as his angel said unto me in my sleep.'

Then Jesus marvelled greatly, and turning to the crowd, he said: 'Behold this stranger, for he hath more faith than all that I have found in Israel.' And turning to the centurion, he said: 'Go in peace, because God, for the great faith that he hath given thee, hath granted health to thy son.'

The centurion went his way, and on the road he met his servants, who announced to him how his son was healed.

The man answered: 'At what hour did the fever leave him?'

They said: 'Yesterday, at the sixth hour, the heat departed from him.'

The man knew that when Jesus said: 'The Lord God of Israel have mercy on thee,' his son received his health. Whereupon the man believed in our God, and having entered into his house, he brake in pieces all his own gods, saying: 'There is only the God of Israel, the true and living God.' Therefore said he: 'None shall eat of my bread that worshippeth not the God of Israel.'

32.

One skilled in the law invited Jesus to supper, in order to tempt him. Jesus came thither with his disciples, and many scribes, to tempt him, waited for him in the house. Whereupon, the disciples sat down to table without washing their hands. The scribes called Jesus, saying: 'Wherefore do not thy disciples observe the traditions[47] of our elders, in not washing their hands before they eat bread?'

Jesus answered; 'And I ask you, for what cause have ye annulled the precept of God to observe your traditions? Ye say to the sons of poor fathers: "Offer and make vows unto the temple." And

---

[47] *do not thy disciples observe the traditions?* It was not for reasons of cleanliness, that the scribes called themselves taking Jesus and his disciples to task, but rather ceremonial observance. The law enjoined washing (Lev. 15:11) after a person had touched anything ceremonially unclean, such as the sick. But as Jesus and his disciples had never even gone to the centurion's home, much less touched him or his son, they were not in violation of the law. But rather the scribes and others, were excessive in their observance of ritual, while lacking in the spirit of the Law. Plus they and their predecessors were guilty of corrupting the Law (Torah) and the "oral law" (*Torah sheb'al peh*) through fabrication of traditions.

they make vows of that little wherewith they ought to support their fathers. And when their fathers wish to take money, the sons cry out: "This money is consecrated to God"; whereby the fathers suffer. O false, scribes, hyprocrites, doth God use this money? Assuredly not, for God eateth not, as he saith by his servant David the prophet: "Shall I then eat the flesh of bulls and drink the blood of sheep? Render unto me the sacrifice of praise,[48] and offer unto me thy vows; for if I should be hungry I will not ask aught of thee, seeing that all things are in my hands, and the abundance of paradise is with me." Hypocrites! ye do this to fill your purse, and therefore ye tithe rue and mint. Oh miserable ones! for unto others ye show the most clear way, by which ye will not go.

'Ye scribes and doctors lay upon the shoulders of others weights of unbearable weight, but ye yourselves the while are not willing to move them with one of your fingers.

'Verily I say unto you, that every evil hath entered into the world under the pretext of the elders. Tell me, who made idolatry to enter into the world, if not the usage of the elders? For there was a king who exceedingly loved his father, whose name was Baal. Whereupon, when the father was dead, his son for his own consolation, caused to be made an image like unto his father, and set it up in the marketplace of the city. And he made a decree that every one who approached that statue within a space of fifteen cubits should be safe, and no one on any account should do him hurt. Hence the malefactors, by reason of the benefit they received therefrom, began to offer to the statue roses and flowers, and in a short time the offerings were changed into money and food, insomuch that they called it god, to Honor it. Which thing from custom was transformed into a law, insomuch that the idol of Baal spread through all the world; and how much doth God lament this by the prophet Isaiah, saying: "Truly this people worshippeth me in vain, for they have

---

[48] *the sacrifice of praise.* The rabbis and scribes had misled the people concerning the importance of burnt offerings and money. Another evil that can be mentioned here, is the pagan doctrine that human sacrifice is necessary to salvation. In II Kings 3:26-27, Mesha, king of Moab sacrificed his first-born son to the god Chemosh. In the Isis-Osirian cult, crucifixion was often a required means of sacrificing the king as the incarnation of the god for the salvation of man. Such bloody sacrifices were usually accompanied by the belief that the savior's flesh and blood had to be eaten and drank in a cannibalistic sacrament. Later symbolic cannibalism was practiced such as that which is still practiced in Christianity today. And of course the notion that Jesus had to be sacrificed for the salvation of man has been traced back to this older barbarism. But the God of Abraham rejects this savagery (Gen. 22:1-14; Sam. 15:22; Ps. 4:5; 5:17.).

annulled my law given to them by my servant Moses, and follow the traditions of their elders."

'Verily I say unto you, that to eat bread with unclean hands defileth not a man, because that which entereth into the man defileth not the man, but that which cometh out of the man defileth the man.'

Thereupon, said one of the scribes: 'If I shall eat pork,[49] or other unclean meats, will they not defile my conscience?"

Jesus answered: 'Disobedience will not enter into the man,[50] but will come out of the man, from his heart; and therefore will he be defiled when he shall eat forbidden food.'

Then said one of the doctors: 'Master, thou hast spoken much against idolatry as though the people of Israel had idols, and so thou hast done us wrong.'

Jesus answered: 'I know well that in Israel to-day there are not statues of wood; but there are statues of flesh.'

Then answered all the scribes in wrath: '"And so we are idolaters?'

Jesus answered: 'Verily I say unto you, the precept saith not "Thou shalt worship," but "Thou shalt love the Lord thy God with all thy soul, and with all thy heart, and with all thy mind." Is this true?' said Jesus.

'It is true,' answered every one.

33.

Then said Jesus: 'Verily all that which a man loveth, for which he leaveth everything else but that, is his god: And so the fornicator hath for his image the harlot, the glutton and drunkard hath for image his own flesh, and the covetous hath for his image silver and gold, and so likewise every other sinner.'

Then said he who had invited him: 'Master, which is the greatest sin?'

Jesus answered: 'Which is the greatest ruin of a house?'

Every one was silent, when Jesus with his finger pointed to the foundation, and said: 'If the foundation give way, immediately the house falleth in ruin, in such wise that it is necessary to build it up

---

[49] *If I shall eat pork.* The Christians being victims of the insidious Nicolaitan conspiracy (Rev. 2:6; 2:15), have in many cases allowed themselves to be duped into ignoring the fact that pork is not edible. Here we have clear evidence that Jesus did not sanction the consumption of pork.

[50] *Disobedience will not enter into the man.* The significance of his words, is that the disobedience to God in eating the pork, and other unclean things, comes from within the person eating the pork, etc., not from the pork itself, though the filthy nature of the pork is unchanged.

anew: but if every other part give way it can be repaired. Even so then say I to you, that idolatry is the greatest sin, because it depriveth a man entirely of faith, and consequently of God; so that he can have no spiritual affection. But every other sin leaveth to man the hope of obtaining mercy: and therefore I say that idolatry is the greatest sin.'

All stood amazed at the speaking of Jesus, for they perceived that it could not in any wise be assailed.

Then Jesus continued? 'Remember that which God spake and which Moses and Joshua wrote in the law, and ye shall see how grave is this sin. Said God, speaking to Israel: "Thous shalt not[51] make to thyself any image of those things which are in heaven nor of those things which are under the heaven, nor shalt thou make it of those things which are above the earth, nor of those which are above the water, nor of those which are under the water. For I am thy God, strong and jealous, who will take vengeance for this sin upon the fathers and upon their children even unto the fourth generation." Remember how,[52] when our people had made the calf, and when they had worshipped it, by commandment of God Joshua and the tribe of Levi took the sword and slew of them one hundred and twenty thousand[53] of those that did not crave mercy of God. Oh, terrible judgment of God upon the idolaters!'

34.

There stood before the door one who had his right hand shrunken in such fashion that he could not use it. Whereupon Jesus, having lift up his heart to God, prayed, and then said: 'In order that ye may know that my words are true, I say, "In the name of God, man, stretch out thine infirm hand."' He stretched it out whole, as if it had never had aught ill with it.

Then with fear of God they began to eat. And having eaten somewhat, Jesus said again: 'Verily I say unto you, that it were better to burn a city than to leave there an evil custom. For on account of

---

[51] *Thou shalt not.* Ex. 20:4-6; and Deut. 5:8-9.

[52] *Remember how.* The calf being a representation of the god Osiris, the making of the golden calf by the Israelites demonstrates just how far many of them had strayed from the Abrahamic faith.

[53] *one hundred and twenty thousand.* In the Exodus version as it is now, the number is 3,000 and Joshua is not mentioned. Once again, as pointed out, Jesus and the Essenes accuse the Jews of having corrupted the Scriptures. (Ex. 32:28)

such is God wroth with the princes and kings of the earth, to whom God hath given the sword to destroy iniquities.[54]

Afterwards said Jesus: 'When thou are invited, remember not to set thyself in the highest place, in order that if a greater friend of the host come the host say not unto thee: "Arise and sit lower down!" which were a shame to thee. But go and sit in the meanest place, in order that he who invited thee may come and say: "Arise, friend, and come and sit here, above!" For then shalt thou have great honor: For every one that exalteth himself shall be humbled, and he that humbleth himself shall be exalted.

'Verily I say unto you, that Satan became not reprobate for other sin than for his pride. Even as saith the prophet Isaiah, reproaching him with these words: "How art thou fallen[55] from heaven, O Lucifer, that wert the beauty of the angels, and didst shine like the dawn: truly to earth is fallen thy pride!"

'Verily I say unto you, that if a man knew his miseries, he would always weep here on earth and account himself most mean, beyond every other thing. For no other cause did the first man with his wife weep for a hundred years without ceasing, craving mercy of God, for they knew truly whither they had fallen through their pride.'

And having said this, Jesus gave thanks; and that day it was published through Jerusalem how great things Jesus, had said, with the miracle he had wrought, insomuch that the people gave thanks to God blessing his holy name.

But the scribes and priests, having understood that he spake against the traditions of the elders, were kindled with greater hatred. And like Pharaoh they hardened their heart; wherefore they sought occasion to slay him, but found it not.

35.

Jesus departed from Jerusalem, and went to the desert beyond Jordan: and his disciples that were seated round him said to Jesus: 'O master, tell us how Satan fell through pride, for we have understood that he fell through disobedience, and because he always tempteth man to do evil.'

Jesus answered: 'God having created a mass of earth, and

---

[54] *to whom God hath given the sword to destroy iniquities.* And they do not do it. With such rulers God is angry. The introduction of evil is an aggression against morality, thus to fight against evil is to fight in defense of morality lest the evil spread and chaos takes hold as it has in North America. Consider the epidemic of AIDS, Drug Abuse, and the appalling crime rate against men, women and *children.*

[55] *How art thou fallen?* Isaiah 15:12.

having left it for twenty-five thousand years without doing aught else; Satan, who was as it were priest and head of the angels, by the great understanding that he possessed, knew that God of that mass of earth was to take one hundred and forty and four thousand signed with the mark of prophecy, and the messenger of God, the soul of which messenger he had created sixty thousand years before aught else. Therefore, being indignant, he instigated the angels, saying: "Look ye, one day God shall will that this earth be revered by us. Wherefore consider that we are spirit, and therefore it is not fitting so to do."

'Many therefore forsook God. Whereupon said God, one day when all the angels were assembled: "Let each one that holds me for his lord straightway do reverence to this earth."

'Many that loved God bowed themselves, but Satan, with them that were of his mind, said: O Lord, we are spirit, and therefore it is not just that we should do reverence to this clay." Having said this, Satan became horrid and of fearsome look, and his followers became hideous; because for their rebellion God took away from them the beauty wherewith he had endued them in creating them. Whereat the holy angels, when, lifting their heads, they saw how terrible a monster Satan had become,[56] and his followers, cast down their face to earth in fear.

'Then said Satan: "O Lord, thou hast unjustly made me hideous,

---

[56] *how terrible a monster Satan had become.* In Jesus' quotation of Isa. 15:12, in chap. 34, Satan is identified with the angels: "O Lucifer, that wert the beauty of the angels." In the Quran (18:50), it says that God commanded the angels to acknowledge Adam, and they obeyed except Iblis (the Devil) and his followers, the Jinn (demons). The evidence of these sources indicates that he and his host had been of the company of angels. But that as they became more rebellious through pride, their nature increasingly changed, and as a result they began to loose their beauty, and in so doing they were evolving into a different specie from the angels.

This change they brought on themselves through their jealousy, bigotry and arrogance, all of which was motivated by pride. The result of their evil was their change into the horrid looking creatures of ugliness that they had become. "Because of their rebellion God took away from them the beauty wherewith he had endued them in creating them." They cannot be identified as angels for they are no longer that, but they can be identified as nephillim (fallen ones) for they have indeed fallen from the angelic state. Because of their hideousness reflecting their evil nature, as an act of mercy, God has hidden them from the perception of our physical sight. Thus they are the Jinn (the hidden ones). Their leader, the Devil, is deemed Shaitan (Satan) because he is the adversary, and leader of adversaries, who are ever in opposition to any good that might befall man. As for their being made of smokeless fire, this is a metaphor signifying that as spirits they are made of a form of something akin to energy.

but I am content thereat, because I desire to annul all that thou shalt do. And the other devils said: "Call him not Lord, O Lucifer, for thou art Lord."

'Then said God to the followers of Satan: "Repent ye, and recognize me as God, your creator."

'They answered: "We repent of having done thee any reverence, for that thou art not just; but Satan is just and innocent, and he is our Lord."

'Then said God: "Depart from me, O ye cursed, for I have no mercy on you."

'And in his departing Satan spat upon that mass of earth, and that spittle the angel Gabriel lifted up with some earth, so that therefore now man has the navel in his belly.'

36.

The disciples stood in great amazement at the rebellion of the angels.

Then said Jesus: 'Verily I say unto you, that he who maketh not prayer is more wicked than Satan, and shall suffer greater torments. Because Satan had, before his fall, no example of fearing, nor did God so much as send him any prophet to invite him to repentance: but man - now that all the prophets are come except the messenger of God who shall come[57] after me, because so God willeth, and that I may prepare his way - and man, I say, albeit he have infinite examples of the justice of God, liveth carelessly without any fear, as though there were no God. Even as of such spake the prophet David: "The fool hath said in his heart, there is no God. Therefore are they corrupt and become abominable, without one of them doing good."[58]

'Make prayer unceasingly, O my disciples, in order that ye may receive. For he who seeketh findeth, and he who knocketh to him it is opened, and he who asketh receiveth. And in your prayer do not look to much speaking, for God looketh on the heart;[59] as he said through Solomon: "O my servant, give me thine heart."[60] Verily I say unto you, as God liveth, the hyprocrites make much prayer in every part of the city in order to be seen and held for saints by the

---

[57] *the messenger of God who shall come.* This prophetic statement made by Jesus, further demonstrates a connection between him, his followers: the Nazarenes, with the Essenes in general, for they too prophesied the advent of two messiahs, identified by them as a Teacher, and a Prophet. (The Dead Sea Scriptures,p.6.)

[58] *without one of them doing good.* Ps. 14:1

[59] *for God looketh on the heart.* I Samuel 16:7.

[60] *give me thine heart.* Prov. 23:26

multitude: but their heart is full of wickedness, and therefore they do not mean that which they ask. It is needful that thou mean thy prayer if thou wilt that God receive it. Now tell me: who would go to speak to the Roman governor or to Herod, except he first have made up his mind to whom he is going, and what he is going to do? Assuredly none. And if man doeth so in order to speak with man, what ought man to do in order to speak with God, and ask of him mercy for his sins, while thanking him for all that he hath given him?

'Verily I say unto you, that very few make true prayer, and therefore Satan hath power over them, because God willeth not those who honor him with their lips: who in the temple ask (with) their lips for mercy, and their heart crieth out for justice.[61] Even as he saith to Isaiah the prophet, saying: "Take away this people that is irksome to me, because with their lips they honor me, but their heart is far from me."[62] Verily I say unto you, that he that goeth to make prayer without consideration mocketh God.

'Now who would go to speak to Herod with his back towards him, and before him speak well of Pilate the governor, whom he hateth to the death? Assuredly none. Yet no less doth the man who goeth to make prayer and prepareth not himself. He turneth his back to God and his face to Satan, and speaketh well of him. For in his heart is the love of iniquity, whereof he hath not repented.

'If one, having injured thee, should with his lips say to thee. "Forgive me," and with his hands should strike thee a blow, how wouldest thou forgive him? Even so shall God have mercy on those who with their lips say: "Lord, have mercy on us," and with their heart love iniquity and think on fresh sins.'

37.

The disciples wept at the words of Jesus and besought him, saying: 'Lord, teach us to make prayer.'

Jesus answered: 'Consider what ye would do if the Roman governor seized you to put you to death, and that same do ye when ye go to make prayer. And let your words be these: "O Lord our God, hallowed be thy holy name, thy kingdom come in us, thy will be done always, and as it is done in heaven so be it done in earth; give us the bread for every day, and forgive us our sins, as we forgive them that

---

[61] *their heart crieth out for justice.* "God desires not people who require [ask for] grace from God in the temples with their mouth, while their hearts are calling for anger [vengeance] from God [against others]." (unknown)

[62] *their hearts is far from me.* Isa. 29:13

sin against us, and suffer us not to fall into temptations, but deliver us from evil, for thou art alone our God, to whom pertaineth glory and Honor for ever.'

38.

Then answered John: 'Master, let us wash ourselves as God commanded by Moses.'

Jesus said: 'Think ye that I am come to destroy the law[63] and the prophets? Verily I say unto you, as God liveth, I am not come to destroy it, but rather to observe it. For every prophet hath observed the law of God and all that God by the other prophets hath spoken. As God liveth, in whose presence my soul standeth, no one that breaketh one least precept can be pleasing to God, but shall be least in the kingdom of God, for he shall have no part there. Moreover I say unto you, that one syllable of the law of God cannot be broken without the gravest sin. But I do you to wit that it is necessary to observe that which God saith by Isaiah the prophet, with these words: "Wash you and be clean,[64] take away your thoughts from mine eyes."

'Verily I say unto you, that all the water of the sea will not wash him who with his heart loveth iniquities. And furthermore I say unto you, that no one will make prayer pleasing to God if he be not washed, but will burden his soul[65] with sin like to idolatry.

'Believe me, in sooth, that if man should make prayer to God as is fitting, he would obtain all that he should ask. Remember Moses the servant of God, who with his prayer scourged Egypt, opened the Red Sea, and there drowned Pharaoh and his host. Remember Joshua, who made the sun stand still, Samuel, who smote with fear the innumerable host of the Philistines, Elijah, who made the fire to rain from heaven, Elisha raised a dead man, and so many other holy prophets, who by prayer obtained all that they

[63] *Think Ye that I am come to destroy the law?* John's statement reflects his failure to have grasped the full meaning of what Jesus said to the scribes concerning the excessive ritual washing of hands (chap. 32). Jesus' response here, is in the way of clarifying the fact, that he had not been sent by God to establish disobedience to the Law, but rather to demonstrate how it should be obeyed (observed), just as all of the prophets had done before him. Thus it was not he who founded Gentile Christianity, a corruption of the faith, but rather Paul and the rest of the Nicolaitans (See, *The Dead Sea Scrolls, The Gospel of Barnabas, and The New Testament*).

[64] *wash you and be clean.* Isaiah. 1:16.

[65] *burden his soul with sin.* "Whosoever intentionally prays without washing is accursed before God like an idolater." (unknown)

asked. But those men[66] truly did not seek their own in their matters, but sought only God and his Honor.'

39.

Then said John: 'Well hast thou spoken, O master, but we lack to know how man sinned through pride.'

Jesus answered? 'When God had expelled Satan, and the angel Gabriel had purified that mass of earth whereon Satan spat, God created everything that liveth, both of the animals that fly and of them that walk and swim, and he adorned the world with all that it hath. One day Satan approached unto the gates of paradise, and, seeing the horses eating grass, he announced to them that if that mass of earth should receive a soul there would be for them grievous labour; and that therefore it would be to their advantage to trample that piece of earth in such wise that it should be no more good for anything. The horses aroused themselves and impetuously set themselves to run over that piece of earth which lay among lilies and roses. Whereupon God gave spirit to that unclean portion of earth upon which lay the spittle of Satan, which Gabriel had taken up from the mass: and raised up the dog,[67] who, barking, filled the horses with fear, and they fled. Then God gave his soul to man,[68] while all the holy angels sang: "Blessed be thy holy name, O God our Lord."

'Adam, having sprung up upon his feet, saw in the air a writing that shone like the sun, which said: "There is only one God, and Mohammed is the messenger of God." Whereupon Adam opened his mouth and said: "I thank thee, O Lord my God, that thou hast deigned to create me; but tell me, I pray thee, what meaneth the message of these words: "Mohammed is messenger of God." Have there been other men before me?"

'Then said God: "Be thou welcome, O my servant Adam, I tell thee that thou art the first man whom I have created. And he whom thou hast seen (mentioned) is thy son, who shall come into the world many years hence, and shall be my messenger, for whom I have

---

[66] *But those men.* Ex. 14:15; Josh. 10:12;
I Sam. 7:5; I Ki. 18:36; and II Ki. 4:32.

[67] *raised up the dog.* The meaning is, that the dog is an unclean animal that nevertheless, served, or serves a purpose. The dog being unclean is referred to in Isa. 66:3. The epithets dog, dead dog, dog's head, were used as terms of reproach or of humility in speaking of one's self. (Peloubet's Bible Dictionary, p. 152.)

[68] God gave his soul to man. Gen. 2:7; and Q. 32:9.

created all things;[69] who shall give light to the world when he shall come; whose soul was set in a celestial splendor sixty thousand years before I made anything."

'Adam besought God, saying: "Lord, grant me this writing upon the nails of the fingers of my hands." Then God gave to the first man upon his thumbs that writing; upon the thumb-nail of the right hand it said: "There is only one God, and upon the thumb-nail of the left it said: "Mohammed is messenger of God." Then with fatherly affection the first man kissed those words, and rubbed his eyes, and said: "Blessed be that day when thou shalt come to the world."

'Seeing the man alone, God said: "It is not well that he should remain alone." Wherefore he made him to sleep, and took a rib from near his heart, filling the place with flesh. Of that rib made he Eve, and gave her to Adam for his wife. He set the twain of them as lords of Paradise, to whom he said: "Behold I give unto you every fruit to eat, except the apples and the corn" whereof he said: "Beware that in no wise ye eat of these fruits, for ye shall become unclean, insomuch that I shall not suffer you to remain here, but shall drive you forth, and ye shall suffer great miseries."

40.

'When Satan had knowledge of this he became mad with indignation. And so he drew near to the gate of paradise, whereat stood on guard a horrid serpent,[70] which had legs like a camel, and the nails of his feet cut like a razor on every side. To him said the enemy: "Suffer me to enter into paradise."

'The serpent answered: 'And how shall I suffer thee to enter, God having commanded me to drive thee out?"

'Satan answered: "Thou seest how much God loveth thee, since he hath set thee outside of paradise to keep guard over a lump of clay, which is man. Wherefore, if thou bring me into paradise I will make thee so terrible that every one shall flee thee, and so at thy pleasure thou shalt go and stay."

---

[69] *for whom I have created all things.* This allegorical statement refers to the ultimate triumph of truth over falsehood, when man's struggle on earth is concluded by the ultimate triumph of monotheism over idolatry, and God's Holy Law over rebelliousness. That this is the meaning is demonstrated in the following statement that he, as one sent by God, would give God's light to the world thereby ultimately expelling the darkness.

[70] *a horrid serpent.* This reptillian is reminiscent of the dinosaurs, extinct long before Jesus' time. Therefore, what he relates here is to something that he saw literally.

'Then said the serpent: "And how shall I set thee within?"

'Said Satan. "Thou art great: therefore open thy mouth, and I will enter into thy belly, and so thou entering into paradise shalt place me near to those two lumps of clay that are newly walking upon the earth."

'Then the serpent did so, and placed Satan near to Eve, for Adam, her husband, was sleeping. Satan presented himself before the woman like a beauteous angel,[71] and said to her "Wherefore eat ye not of those apples and of corn?"

"Eve answered: "Our God hath said to us that eating thereof we shall be unclean, and therefore he will drive us from paradise."

'Satan answered: "He saith not the truth. Thou must know that God is wicked and envious, and therefore he brooketh no equals, but keepeth every one for a slave. And so he hath thus spoken unto you, in order that ye may not become equal to him. But if thou and thy companion do according to my counsel, ye shall eat of those fruits even as of the others, and ye shall not remain subject to others, but like God ye shall know good and evil, and ye shall do that which ye please, because ye shall be equal to God."

'Then Eve took and ate of those (fruits). And when her husband awoke she told all that Satan had said; and he took of them, his wife offering them, and did eat. Whereupon, as the food was going down, he remembered the words of God; wherefore, wishing to stop the food, he put his hand into his throat, where every man has the mark.

41.

'Then both of them knew that they were naked: wherefore, being ashamed, they took fig leaves and made a clothing for their secret parts. When midday was passed, behold God appeared to them, and called Adam, saying: "Adam, where art thou?"

'He answered: "Lord, I did hide myself from thy presence because I and my wife are naked, and so we are ashamed to present ourselves before thee."

'Then said God: "And who hath robbed you of your innocence, unless ye have eaten[72] the fruit by reason of which ye are unclean, and will not be able to abide longer in paradise?"

---

[71] *like a beauteous angel.* The demons are able to temporarily assume various forms.

[72] *unless ye have eaten.* Satan the arch deceiver cast an evil suggestion into the minds of both Adam and Eve (as he casts evil suggestions into the minds of their descendants). And caused them to commit a fault unintentionally, the result of which, was that as he fell, so they fell also, but not as far as he, for their misdeed was the

'Adam answered: "O Lord, the wife whom thou hast given me besought me to eat, and so I have eaten thereof."

'Then said God to the woman: "Wherefore gavest thou such food to thy husband?"

'Eve answered: "Satan deceived me, and so I did eat."

"'And how did that reprobate enter in hither?" said God.

'Eve answered: "A serpent that standeth at the northern gate brought him near to me."

'Then said God to Adam: "Because thou hast hearkened to the voice of thy wife and hast eaten the fruit, cursed be the earth in thy works; it shall bring forth for thee brambles and thorns, and in the sweat of thy face shalt thou eat bread. And remember that thou art earth, and to earth shalt thou return."

'And he spake to Eve, saying: "And thou who didst hearken to Satan, and gavest the food to thy husband, shalt abide under the dominion of man, who shall keep thee as a slave, and thou shalt bear children with travail."

'And having called the serpent, God called the angel Michael, him who holdeth the sword of God, (and) said: "First drive forth from paradise this wicked serpent, and when outside cut off his legs: for if he shall wish to walk, he must trail his body upon the earth." Afterwards God called Satan, who came laughing, and he said to him: "Because thou reprobate, hast deceived these and hast made them to become unclean, I will that every uncleanness of them and of all their children, whereof they shall be truly penitent and shall serve me, in going forth from their body shall enter through thy mouth, and so shalt thou be satiated with uncleanness."

'Satan then gave a horrible roar, and said: "Since thou willest to make me ever worse, I yet will make me that which I shall be able!"

'Then said God: "Depart, cursed one, from my presence!: Then Satan departed: whereupon God said to Adam (and) Eve, who were both weeping: "Go ye forth from paradise, and do penance, and let

result of a mistake in judgment, whereas he was, and is, openly rebellious. They had been warned: "Beware that in no wise ye eat of these fruits, for ye shall become [spiritually] unclean insomuch that I shall not suffer you to remain here, but shall drive you forth, and ye shall suffer great miseries [as chastisement, and as part of the means of regaining your lost state]. In accordance with His warning, God cut them off from the blissful awareness of His presence from whence all spiritual joy abounds. Thus we are told: God hid himself, and the angel Michael drove them forth from Paradise." Thereafter, man's awareness of God has been by virtue of a dim memory (God consciousness), and logic and reasoning in response to God's handiwork.

not your hope fail, for I will send your son to such wise that your seed shall lift the dominion of Satan from off the human race: for he who shall come, my messenger, to him will I give all things."

'God hid himself, and the angel Michael drove them forth from paradise. Whereupon Adam, turning him round, saw written above the gate, "There is only one God, and Mohammed is messenger of God." Whereupon, weeping, he said: "May it be pleasing to God, O my son, that thou come quickly and draw us out of misery."

'And thus,' said Jesus, 'sinned Satan and Adam through pride, the one by despising man, the other by wishing to make himself equal with God.'

42.

Then the disciples wept after this discourse, and Jesus was weeping, when they saw many who came to find him, for the chiefs of the priests took counsel among themselves to catch him in his talk. Wherefore they sent the Levites and some of the scribes to question him, saying: 'Who art thou?"

Jesus confessed, and said the truth: 'I am not the Messiah.'

They said: 'Art thou Elijah or Jeremiah, or any of the ancient prophets?"

Jesus answered: 'No.'

Then said they: 'Who art thou? Say, in order that we may give testimony to those who sent us.'

Then said Jesus: 'I am a voice that crieth through all Judea,[73] and crieth: "Prepare ye the way for the messenger of the Lord," even as it is written in Isaiah.'[74]

They said: 'If thou be not the Messiah nor Elijah, or any prophet, wherefore dost thou preach new doctrine, and make thyself of more account than the Messiah?'

Jesus answered: 'The miracles which God worketh by my hands show that I speak that which God willeth; nor indeed do I make myself to be accounted as him of whom ye speak. For I am not worthy to unloose the ties of the hosen or the latchets of the shoes of the messenger of God whom ye call "Messiah,"[75] who was made before

---

[73] *I am a voice that crieth through all Judea.* Here Jesus identifies his role as the Israelite Messiah with that of the Essene 'Teacher of Righteousness' (The Dead Sea Scrolls, pp. 104, 158). And it is this statement and accompanying circumstances, that Cerinthus, the author of John's gospel associated with John the Baptist.

[74] *written in Esaias.* Isa. 40:3

[75] *The messenger of God whom ye call "Messiah."* It was the Israelites themselves that applied this title to the prophet that was yet to come. There was nothing wrong

me, and shall come after me, and shall bring the words of truth, so that his faith shall have no end.'

The Levites and scribes departed in confusion, and recounted all to the chiefs of the priests, who said: 'He hath the devil on his back who recounteth all to him.'

Then said Jesus to his disciples: 'Verily I say unto you, that the chiefs and the elders of our people seek occasion against me.'

Then said Peter: 'Therefore go not thou any more into Jerusalem.'

Therefore said Jesus unto him: 'Thou art foolish, and knowest not what thou sayest, for it is necessary that I should suffer many persecutions, because so have suffered [76] all the prophets and holy ones of God. But fear not, for there be that are with us and there be that are against us.'

And having said this, Jesus departed and went to the mount Tabor, and there ascended with him Peter and James and John his brother, with him who writeth this. Whereupon there shone a great light above him, and his garments became white like snow and his face glistened as the sun, and lo! there came Moses and Elijah speaking with Jesus concerning all that needs must come upon our race and upon the holy city.'

Peter spake, saying: 'Lord, it is good to be here. Therefore, if thou wilt, we will make here three tabernacles, one for thee and one for Moses and the other for Elijah.'' And while he spake they were covered with a white cloud, and they heard a voice saying: 'Behold my servant, in whom I am well pleased; hear ye him.'

The disciples were filled with fear, and fell with their face upon the earth as dead. Jesus went down and raised up his disciples, saying: 'Fear not, for God loveth you, and hath done this in order that ye may believe on my words.'

43.

Jesus went down to the eight disciples who were awaiting him below. And the four narrated to the eight all that they had seen: and so there departed that day from their heart all doubt of Jesus, save (from) Judas Iscariot, who believed naught. Jesus seated himself at

with that, as long as they continued to realize that this prophet would not be an Israelite. Thus Jesus used the term for the sake of their understanding.

[76] *so have suffered.* Not only did the Essenes identify themselves as the "holy ones of God' but they also identified themselves as the suffering servants of God," after their founder, the "Teacher of Righteousness," whom they identified with the suffering servant of Isaiah (The Dead Sea Scrolls, p. 161.), and here, Jesus is identifying himself in like manner.

the foot of the mountain, and they ate of the wild fruits, because they had not bread.

Then said Andrew: 'Thou has told us many things of the Messiah, therefore of thy kindness tell us clearly all.' And in like manner the other disciples besought him.

Accordingly Jesus said: 'Everyone that worketh worketh for an end in which he findeth satisfaction. Wherefore I say unto you that God, verily because he is perfect, hath not need of satisfaction, seeing that he hath satisfaction himself. And so, willing to work, he created before all things the soul of his messenger, for whom he determined to create the whole, in order that the creatures should find joy and blessedness in God, whence his messenger should take delight in all his creatures which he hath appointed to be his slaves. And wherefore is this so, save because thus he hath willed?

'Verily I say unto you, that every prophet when he is come hath borne to one nation only the mark of the mercy of God. And so their words were not extended save to that people to which they were sent. But the messenger of God, when he shall come, God shall give to him as it were the seal of his hand, insomuch that he shall carry salvation and mercy to all the nations of the world that shall receive his doctrine. He shall come with power upon the ungodly, and shall destroy idolatry, insomuch that he shall make Satan confounded; for so promised God to Abraham, saying: "Behold, in thy seed I will bless all the tribes of the earth; and as thou hast broken in pieces the idols, O Abraham, even so shall thy seed do."'

James answered: 'O master, tell us in whom this promise was made; for the Jews say "in Isaac," and the Ishmaelites say "in Ishmael."'

Jesus answered: 'David, whose son was he, and of what lineage?'

James answered: 'Of Isaac; for Isaac was father of Jacob and Jacob was father of Judah, of whose lineage is David.'

Then said Jesus: 'And the messenger of God when he shall come, of what lineage will he be:'

The disciples answered: 'Of David.'

Whereupon Jesus said: 'Ye deceive yourselves; for David in spirit calleth him lord,[77] saying thus: "God said to my lord, sit thou on my right hand until I make thine enemies thy footstool. God shall send forth thy rod which shall have lordship in the midst of thine enemies? If the messenger of God whom ye call Messiah were son of

---

[77] *David in spirit calleth him Lord.* Ps. 110:1-2.

David, how should David call him lord? Believe me, for verily I say to you, that the promise was made in Ishmael,[78] not in Isaac.'

44.

Thereupon said the disciples: 'O master, it is thus written in the book of Moses, that in Isaac was the promise made.'

Jesus answered, with a groan: 'It is so written, but Moses wrote it not, nor Joshua, but rather our rabbis, who fear not God. Verily I say unto you, that if ye consider the words of the angel Gabriel, ye shall discover the malice of our scribes and doctors. For the angel said: "Abraham, all the world shall know how God loveth thee; but how shall the world know the love that thou bearest to God? Assuredly it is necessary that thou do something for love of God." Abraham answered: "Behold the servant of God, ready to do all that which God shall will."

'Then spake God, saying to Abraham: "Take thy son, thy firstborn Ishmael, and come up the mountain to sacrifice him." How

---

[78] *the promise was made in Ishmael.* First of all, as already shown, Hagar in accordance with the law, was the legitimate wife of Abraham as was Sarah, which is why their names do not appear in I Chr. 1:1-34; but rather their sons as the heirs of their father and progenitors of his descendants. Furthermore, Gen. 12:1-3, shows that the covenant was made not with Isaac, but with Abraham, signifying that Ishmael, his first-born, and Isaac, were equally to be blessed initially. The promise to bless Abraham and his seed being made long before his sons were born. However, that the promise (the desire of all nations) would come forth from Ishmael, the firstborn, is demonstrated in a number of additional factors: 1) The promise given by God to Abraham that He would greatly multiply Abraham's seed (Gen. 15:5), is the same promise God made to Abraham's wife: Hagar (Gen. 16:10). And indeed, the Arabs greatly outnumber the Israelites, and always have. And the Muslims as Abraham's spiritual descendants through Ishmael, exceedingly outnumber the Jews; 2) The covenant was made again by God with Abraham after Ismael was born, while Abraham had no reason to hope for another son, for there had ben no promise that Sarah would bear him a son. The promise in Gen. 15:4, having been fulfilled in the birth of Ishmael, whose very name pertains to the promise. In Gen. 17:2-6; God promised that in addition to a great multitude of descendants, nations and rulers of nations would come forth from Abraham. History bears out the fact that this promise has ever been fulfilled in Ishmael, rather than in Isaac; 3) The covenant was renewed with Ishmael after Isaac was promised: "And as for Ishmael I have heard thee; behold I have blessed him and will make him fruitful, and will multiply him exceedingly; twelve princes shall he beget, and I will make him a great nation" (Gen. 17:20). God's hearing Abraham regarding Ishmael, refers to Gen. 17:18. Ishmael's very name signifies that the promise was in his line, it means "he whom the Lord God hears." The promise was in Ishmael, the first-born, not in Isaac.

is Isaac firstborn,[79] if when Isaac was born Ishmael was seven years old?

Then said the disciples: 'Clear is the deception of our doctors: Therefore tell us thou the truth, because we know that thou art sent from God.'

Then answered Jesus: 'Verily I say unto you, that Satan ever seeketh to annul the laws of God; and therefore he with his followers, hypocrites and evil-doers, the former with false doctrine, the latter with lewd living, to-day have contaminated almost all things, so that scarcely is the truth found. Woe to the hypocrites! For the praises of this world shall turn for them into insults and torments in hell.

'I therefore say unto you that the messenger of God is a splendor that shall give gladness to nearly all that God hath made, for he is adorned with the spirit of understanding and of counsel, the spirit of wisdom and might, the spirit of fear and love, the spirit of prudence and temperance, he is adorned with the spirit of charity and mercy, the spirit of justice and piety, the spirit of gentleness and patience, which he hath received from God three times more than he hath given to all his creatures. O blessed time, when he shall come to the world! Believe me that I have seen him and have done him reverence, even as every prophet hath seen him: Seeing that of his spirit God giveth to them prophecy. And when I saw him my soul was filled with consolation, saying: "O Mohammed, God be with thee, and may he make me worthy to untie thy shoelatchet, for obtaining this I shall be a great prophet and holy one of God."'

And having said this, Jesus rendered his thanks to God.

45.

Then came the angel Gabriel to Jesus, and spake to him in such wise that we also heard his voice, which said: 'Arise, and go unto Jerusalem!'

Accordingly Jesus departed and went up to Jerusalem. And on

[79] *How is Isaac firstborn?* Gen. 17:25, says that Ishamel was 14 years old when circumcised, which would make him about 14 years old when Isaac was born. But in Gen. 21:14, the picture we are given is not that of a man handing up to his wife Hagar, sitting on a riding animal, a 14 year old teenager. The picture given, is that of a man handing up to his wife, a young boy. Further evidence of this discrepancy in Genesis, is in Gen. 21:15 where we are told that Hagar cast the child Ishamel, under a bush. A woman might cast a young boy of 7, under a shrub, but certainly not a young man 14 years old. Not only was Ishmael 7 years old when Isaac was born, as Jesus has pointed out, but Ishmael was the firstborn with all rights of the first-born.

the Sabbath day he entered into the temple, and began to teach the people. whereupon the people ran together to the temple with the high priest and priests, who drew nigh to Jesus, saying: 'O master, it hath been said to us that thou sayest evil of us; therefore beware lest some evil befall thee.'

Jesus answered: 'Verily I say unto you, that I speak evil of the hypocrites; therefore if ye be hypocrites I speak against you.'

They answered: 'Who is a hypocrite? Tell us plainly.'

Said Jesus: 'Verily I say to you, that he who doeth a good thing in order that men may see him, even he is a hypocrite, forasmuch as his work penetrateth not the heart which men cannot see, and so leaveth therein every unclean thought and every filthy lust. Know ye who is hypocrite? He who with his tongue serveth God, but with his heart serveth men. O wretched man! For dying loseth all his reward. For on this matter saith the prophet David:[80] "Put not your confidence in princes, (nor) in the children of men, in whom is no salvation; for at death their thoughts perish:" nay, before death they find themselves deprived of reward, for "Man is," as said Job the prophet[81] of God, "unstable, so that he never continueth in one stay." So that if today he praiseth thee, tomorrow he will abuse thee, and if today he willeth to reward thee, tomorrow he will be fain to despoil thee. Woe, then, to the hypocrites, because their reward is vain. As God liveth, in whose presence I stand, the hypocrite is a robber and committeth sacrilege inasmuch as he maketh use of the law to appear good, and thieveth the honor of God, to whom alone pertaineth praise and honor forever.

'Furthermore I say to you, that the hypocrite hath not faith, forasmuch as if he believed that God seeth all and with terrible judgment would punish wickedness, he would purify his heart, which, because he hath not faith, he keepeth full of iniquity. Verily I say unto you, that the hypocrite is as a sepulchre, that without is white, but within is full of corruption and worms. So then if ye, O priests, do the service of God because God hath created you and asketh it of you, I speak not against you, for ye are servants of God; but if ye do all for gain, and so buy and sell in the temple as in a market-place, not regarding that the temple of God is a house of prayer and not of merchandise, which ye convert into a cave of robbers: If ye do all to please men, and have put God out of your mind; then cry I against you that ye are sons of the devil, and not sons of Abraham, who left his father's house for love of God, and was willing

---

[80] *saith the prophet David:* Ps. 146:3-4.
[81] *as said Job the prophet.* Job 14:2.

to slay his own son. Woe unto you, priests and doctors, if ye be such for God will take away from you the priesthood!'

46.

Again spake Jesus, saying: 'I set before you an example. There was a householder who planted a vineyard, and made a hedge for it in order that it should not be trampled down of beasts. And in the midst of it he built a press for the wine, and thereupon let it out to husbandmen. Whereupon, when the time was come to collect the wine he sent his servants; whom when the husbandmen saw, they stoned some and burned some, and others they ripped open with a knife. And this they did many times. Tell me, what will the lord of the vineyard do to the husbandmen?'

Every one answered: 'In evil wise will he make them to perish, and his vineyard will he give to other husbandmen.'

Therefore said Jesus: 'Know ye not that the vineyard is the house of Israel, and the husbandmen are the people of Judah and Jerusalem? Woe to you; for God is wroth with you, having ripped open so many prophets of God; so that at the time of Ahab[82] there was not found one to bury the holy ones of God!'

And when he had said this the chief priests wished to seize him, but they feared the common people, which magnified him.

Then Jesus, seeing a woman who from her birth had remained with her head bent toward the ground, said: 'Raise thy head, O woman, in the name of our God, in order that these may know that I speak truth, and that he willeth that I announce it.'

Then the woman raised herself up whole, magnifying God.

The chief of the priests cried out, saying: 'This man is not sent of God, seeing he keepeth not the Sabbath; for today he hath healed an infirm person.'

Jesus answered: 'Now tell me, is it not lawful to speak on the Sabbath day, and to make prayer for the salvation of others? And who is there among you who, if on the Sabbath his ass or his ox fell into the ditch, would not pull him out on the Sabbath? Assuredly none. And shall I then have broken the Sabbath day by having given health to a daughter of Israel? Of a surety, here is known thy

---

[82] *the time of Ahab*. The Essenes held the doctrine that throughout Israelite history the Abrahamic covenant - renewed on Mount Sinai - had been maintained and preserved throughout history by a succession of "pious remnants," who remained faithful to the law. (*The Dead Sea Scriptures*, p.4) Thus when Jesus spoke of the "holy ones of God" living back during the time of Ahab (r. 919-896 B.C.), this was in character with this Essene belief.

hypocrisy! Oh, how many are there today that fear the smiting of a straw in another's eye, while a beam is ready to cut off their own head? Oh, how many there are that fear an ant, but reck not of an elephant!'

And having said this, he went forth from the temple. But the priests chafed with rage among themselves, because they were not able to seize him and to work their will upon him, even as their fathers have done against the holy ones of God.

47.

Jesus went down, in the second year of his prophetic ministry, from Jerusalem, and went to Nain. Whereupon, as he drew nigh to the gate of the city, the citizens were bearing to the sepulchre the only son of his mother, a widow, over whom every one was weeping. Whereupon, when Jesus had arrived, the men understood how that Jesus, a prophet of Galilee, was come: and so they set themselves to beseech him for the dead man, that he being a prophet should raise him up; which also his disciples did. Then Jesus feared greatly, and turning himself to God, said: 'Take me from the world, O Lord, for the world is mad, and they wellnigh call me God!' And having said this, he wept.

Then came the angel Gabriel, and said: 'O Jesus, fear not, for God hath given thee power over every infirmity, insomuch that all that thou shalt grant in the name of God shall be entirely accomplished.' Hereupon Jesus gave a sigh, saying: 'Thy will be done, Lord God almighty and merciful.' And having said this, he drew near to the mother of the dead, and with pity said to her: 'Woman, weep not,' And having taken the hand of the dead, he said: 'I say unto thee, young man, in the name of God arise up healed!'

Then the boy revived, whereupon all were filled with fear, saying: 'God hath raised up a great prophet amongst us, and he hath visited his people.'

48.

At that time the army of the Romans was in Judea, our country being subject to them for the sins of our forefathers. Now it was the custom of the Romans to call god and to worship him that did any new thing of benefit to the common people. And so (some) of these soldiers finding themselves in Nain, they rebuked now one, now another, saying: 'One of your gods hath visited you, and ye make no account of it. Assuredly if our gods should visit us we should give them all that we have. And ye see how much we fear our gods, since to their images we give the best of all we have.' Satan did so instigate this manner of speaking that he aroused no small sedition among the people of Nain. But Jesus tarried not at all in Nain, but turned to go into Capernaum. The discord of Nain was such that some said: 'He is our God who hath visited us'; others said: 'God is invisible, so that none hath seen him, not even Moses, his servant; therefore it is not God, but rather his son.' Others said: 'He is not God, nor son of God,[83] for God hath not a body to beget withal; but he is a great prophet of God.'

And so did Satan instigate that, in the third year of the prophetic ministry of Jesus, great ruin to our people was like to arise therefrom.

Jesus went into Capernaum: whereupon the citizens, when they knew him, assembled together all the sick folk they had, and placed them in front of the porch (of the house) where Jesus was lodging with his disciples. And having, called Jesus forth, they besought him for the health of them. Then Jesus laid his hands upon each of them, saying: 'God of Israel, by thy holy name, give health to this sick person.' Whereupon each one was healed.

On the Sabbath Jesus entered into the synagogue, and thither ran together all the people to hear him speak.

49.

The scribe that day read the psalm of David,[84] where saith David: 'When I shall find a time, I will judge uprightly.' Then, after the reading of the prophets, arose Jesus, and made sign of silence with his hands, and opening his mouth he spake thus: 'Brethren, ye have heard the words spoken by David the prophet, our father, that when he should have found a time he would judge uprightly. I tell

---

[83] *He is not God, nor son of God.* Two things typically characterized the gods of the pagans, first, their requirement of bloody human sacrifice for the remission of sin; and second, the representation of them as the sons of themselves, and therefore the representation of them - according to their theologies - as the "son of God." Thus the rejection of human sacrifices by the God of Abraham (Gen. 22:10-14.), clearly demonstrated to Abraham and to us, that the true God is not to be confused with the savage representations of deity presented by the pagans. Another characteristic of the God of Abraham, says Professor Albright, is that He is One and alone, He has no fathers, sons, daughters, or female companions. Therefore no being, human or otherwise, is the son of the God of Abraham. The Israelites knew this, but through the adoption of pagan thought and ways some of them at Nain uttered such blasphemy while others tried to correct them. (From The Stone Age To Christianity, p. 261.)

[84] *read the psalm of David.* Ps. 75:2

you in truth that many judge, in which judgment they fall for no other reason than because they judge that which is not meet for them, and that which is meet for them they judge before the time. Wherefore the God of our fathers crieth to us by his prophet David, saying: 'Justly judge,[85] O sons of men'. Miserable therefore are those who set themselves at street corners, and do nothing but judge all those who pass by, saying: "That one is fair, this one is ugly, that one is good, this one is bad." Woe unto them, because they lift the scepter of his judgment from the mind of God, who saith: "I am witness and judge, and my honor I will give to none." Verily I tell you that these testify of that which they have not seen nor really heard, and judge without having been constituted judges. Therefore are they abominable on the earth before the eyes of God, who will pass tremendous judgment upon them in the last day. Woe to you, woe to you who speak good of the evil, and call the evil good,[86] for ye condemn as a malefactor God, who is the author of good, and justify as good Satan, who is the origin of all evil. Consider what punishment ye shall have, and that it is horrible to fall into the judgment of God, which shall be then upon those who justify the wicked for money, and judge not the cause of the orphans and widows.[87] Verily I say unto you, that the devils shall tremble at the judgment of such, so terrible shall it be. Thou man who art set as a judge, regard no other thing; neither kinsfolk nor friends, neither honor nor gain, but look solely with fear of God to the truth, which thou shalt seek with greatest diligence, because it will secure thee in the judgment of God. But I warn thee that without mercy shall he be judged who judgeth without mercy.'

50.

'Tell me, O man, thou that judgest another man, dost thou not know that all men had their origin in the same clay? Dost thou not know that none is good save God alone? wherefore every man is a liar and a sinner. Believe me, man, that if thou judge others of a fault thine own heart hath whereof to be judged. Oh, how dangerous it is to judge! Oh, how many have perished by their false judgment! Satan judged man to be more vile than himself; therefore he rebelled against God, his creator: whereof he is impenitent, as I have knowledge by speaking with him. Our first parents judged the speech of Satan to be good, therefore they were cast out of paradise, and

---

[85] *justly judge.* Ps. 58:16.
[86] *and call the evil good.* Isa. 5:20.
[87] *orphans and widows.* Isa. 1:23.

condemned all their progeny.[88] Verily I say unto you, as God liveth in whose presence I stand, false judgment is the father of all sins. Forasmuch as none sinneth without will, and none willeth that which he doth not know. Woe, therefore, to the sinner who with the judgment judgeth sin worthy and goodness unworthy, who on that account rejecteth goodness and chooseth sin. Assuredly he shall bear an intolerable punishment when God shall come to judge the world. Oh, how many have perished through false judgment, and how many have been nigh to perishing! Pharaoh judged Moses and the people of Israel to be impious, Saul judged David to be worthy of death, Ahab judged Elijah, Nebuchadnezzar the three children who would not worship their lying gods. The two elders judged Susanna, and all the idolatrous princes judged the prophets. Oh, tremendous judgment of God! The judge perisheth, the judged is saved. And wherefore this, O man, if not because (in) rashness they falsely judge the innocent? How nearly then the good approached to ruin by judging falsely, is shown by the brethren of Joseph, who sold him to the Egyptians, by Aaron and Miriam, sister of Moses, who judged their brother. Three friends of Job judged the innocent friend of God, Job. David judged Mephibosheth and Uriah. Cyrus judged Daniel to be meat for the lions; and many others, the which were nigh to their ruin for this. Therefore I say to you, Judge not and ye shall not be judged.' And then, Jesus having finished his speech, many forthwith were converted to repentance, bewailing their sins; and they would fain have forsaken all to go with him. But Jesus said: 'Remain in your homes, and forsake sin and serve God with fear, and thus shall ye be saved; because I am not come to receive service, but rather to serve.'

---

[88] *condemned all their progeny.* In his innocence, before man's fall, he was unaware that he could do wrong. In the Biblical account man's freewill is symbolized by "the tree of knowledge of good and evil" (Gen. 2:17; 3:9). While in the Quranic account the Devil calls it: "the tree of immortality" (Q. 20:120), because he sought to deceive them into bringing about the termination of their innocence by making them aware of their ability to do evil, just as they could do good. As a result of their mistake in judgement, in listening to Satan, they initiated man's struggle through the ages with the negative side of his nature. That side which he must now overcome to regain the state he once enjoyed before the fall. In chapter 39, Jesus used apples and corn (grain) as symbols, instead of the tree. The symbols used by him relate to the agricultural based rituals of Canaanite idolatry which focussed on the earth-mother goddess, Astarte and her consort, Baal. These rituals were aimed at promoting fertility in the soil to provide abundant harvests of grain and other foodstuffs. The tendency of his people after settling in Canaan, to adopt such cults, and/or to worship God by such immoral rites, is that which he is specifically focusing on. For the apple was sacred to Astarte, and therefore, like the corn (grain), symbolic of Canaanite idolatry.

And having said thus, he went out of the synagogue and the city, and retired into the desert to pray, because he loved solitude greatly.

51.

When he had prayed to the Lord, his disciples came to him and said: 'O master, two things we would know; one is, how thou talkest with Satan, who nevertheless thou sayest is impenitent; the other is, how God shall come to judge in the day of judgment.' Jesus replied: 'Verily I say unto you I had compassion on Satan, knowing his fall, and I had compassion on mankind whom he tempteth to sin. Therefore I prayed and fasted to our God, who spake to me by his angel Gabriel: "What seekest thou, O Jesus, and what is thy request?" I answered: "Lord, thou knowest of what evil Satan is the cause, and that through his temptations many perish; he is thy creature, Lord, whom thou didst create; therefore, Lord, have mercy upon him."

'God answered: "Jesus, behold I will pardon him. Only cause him to say, 'Lord, my God, I have sinned, have mercy upon me,' and I will pardon him and restore him to his first state."

'I rejoiced greatly,' said Jesus, 'when I heard this, believing that I had made this peace. Therefore I called Satan, who came, saying: "What must I do for thee, O Jesus?"

'I answered: "Thou shalt do it for thyself, O Satan, for I love not thy services, but for thy good have I called thee."

'Satan replied: "If thou desirest not my services, neither desire I thine; for I am nobler than thou,[89] therefore thou art not worthy to serve me - thou who art clay, while I am spirit."

'Let us leave this,' I said, 'and tell me if it were not well thou shouldst return to thy first beauty and thy first state. Thou must know that the angel Michael must needs on the day of judgement strike thee with the sword of God one hundred thouand times, and each blow will give thee the pain of ten hells.'

'Satan replied: "We shall see in that day who can do most; certainly I shall have on my side many angels[90] and most potent idolaters who will trouble God, and he shall know how great a mistake he made to banish me for the sake of a vile (piece of) clay."

---

[89] *I am nobler than thou.* (i.e., I am better than you.) These are the words and thoughts of the bigot, whether he bases this notion on his national identity, class or caste; his wealth, religious affiliation, or the color of his skin, he or she, bears the mark of Satan.

[90] *on my side many angels.* Here the arch deceiver is actually referring to the Jinn.

'Then I said: "O Satan, thou art infirm in mind, and knowest not what thou sayest."

'Then Satan, in a derisive manner, wagged his head, saying: "Come now, let us make up this peace between me and God; and what must be done say thou, O Jesus, since thou art sound in mind."

'I answered: "Two words only need be spoken."

'Satan replied: "What words?"

'I answered: "These: I have sinned; have mercy on me."

'Said Satan then: "Now willingly will I make this peace if God will say these words to me."

'"Now depart from me," I said, "O cursed one, for thou art the wicked author of all injustice and sin, but God is just and without any sin."

'Satan departed shrieking, and said: "It is not so, O Jesus, but thou tellest a lie to please God.'

'Now consider,' said Jesus to his disciples, 'how he will find mercy.'

They answered: 'Never, Lord, because he is impenitent. Speak to us now of the judgment of God.'

52.

'The judgment day of God will be so dreadful[91] that, verily I say unto you, the reprobates would sooner choose ten hells than go to hear God speak in wrath against them. Against whom all things created will witness. Verily I say unto you, that not alone shall the reprobates fear, but the saints and the elect of God, so that Abraham, shall not trust in his righteousness, and Job shall have no confidence in his innocence. And what say I? Even the messenger of God shall fear, for that God, to make known his majesty, shall deprive his messenger of memory, so that he shall have no remembrance how that God hath given him all things. Verily I say unto you that, speaking from the heart, I tremble because by the world I shall be called God,[92] and for this I shall have to render an account. As God liveth, in whose presence my soul standeth, I am a mortal man as other men are, for although God has placed me as prophet over the

[91] *will be dreadful.* Whether Jesus is speaking throughout this chapter metaphorically or literally, and in the several others that follow, it stands to reason that God being the knower of all things, knew that the true teachings of Jesus would come to light in this document; and that those who read it would better understand many things. Consider the words of the Quran 22:1-4.

[92] *by the world I shall be called God.* Here Jesus prophesies concerning the Nicolaitan conspiracy which led to the establishment of Gentile Christianity. (See *The Dead Sea Scrolls, The Gospel of Barnabas,* and *The New Testament.*)

house of Israel for the health of the feeble and the correction of sinners, I am the servant of God, and of this ye are witness, how I speak against those wicked men who after my departure from the world shall annul the truth of my gospel by the operation of Satan. But I shall return towards the end, and with me shall come Enoch and Elijah, and we will testify against the wicked, whose end shall be accursed.' And having thus spoken, Jesus shed tears, whereat his disciples wept aloud, and lifted their voices, saying: 'Pardon, O Lord God, and have mercy on thy innocent servant.' Jesus answered: 'Amen, Amen.'

53.

'Before that day shall come,' said Jesus, 'great destruction shall come upon the world, for there shall be war so cruel and pitiless that the father shall slay the son, and the son shall slay the father by reason of the factions of peoples. Wherefore the cities shall be annihilated, and the country shall become desert. Such pestilences shall come that none shall be found to bear the dead to burial, so that they shall be left as food for beasts. To those who remain upon the earth God shall send such scarcity that bread shall be valued above gold, and they shall eat all manner of unclean things. O miserable age, in which scarce any one shall be heard to say: "I have sinned, have mercy on me, O God"; but with horrible voices they shall blaspheme him who is glorious and blessed for ever. After this, as that day draweth nigh, for fifteen days, shall come every day a horrible sign over the inhabitants of the earth. The first day the sun shall run its course in heaven without light but black as the dye of cloth; and it shall give groans as a father who groaneth for a son nearing to death. The second day the moon shall be turned into blood, and blood shall come upon the earth like dew. The third day the stars shall be seen to fight among themselves like an army of enemies. The fourth day the stones and rocks shall dash against each other as cruel enemies. The fifth day every plant and herb shall weep blood. The sixth day the sea shall rise without leaving its place to the height of one hundred and fifty cubits, and shall stand all day like a wall. The seventh day it shall on the contrary sink so low as scarcely to be seen. The eighth day the birds and the animals of the earth and of the water shall gather themselves close together, and shall give forth roars and cries. The ninth day there shall be a hailstorm so horrible that it shall kill in such wise that scarcely the tenth part of the living shall escape. The tenth day shall come such horrible lightning and thunder that the third part of the mountains shall be split and scorched. The eleventh day every river shall run backwards, and shall run blood and not water. The twelfth day every created thing shall groan and cry. The thirteenth day the heaven shall be rolled up like a book, and it shall rain fire, so that every living thing shall die. The fourteenth day there shall be an earthquake so horrible that the tops of the mountains shall fly through the air like birds, and all the earth shall become a plain. The fifteenth day the holy angels shall die, and God alone shall remain alive; to whom be honor and glory.'

And having said this, Jesus smote his face with both his hands, and then smote the ground with is head. And having raised his head, he said: 'Cursed be every one who shall insert into my sayings that I am the son of God.' At these words the disciples fell down as dead, whereupon Jesus lifted them up, saying: 'Let us fear God now, if we would not be affrighted in that day.'

54.

'When these signs be passed, there shall be darkness over the world forty years, God alone being alive, to whom be honor and glory for ever. When the forty years be passed, God shall give life to his messenger, who shall rise again like the sun, but resplendent as a thouand suns. He shall sit, and shall not speak, for he shall be as it were beside himself. God shall raise again the four angels favoured of God, who shall seek the messenger of God,[93] and, having found him, shall station themselves on the four sides of the place to keep watch upon him. Next shall God give life to all the angels, who shall come like bees circling round the messenger of God. Next shall God give life to all his prophets, who, following Adam, shall go every one to kiss the hand of the messenger of God, committing themselves to his protection. Next shall God give life to all the elect, who shall cry out: "O Mohammed, be mindful of us!" At whose cries pity shall awake in the messenger of God, and he shall consider what he ought to do, fearing for their salvation. Next shall God give life to every

---

[93] *the messenger of God.* "I will raise them [the Israelites] up a Prophet from among [not themselves, but] their brethren [the Ishmaelites], like unto thee [Moses, a husband, a father, lawgiver, statesman and general] and will put my words in his mouth, and he shall speak unto them all that I shall command him. And it shall come to pass, that whosoever will not hearken unto my words which he shall speak in my name, [In the name of God, the Beneficent, the Merciful; is the opening declaration of the Quran], I will require it of him." (Deut. 18:18-19). Not only was Prophet Muhammad all the above things Moses was, but both of them were Arabs. Moses through marriage, and thus naturalization, having also adopted the culture (Ex. 2:21), while Muhammad was Ishmaelite by birth, and culture. No other Prophet is so much like Moses as Muhammad. Those who will seek his protection, will be those who have heeded his message.

created thing, and they shall return to their former existence, but every one shall besides possess the power of speech. Next shall God give life to all the reprobates, at whose resurrection, by reason of their hideousness, all the creatures of God shall be afraid, and shall cry: "Let not thy mercy forsake us, O Lord our God." After this shall God cause Satan to be raised up, at whose aspect every creature shall be as dead, for fear of the horrid form of his appearance. May it please God,' said Jesus, 'that I behold not that monster on that day. The messenger of God alone shall not be affrighted by such shapes because he shall fear God only.

'Then the angel, at the sound of whose trumpet all shall be raised, shall sound his trumpet again, saying: "Come to the judgment, O creatures, for your Creator willeth to judge you." Then shall appear in the midst of heaven over the valley of Jehoshaphat a glittering throne, over which shall come a white cloud, whereupon the angels shall cry out: "Blessed be thou our God, who hast created us, and saved us from the fall of Satan." Then the messenger of God shall fear, for that he shall perceive that none hath loved God as he should. For he who would get in change a piece of gold must have sixty mites; wherefore, if he have but one mite he cannot change it. But if the messenger of God shall fear, what shall the ungodly do who are full of wickedness?'

55.

'The messenger of God shall go to collect all the prophets, to whom he shall speak, praying them to go with him to pray God for the faithful. And everyone shall excuse himself for fear; nor, as God liveth, would I go there, knowing what I know. Then God, seeing this, shall remind his messenger how he created all things for love of him, and so his fear shall leave him, and he shall go nigh unto the throne with love and reverence, while the angels sing: "Blessed be thy holy name, O God, our God."

'And when he hath drawn nigh unto the throne, God shall open (his mind) unto his messenger, even as a friend unto a friend when for a long while they have not met. The first to speak shall be the messenger of God, who shall say: "I adore and love thee, O my God, and with all my heart and soul I give thee thanks for that thou didst vouchsafe to create me to be thy servant, and madest all for love of me, so that I might love thee for all things and in all things and above all things; therefore let all thy creatures praise thee, O my God." Then all things created by God shall say: "We give thee thanks, O Lord, and bless thy holy name." Verily I say unto you, the demons and reprobates with Satan shall then weep so that more water shall flow from the eyes of one of them than is in the river of Jordan. Yet shall they not see God.

'And God shall speak unto his messenger, saying: "Thou art welcome, O my faithful servant; therefore ask what thou wilt, for thou shalt obtain all." The messenger of God shall answer, "O Lord, I remember that when thou didst create me, thou saidst that thou hadst willed to make for love of me the world and paradise, and angels and men, that they might glorify thee by me thy servant. Therefore, Lord God, merciful and just. I pray thee that thou recollect thy promise made unto thy servant."

'And God shall make answer even as a friend who jesteth with a friend, and shall say: "Hast thou witnesses of this, my friend Mohammed?" And with reverence he shall say: "Yes, Lord." Then God shall answer: "Go, call them, O Gabriel." The angel Gabriel shall come to the messenger of God, and shall say: "Lord, who are thy witnesses?" The messenger of God shall answer: "They are Adam, Abraham, Ishmael, Moses, David, and Jesus son of Mary."

'Then shall the angel depart, and he shall call the aforesaid witnesses, who with fear shall go thither. And when they are present God shall say unto them: "Remember ye that which my messenger affirmeth?" They shall reply: "What thing, O Lord?" God shall say: "That I have made all things for love of him, so that all things might praise me by him." [94] Then every one of them shall answer: "There are with us three witnesses better than we are, O Lord." And God shall reply: "Who are these three witnesses?" Then Moses shall say "The book that thou gavest to me is the first"; and David shall say: "The book that thou gavest to me is the second": and he who speaketh to you shall say: "Lord, the whole world, deceived by Satan, said that

---

[94] *so that all things might praise me by him.* In allegory we are being told in this chapter, that all of creation was preordained to benefit mankind, even in the ultimate triumph of man's struggle to subdue the negative side of his nature which leads him to rebel against God. In this struggle man has been directed and aided by the messages entrusted to the prophets by God, the best of which have culminated in the final message entrusted to Prophet Muhammad, the essence of which is that: "There is no God, but God." The culmination of all that has thus far occurred, beginning with creation, will come about with the Day of Judgement. In that day will be the final triumph of truth over falsehood, and good over evil. From that day forward submission to the will of God will ever be mankind's way of life. And thus the drama that began with creation, and has come to pass through stages, will reach its conclusion on that final day. Every prophet has had a major role as events unfolded leading up to the advent and role of the universal prophet, whose mission was to propagate the final message which will lead up to the ultimate triumph. Of his message, the last message, we are told by God in the Quran: "This day have I perfected for you your religion and completed My favor to you and chosen for you Islam (submission to God) as a religion (way of life)" (Quran: 5:4).

I was thy son and thy fellow, but the book that thou gavest me said truly that I am thy servant; and that book confesseth[95] that which thy messenger affirmeth." Then shall the messenger of God speak, and shall say: "Thus saith the book that thou gavest me, O Lord." And when the messenger of God hath said this, God shall speak, saying: "All that I have now done, I have done in order that every one should know how much I love thee." And when he hath thus spoken, God shall give unto his messenger a book, in which are written all the names of the elect of God. Wherefore every creature shall do reverence to God, saying: "To thee alone, O God, be glory and honor, because thou hast given us to thy messenger."

56.

'God shall open the book in the hand of his messenger, and his messenger reading therein shall call all the angels and prophets and all the elect, and on the forehead of each one[96] shall be written the mark of the messenger of God. And in the book shall be written the glory of paradise.

'Then shall each pass to the right hand of God: next to whom shall sit the messenger of God, and the prophets shall sit near him, and the saints, and the angel shall then sound the trumpet, and shall call Satan to judgment.

57.

'Then that miserable one shall come, and with greatest contumely shall be accused of every creature. Wherefore God shall call the angel Michael, who shall strike him one hundred thouand times with the sword of God. He shall strike Satan, and every stroke is heavy as ten hells, and he shall be the first to be cast into the abyss. The angel shall call his followers, and they shall in like manner be abused and accused. Wherefore the angel Michael, by commission from God, shall strike some a hundred times, some fifty, some twenty, some ten, some five. And then shall they descend into the abyss,

---

[95] *that book that confesseth.* The book of Jesus described in the Acts of Barnabas, as the scroll that was the "Word of God," and in the heading to chapter ten as the "Gospel."

The book of David, referred to here is the original unadulterated book from whence the current version was derived. The same applies to the book of Moses (The Torah).

[96] *on the forehead of each one.* Angels, prophets and all the elect, all who serve God in sincerity and understanding hold dear the awareness of God in their hearts and *minds.* The mark written on the forehead is not literal, but metaphoric. It is: "There is no God, but God."

because God shall say to them: "Hell is your dwelling-place, O cursed ones."

'After that shall be called to judgment all the unbelievers and reprobates, against whom shall first arise all creatures inferior to man, testifying before God how they have served these men, and how the same have outraged God and his creatures. And the prophets every one shall arise, testifying against them; wherefore they shall be condemned by God to infernal flames. Verily I say unto you, that no idle word or thought shall pass unpunished in that tremendous day. Verily I say unto you, that the hair-shirt shall shine like the sun, and every louse a man shall have borne for love of God shall be turned into pearl. O, thrice and four times blessed are the poor, who in true poverty shall have served God from the heart, for in this world are they destitute of worldly cares, and shall therefore be freed from many sins, and in that day they shall not have to render an account of how they have spent the riches of the world, but they shall be rewarded for their patience and their poverty. Verily I say unto you, that if the world knew this it would choose the hair-shirt sooner than purple, lice sooner than gold, fasts sooner than feasts.

'When all have been examined, God shall say unto his messenger: "Behold, O my friend, their wickedness, how great it has been, for I their creator did employ all created things in their service, and in all things have they dishonored me.[97] It is most just, therefore, that I have no mercy on them." The messenger of God shall answer: "It is true, Lord, our glorious God, not one of thy friends and servants could ask thee to have mercy on them; nay, I thy servant before all ask justice against them."

'And he having said these words, all the angels and prophets, with all the elect of God - nay, why say I the elect? - verily I say unto you, that spiders and flies, stones and sand shall cry out against the impious, and shall demand justice.

'Then shall God cause to return to earth every living soul inferior to man, and he shall send the impious to hell. Who, in going, shall see again that earth, to which dogs and horses and other vile animals shall be reduced. Wherefore shall they say: "O Lord God, cause us also to return to that earth." But that which they ask shall not be granted to them.'

---

[97] *they have dishonored me.* This addresses man's abuse of the environment and lower creatures in addition to all his other evils. It also addresses the evil of the polytheists, for they have made gods out of the forces of nature, while the humanists have made a god out of nature, by attributing to nature the creative attributes of deity.

58.

While Jesus was speaking the disciples wept bitterly. And Jesus wept many tears.

Then after he had wept, John spake: O master, two things we desire to know. The one is, how it is possible that the messenger of God, who is full of mercy and pity, should have no pity on reprobates that day, seeing that they are of the same clay as himself? The other is, how is it to be understood that the sword of Michael is heavy as ten hells then is there more than one hell?' Jesus replied: 'Have ye not heard what David the prophet saith[98] how that the just shall laugh at the destruction of sinners, and shall deride him with these words, saying: "I saw the man who put his hope in his strength and his riches, and forgot God." Verily, therefore, I say unto you, that Abraham shall deride his father, and Adam all reprobate men: and this shall be because the elect, shall rise again so perfect and united to God that they shall not conceive in their minds the smallest thought against his justice; therefore shall each of them demand justice, and above all the messenger of God. As God liveth, in whose presence I stand, though now I weep for pity of mankind, on that day I shall demand justice without mercy against those who despise my words, and most of all against those who defile my gospel.[99]

59.

'Hell is one, O my disciples, and in it the damned shall suffer punishment eternally. Yet hath it seven rooms or regions, one deeper than the other, and he who goeth to the deepest shall suffer greater punishment. Yet are my words true concerning the sword of the angel Michael, for he that committeth but one sin meriteth hell, and he that committeth two sins meriteth two hells. Therefore in one hell shall the reprobates feel punishment as though they were in ten, or in a hundred or in a thouand, and the omnipotent God, through his power and by reason of his justice, shall cause Satan to suffer as though he were in ten hundred thouand hells, and the rest each one according to his wickedness.'

Then answered Peter: 'O master, truly the justice of God is great, and today this discourse hath made thee sad; therefore, we pray thee, rest, and to-morrow tell us what hell is like.'

Jesus answered: 'O Peter, thou tellest me to rest; O Peter, thou knowest not what thou sayest, else thou hadst not spoken thus. Verily

---

[98] *David the prophet saith.* Ps. 52:7.
[99] *my gospel.* See chapter ten.

I say unto you, that rest in this present life is the poison of piety and the fire which consumeth every good work. Have ye then forgotten how Solomon, God's prophet, with all the prophets, hath reproved sloth? True it is that he saith "The idle will not work the soil for fear of the cold, therefore in summer shall he beg!'[100] Wherefore he said: "All that thy hand can do, do it without rest." And what saith Job,[101] the most innocent friend of God: "As the bird is born to fly, man is born to work." Verily I say unto you, I hate rest above all things.'

60.

'Hell is one, and is contrary to paradise, as winter is contrary to summer, and cold to heat. He therefore who would describe the misery of hell must needs have seen the paradise of God's delights.

'O place accursed by God's justice for the malediction of the faithless and reprobate, of which said Job, the friend of God: "There is no order there, but everlasting fear!" And Isaiah the prophet, against the reprobate, saith: "Their flame shall not be quenched nor their worm die." [102] And David our father,[103] weeping, said: "Then shall rain upon them lightning and bolts and brimstone and great tempest." O miserable sinners, how loathsome then shall seem to them delicate meats, costly raiment, soft couches, and concord of sweet song! how sick shall make them raging hunger, burning flames, scorching cinders, and cruel torments with bitter weeping!"

And then Jesus uttered a lamentable groan, saying: 'Truly it were better never to have been formed than to suffer such cruel torments. For imagine a man suffering torments in every part of his body, who hath no one to show him compassion, but is mocked of all; tell me, would not this be great pain?'

The disciples answered: 'The greatest.'

Then said Jesus : Now this is a delight (in comparison) of hell. For I tell you in truth, that if God should place in one balance all the pain which all men have suffered in this world and shall suffer till the day of judgment, and in the other one single hour of the pain of hell, the reprobates would without doubt choose the worldly tribulations, for the worldly come from the hand of man, but the others from the hand of devils, who are utterly without compassion. O what cruel fire they shall give to miserable sinners! O what bitter cold, which

---

[100] *in summer shall he beg.* Prov. 20:4.

[101] *what saith Job* . 5:7.

[102] *nor their worms die.* The reference here, is to Isa. 66:24; in which the chastisement of the reprobates in hell is likened to being eaten alive by worms (insect larvae).

[103] *David our father.* Ps. 11:6.

yet shall not temper their flames! What gnashing of teeth and sobbing and weeping! For the Jordan has less water than the tears which every moment shall flow from their eyes. And here their tongues shall curse all things created, with their father and mother, and their Creator, who is blessed for ever.'

61.

Having thus said, Jesus washed himself, with his disciples, according to the law of God written in the book of Moses; and then they prayed. And the disciples seeing him thus sad spake not at all to him that day, but each stood terror-struck at his words.

Then Jesus opening his mouth after the evening (prayer), said: 'What father of a family if he knew that a thief meant to break into his house, would sleep? None assuredly; for he would watch and stand prepared to slay the thief. Do ye not know then that Satan is as a roaring lion that goeth about seeking whom he may devour. Thus he seeketh to make man sin. Verily I say unto you, that if man would act as the merchant he should have no fear in that day, because he would be well prepared. There was a man who gave money to his neighbors that they might trade with it, and the profit should be divided in a just proportion. And some traded well, so that they doubled the money. But some used the money in the service of the enemy of him who gave them the money, speaking evil of him. Tell me now, when the neighbor shall call the debtors to account how shall the matter go? Assuredly he will reward those who traded well, but against the others his anger shall vent itself in reproaches. And then he will punish them according to the law. As God liveth, in whose presence my soul standeth, the neighbor is God, who has given to man all that he hath, with life itself, so that, (man) living well in this world, God may have praise, and man the glory of paradise. For those who live well double their money by their example, because sinners, seeing their example, are converted to repentance; wherefore men who live well shall be rewarded with a great reward. But wicked sinners, who by their sins halve what God has given them, by their lives spent in the service of Satan the enemy of God, blaspheming God and giving offence to others, - tell me what shall be their punishment?'

'It shall be without measure,' said the disciples.

62.

Then said Jesus: 'He who would live well should take example from the merchant who locketh up his shop, and guardeth it day and night with great diligence. And selling again the things which he buyeth he is fain to make a profit; for if he perceiveth that he will lose thereby he will not sell, no, not to his own brother. Thus then should ye do; for in truth your soul is a merchant, and the body is the shop: wherefore what it receiveth from outside, through the senses, is bought and sold by it. And the money is love. See then that with your love ye do not sell nor buy the smallest thought by which ye cannot profit. But let thought, speech, and work be all for love of God; for so shall ye find safety in that day. Verily I say unto you, that many make ablutions and go to pray, many fast and give alms, many study and preach to others, whose end is abominable before God; because they cleanse the body and not the heart, they cry with the mouth not with the heart; they abstain from meats, and fill themselves with sins; they give to others things not good for them, in order that they may be held good; they study that they may know to speak, not to work; they preach to others against that which they do themselves, and thus are condemned by their own tongue. As God liveth, these do not know God with their hearts; for if they knew him they would love him; and since whatsoever a man hath he hath received it from God, even so should he spend all for the love of God.'

63.

After certain days Jesus passed near unto a city of the Samaritans; and they would not let him enter the city, nor would they sell bread to his disciples. Wherefore said James and John: Master may it please thee that we pray God that he send down fire from heaven upon these people?'

Jesus answered; 'Ye know not by what spirit ye are led, that ye so speak. Remember that God determined to destroy Nineveh because he did not find one who feared God in that city; the which was so wicked[104] that God, having called Jonah the prophet to send him to that city, he would fain for fear of the people have fled to Tarsus, wherefore God caused him to be cast into the sea, and received by a fish and cast up nigh to Nineveh. And he preaching there, that people was converted to repentance, so that God had mercy on them.

Woe unto them that call for vengeance; for on themselves it shall come, seeing that every man hath in himself cause for the vengeance of God. Now tell me, have ye created this city with this people? O madmen that ye are, assuredly no. For all creatures united together could not create a single new fly from nothing, and this it is to create. If the blessed God who hath created this city now sustaineth

---

[104] *the [inhabitants of] which was so wicked.* See Jonah 1 - 3.

it, why desire ye to destroy it? Why didst thou not say: "May it please thee, master, that we pray to the Lord our God that this people may be converted to penitence?" Assuredly this is the proper act of a disciple of mine, to pray to God for those who do evil. Thus did Abel when his brother Cain, accursed of God, slew him. Thus did Abraham[105] for Pharaoh, who took from him his wife, and whom, therefore, the angel of God did not slay, but only struck with infirmity. Thus did Zechariah[106] when, by decree of the impious king, he was slain in the temple. Thus did Jeremiah, Isaiah, Ezekiel, Daniel, and David, with all the friends of God and holy prophets. Tell me, if a brother were stricken with frenzy, would you slay him because he spoke evil and struck those who came near him? Assuredly ye would not do so; but rather would ye endeavor to restore his health with medicines suitable to his infirmity.'

64.

'As God liveth, in whose presence my soul standeth, a sinner is of infirm mind when he persecuteth a man. For tell me, is there anyone who would break his head for the sake of tearing the cloak of his enemy? Now how can he be of sane mind who separateth himself from God, the head of his soul, in order that he may injure the body of his enemy?

'Tell me, O man, who is thy enemy? Assuredly thy body, and every one who praiseth thee. Wherefore if thou wert of sane mind thou wouldst kiss the hand of those who revile thee, and present gifts to those who persecute thee and strike thee much; because, O man, because the more that for, thy sins thou art reviled and persecuted in this life the less shalt thou be in the day of judgment. But tell me, O man, if the saints and prophets of God have been persecuted and defamed by the world even though they were innocent, what shall be done to thee, O sinner? And if they endured all with patience, praying for their persecutors, what shouldst thou do, O man, who art worthy of hell? Tell me, O my disciples, do ye not know that Shimei[107] cursed the servant of God, David the prophet, and threw stones at him? Now what said David to those who would fain have killed Shimei? "What is it to thee, O Joab, that thou wouldst kill Shimei? let him curse me, for this is the will of God, who will turn this curse into a blessing." And thus it was; for God saw the patience of David and delivered him from the persecution of his own son, Absalom.

---

[105] *Thus did Abraham.* Gen. 12:15-20.
[106] *Thus did Zachariah.* II Chron. 24:20-22.
[107] *that Shimei.* II Sam. 14:5-12.

Assuredly not a leaf stirreth without the will of God. Wherefore, when thou art in tribulation do not think of how much thou hast borne, nor of him who afflicted thee; but consider how much for thy sins thou art worthy to receive at the hand of the devils of hell. Ye are angry with this city because it would not receive us, nor sell bread to us. Tell me, are these people your slaves? Have ye given them this city: Have ye given them their corn? Or have ye helped them to reap it? Assuredly no; for ye are strangers in this land, and poor men. What thing is this then that thou sayest?'

The two disciples answered: 'Lord, we have sinned; may God have mercy on us.'

And Jesus answered: 'So be it.'

65.

The Passover drew near, wherefore Jesus, with his disciples, went up to Jerusalem. And he went to the pool call 'Probatica.' And the bath was so called because the angel of God every day troubled the water, and whosoever first entered the water after its movement was cured of every kind of infirmity. Wherefore a great number of sick persons remained beside the pool, which had five porticoes. And Jesus saw there an impotent man, who had been there thirty-and-eight years, sick with a grievous infirmity. Whereupon Jesus, knowing this by divine inspiration, had compassion on the sick man, and said to him: 'Wilt thou be made whole?'

The impotent man answered: 'Sir, I have no man when the angel troubleth the water to put me into it, but while I am coming another steppeth down before me and entereth therein.'

Then Jesus lifted up his eyes to heaven and said: 'Lord our God, God of our fathers, have mercy upon this impotent man.'

And having said this, Jesus said: 'In God's name, brother, be thou whole; rise and take up thy bed.'

Then the impotent man arose, praising God, and carried his bed upon his shoulders, and went to his house praising God.'

Those who saw him cried: 'It is the Sabbath day; it is not lawful for thee to carry thy bed.'

He answered: 'He that made whole said unto me, "Pick up thy bed, and go thy way to thy home."'

Then asked they him: 'Who is he?'

He answered: 'I know not his name.'

Whereupon, among themselves they said: 'It must have been Jesus the Nazarene.'[108] Others said: 'Nay, for he is a holy one of God,

---

[108] *It must have been Jesus the Nazarene.* Of the Essenes, Josephus says: "They

whereas he who has done this thing is a wicked man, for he causeth the Sabbath to be broken.'

And Jesus went into the temple, and a great multitude drew nigh unto him to hear his words; whereat the priests were consumed with envy.

66.

One of them came to him, saying: 'Good master, thou teachest well and truly; tell me therefore, in paradise what reward shall God give us?'

Jesus answered; 'Thou callest me good, and knowest not that God alone is good, even as said Job,[109] the friend of God: "A child of a day old is not clean; yea, even the angels are not faultless in God's presence." Moreover he said: "The flesh attracteth sin, and sucketh up iniquity even as a sponge sucketh up water."

Wherefore the priest was silent, being confounded. And Jesus said: 'Verily I say unto you, naught is more perilous than speech. For so said Solomon: [110]"Life and death are in the power of the tongue."'

And he turned to his disciples, and said: 'Beware of those who bless you, because they deceive you. With the tongue Satan blessed our first parents, but miserable was the outcome of his words. So did the sages of Egypt bless Pharaoh. So prophets bless Ahab,[111] but false were their praises, so that the praised one perished with the praisers. Wherefore not without cause did God say by Isaiah the prophet: "My people, those that bless thee deceive thee."

'Woe unto you, scribes and Pharisees; woe unto you, priests and Levites, because ye have corrupted the sacrifice of the Lord, so that those who come to sacrifice believe that God eateth cooked flesh like unto a man.'

67.

'For ye say unto them: "Bring of your sheep and bulls and lambs to the temple of your God, and eat not all, but give a share to your

---

are stricter than any other of the Jews in resting from their labors on the seventh day." (Wars of the Jews, Book II 8:2-14.) And this is precisely what Jesus' defenders here, are saying about him: "Nay, for he is a 'holy one of God' (i.e., an Essene), whereas he who has done this thing is a wicked man, for he causeth the sabbath to be broken.: The Nazarenes (preservers and maintainers of the Law) were, according to the evidence, identified as a part of the overall Essene movement for reform.

[109] *as said Job.* Job. 15:14-16.

[110] *For so said Solomon.* Prov. 18:21.

[111] *false prophets bless Ahab.* I Kings 22:6.

God of that which he hath given you''; and ye do not tell them of the origin of sacrifice,[112] that it is for a witness of the life granted to the son of our father Abraham, so that the faith and obedience of our father Abraham, with the promises made to him by God and the blessing given to him, should never be forgotten. But by Ezekiel the prophet[113] saith God: "Remove from me these your sacrifices, your victims are abominable to me.'' For the time draweth near when that shall be done of which our God spake by Hosea the prophet,[114] saying: "I will call chosen the people not chosen.'' And as he saith in Ezekiel the prophet: "God shall make a new covenant with his people, not according to the covenant which he gave to your fathers, which they observed not [115] and he shall take from them a heart of stone, and give them a new heart'': and all this shall be because ye walk not now in his law. And ye have the key and open not: rather do ye block the road for those who would walk in it.'

The priest was departing to report all to the high priest, who stood nigh unto the sanctuary, but Jesus said: 'Stay, for I will answer thy question.'

68.

'Thou askest me to tell thee what God will give us in paradise. Verily I say unto you, that those who think of the wages love not the master. A shepherd who hath a flock of sheep, when he seeth the wolf coming, prepareth to defend them; contrariwise, the hireling when he seeth the wolf leaveth the sheep and fleeth. As God liveth, in whose presence I stand, if the God of our fathers were your God ye would not have thought of saying: "What will God give me?'' But ye would have said, as did David his prophet:[116] "What shall I give unto God for all that he hath given unto me?''

---

[112] *the origin of sacrifice.* The explanation here is that the practice of animal sacrifice unto God amongst the descendants of Abraham, was initiated with the sacrifice of the ram in place of Ishmael, as a reminder of all the blessings He had bestowed upon him. It is also a reminder that God, being the true God, totally rejects the abominable notion that characterizes idolatry, that a man as the supposed incarnation of deity, must be slain as a sacrifice for the redemption of mankind from sin. Such barbarism, and barbaric belief denies the mercy and grace of God.

[113] *Ezekiel the prophet.* Here Jesus quotes from what must have been the original book of this prophet, before any corruption of its text occurred. A similar statement is found in both Isaiah 1:11; and Jeremiah 6:20.

[114] *Hosea the prophet.* Hosea 11:23.

[115] *they observed not.* Once again he is quoting from the aforementioned manuscript. However, a similar statement of condemnation is to be found in Jer.31:31-32.

[116] *David his prophet.* Ps. 116:12.

'I will speak to you by a parable that ye may understand. There was a king who found by the wayside a man stripped by thieves, who had wounded him unto death. And he had compassion on him, and commanded his slaves to bear that man to the city and tend him; and this they did with all diligence. And the king conceived a great love for the sick man, so that he gave him his own daughter in marriage, and made him his heir. Now assuredly this king was most merciful; but the man beat the slaves, despised the medicines, abused his wife, spake evil of the king, and caused his vassals to rebel against him. And when the king required any service, he was wont to say: "What will the king give me as reward?" Now when the king heard this, what did he do to so impious a man?'

They all replied: 'Woe to him, for the king deprived him of all, and cruelly punished him.' Then said Jesus: 'O priests, and scribes, and Pharisees, and thou high-priest that hearest my voice, I proclaim to you what God hath said to you by his prophet Isaiah:[117] "I have nourished slaves and exalted them, but they have despised me."

'The king is our God, who found Israel in this world full of miseries, and gave him therefore to his servants Joseph, Moses and Aaron, who tended him. And our God conceived such love for him that for the sake of the people of Israel he smote Egypt, drowned Pharaoh, and discomfited an hundred and twenty kings[118] of the Canaanites and Madianites; he gave him his laws, making him heir of all that (land) wherein our people dwelleth.

'But how doth Israel bear himself: How many prophets hath he slain; how many prophecies hath he contaminated; how hath he violated the law of God: how many for that cause have departed from God and gone to serve idols, through your offence, O priests! And how do ye dishonor God with your manner of life! And now ye ask me: "What will God give us in paradise?" Ye ought to have asked me: What will be the punishment that God will give you in hell; and then what ye ought to do for true penitence in order that God may have mercy on you: for this I can tell you, and to this end am I sent to you.'

69.

'As God liveth, in whose presence I stand, ye will not receive adulation from me, but truth. Wherefore I say unto you, repent and

---

[117] *by his prophet Isaiah.* Isa. 1:2.

[118] *an hundred and twenty kings.* Joshua, 12:24, alone, accounts for 31 of these kings during the Israelite penetration of Canaan. As for the Midianites, the reference here is to the non-Ishmaelite tribes of Midian who were idolatrous and hostile toward the Israelites.

turn to God even as our fathers did after sinning, and harden not your heart.'

The priests were consumed with rage at this speech, but for fear of the common people they spake not a word.

And Jesus continued, saying: 'O doctors, O scribes, O pharisees, O priests, tell me. Ye desire horses like knights, but ye desire not to go forth to war; ye desire fair clothing like women, but ye desire not to spin and nurture children; ye desire the fruits of the field, and ye desire not to cultivate the earth; ye desire the fishes of the sea, but ye desire not to go a fishing; ye desire honor as citizens, but ye desire not the burden of the republic; and ye desire tithes and first fruits as priests, but ye desire not to serve God in truth. What then shall God do with you, seeing ye desire here every good without any evil? Verily I say to you that God will give you a place where ye will have every evil without any good.'

And when Jesus had said this, there was brought unto him a demoniac who could not speak nor see, and was deprived of hearing. Whereupon Jesus, seeing their faith, raised his eyes to heaven and said: 'Lord God of our fathers, have mercy on this sick man and give him health, in order that this people may know that thou hast sent me.'

And having said this Jesus commanded the spirit to depart, saying: 'In the power of the name of God our Lord, depart, evil one, from the man!'

The spirit departed and the dumb man spoke, and saw with his eyes. Whereupon every one was filled with fear, but the scribes said: 'In the power of Beelzebub, prince of the demons, he casteth out the demons'

Then said Jesus: 'Every kingdom divided against itself destroyeth itself, and house falleth upon house. If in the power of Satan, Satan be cast out, how shall his kingdom stand? And if your sons cast out Satan with the scripture that Solomon the prophet gave them,[119] they testify that I cast out Satan in the power of God. As God liveth, blasphemy against the Holy Spirit[120] is without remission in

---

[119] *Solomon the prophet gave them.* The reference here, is to that which Josephus perhaps best describes: "God also enabled him [Solomon] to learn that skill [prayers and incantations calling upon the power of God] which expels demons, which is a science useful and sanative to men. He composed such incantations also by which distempers are alleviated. And he left behind him the manner of using exorcisms, by which they drive away demons, so that they never return; and this method of cure is of great force unto this day." (Antiquities of the Jews, Book 8, chap. 2:5).

[120] *Holy Spirit.* In this instance the Holy Spirit is "the power of the Most High" acting through the prophet Jesus enabling him to expel the demon, for only by the power of God are such men: prophets and sages, able to do great works.

this and in the other world; because the wicked man of his own will reprobates himself, knowing the reprobation.'

And having said this Jesus went out of the temple. And the common people magnified him, for they brought all the sick folk whom they could gather together, and Jesus having made prayer gave to all their health: whereupon on that day in Jerusalem the Roman soldiery, by the working of Satan, began to stir up the common people, saying that Jesus was the God of Israel, who was come to visit his people.

70.

Jesus departed from Jerusalem after the Passover, and entered into the borders of Caesarea Philippi. Whereupon, the angel Gabriel having told him of the sedition which was beginning among the common people, he asked his disciples, saying: 'What do men say of me?'

They said: 'Some say that thou art Elijah, others Jeremiah, and others one of the old prophets.'

Jesus answered: 'And ye; what say ye that I am?'

Peter answered: 'Thou art Christ, son of God.'

Then was Jesus angry, and with anger rebuked him, saying: 'Begone and depart from me, because thou art the devil and seekest to cause me offence!'

And he threatened the eleven, saying: 'Woe to you if ye believe this, for I have won from God a great curse against those who believe this.'

And he was fain to cast away Peter; whereupon the eleven besought Jesus for him, who cast him not away, but again rebuked him, saying: 'Beware that never again thou say such words, because God would reprobate thee!'

Peter wept, and said: 'Lord, I have spoken foolishly: beseech God that he pardon me.'

Then said Jesus: 'If our God willed not to show himself to Moses his servant, nor to Elijah whom he so loved, nor to any prophet, will ye think that God should show himself to this faithless generation? But know ye not that God hath created all things of nothing with one single word, and all men have had their origin out of a piece of clay? Now, how shall God have likeness to man?[121] Woe to those who suffer themselves to be deceived of Satan!'

---

[121] *Now how shall God have likeness to man?* The notion that God incarnated himself into a man held to be the Son of God, is rooted in the worship of fertility, which characterizes ancient and contemporary idolatry. A classic example of this

And having said this, Jesus besought God for Peter, the eleven and Peter weeping, and saying: 'So be it, so be it, O blessed Lord our God.'

Afterwards Jesus departed and went into Galilee, in order that this vain opinion which the common folk began to hold concerning him might be extinguished.

71.

Jesus having arrived in his own country, it was spread through all the region of Galilee[122] how that Jesus the prophet was come to Nazareth.[123] Whereupon with diligence sought they the sick and brought them to him, beseeching him that he would touch them with his hands. And so great was the multitude that a certain rich man sick of the palsy, not being able to get himself carried through the door, had himself carried up to the roof of the house in which Jesus was, and having caused the roof to be uncovered, and himself let down by sheets in front of Jesus. Jesus stood for a moment in hesitation, and then he said: 'Fear not, brother, for thy sins are forgiven thee.'

---

belief from whence the idea in Christianity was derived, is described by Professor Margaret Murray in her book entitled: *The Splendor That Was Egypt,* in which she says: "It (the Osirian cult) is perhaps the most perfect example of that belief which is found in so many countries, viz. that God (Fertility) is incarnate in man, which belief is usually accompanied by the rite of killing the Divine Man.

The chosen man is almost invariably the king. In him dwells the Spirit of God, and he thus becomes God incarnate. The indwelling Spirit is that of the Creator, the Giver of Life, and to the Incarnate God was therefore ascribed the power to give *fertility* to his people and land. In the eyes of his subjects the king was actually God (Fertility)." (p.164).

But the true God is not fertility, nor does He incarnate himself into man. For what flesh could withstand the awesome majesty of God? It was through the influence of Satan that Peter forgot the words of God: "God is not man, that he should lie; neither the son of man, that he should repent. Hath he said, and shall he not do it: or hath he spoken, and shall he not make it good?" (Num. 23:19). Consider the words of Paul, who himself became guilty of participation in the Nicolaitan conspiracy: "Because when they [the Gentiles] knew God, they glorified him not as God, neither were thankful, but became vain in their imaginations, and their foolish heart was darkened. Professing themselves to be wise, they became fools, and changed the glory of the incorruptible God into an image made like corruptible man, etc." (Rom.1:21-23). Indeed what he says here is applicable to the Nicolaitans who gave the world Christianity.

[122] *all the region of Galilee.* There prevailed throughout Galilee a purer form of the Abrahamic religion than in Judea, despite Judean attempts to destroy it. As Dr. Schonfield points out, it was in this purer form of the faith, that so strongly influenced the communities of Essenes spread across Galilee, that Jesus and his forebears were nurtured (*Passover Plot,* p. 31).

[123] *Nazareth.* Compare the statement here: "It was spread through all the region of

Every one was offended hearing this, and they said: 'And who is this who forgiveth sins?'[124]

Then said Jesus: 'As God liveth, I am not able to forgive sins, nor is any man, but God alone forgiveth. But as servant of God I can beseech him for the sins of others: and so I have besought him for this sick man, and I am sure that God hath heard my prayer. Wherefore, that ye may know the truth, I say to this sick man: "In the name of the God of our fathers, the God of Abraham and his sons, rise up healed!"' And when Jesus had said this the sick man rose up healed, and glorified God.

Then the common people besought Jesus that he would beseech God for the sick who stood outside. Whereupon Jesus went out unto them, and, having lifted up his hands, said: 'Lord God of hosts, the living God, the true God, the holy God, that never will die; have mercy upon them!' Whereupon every one answered: 'Amen.' And this having been said, Jesus laid his hands upon the sick folk, and they all received their health.

Thereupon they magnified God, saying: 'God hath visited us by his prophet,[125] and a great prophet hath God sent unto us.'

72.

At night Jesus spake in secret with his disciples, saying: 'Verily I say unto you that Satan desireth to sift you as wheat; but I have besought God for you, and there shall not perish of you save he that layeth snares for me.' And this he said of Judas, because the angel Gabriel said to him how that Judas had hand with the priests, and reported to them all that Jesus spake.

Galilee how that Jesus the prophet was come to Nazareth," with the statement in chapter twenty: "Jesus went to the sea of Galilee, and having embarked in a ship sailed to his city of Nazareth." The two statements plus the description of events upon Jesus' arrival in both incidents, shows that Jesus' city of Nazareth is not the same as the one mentioned here. (See note to chapter 20). Here we seem to be dealing with the city described by Werner Keller: "Old Nazareth with its little houses of clay walls clustered together, has left many traces behind. Resting 1200 feet above sea level, it lay farther up the hill than the modern village bearing that name." (The Bible as History, P. 402).

[124] *And who is this who forgiveth sins?* This reaction of the inhabitants, and Jesus' speedy reply, characterizes what one would expect from those who still followed a purer form of the faith, and a stricter observance than the Jews.

[125] *God hath visited us by his prophet.* Consider the statement attributed to Peter in *Acts:* "Ye men of Israel, hear these words: Jesus of Nazareth, *a man* approved of God among you by miracles and wonders and signs, *which God did by him* in the midst of you, as ye yourselves know." (*Acts* 2:22) Indeed, in this the Christians fail to perceive the obvious.

With tears drew near unto Jesus he who writeth this, saying: 'O master, tell me, who is he that should betray thee:'

Jesus answered, saying : 'O Barnabas, this is not the hour for thee to know him, but soon will the wicked one reveal himself, because I shall depart from the world.'

Then wept the apostles, saying: 'O master, wherefore wilt thou forsake us? It is much better that we should die than be forsaken of thee!'

Jesus answered: 'Let not your heart be troubled, neither be ye fearful: for I have not created you, but God our creator who hath created you will protect you. As for me, I am now come to the world to prepare the way for the messenger of God, who shall bring salvation to the world. But beware that ye be not deceived, for many false prophets shall come,[126] who shall take my words and contaminate my gospel.'

Then said Andrew: 'Master, tell us some sign, that we may know him.'

Jesus answered: 'He will not come in your time, but will come some years after you, when my gospel shall be annulled, insomuch that there shall be scarcely thirty faithful. At that time God will have mercy on the world, and so he will send his messenger, over whose head will rest a white cloud, whereby he shall be known of one elect of God, and shall be by him manifested to the world. He shall come with great power against the ungodly, and shall destroy idolatry upon the earth. And it rejoiceth me because that through him our God shall be known and glorified, and I shall be known to be true;

---

[126] *false prophets shall come.* Consider the implication of the words of Paul of Tarsus, in his epistle to the Galatians where he says: "But I make known to you brethren, that *the gospel which was preached by me* is not after man, neither was I taught it, but by the revelation of Jesus Christ." (Gal. 1:11-12.) Paul' assertion is that the gospel that he preached was not derived from any human source, but rather that it had been communicated to him by God through Jesus, who was no longer upon the earth. In other words, he had received divine revelation. But in his alleged case, it is Jesus, instead of Gabriel, who supposedly brought him this message from God to take unto men. And as the power of God (the Holy Spirit) enabled the prophets to carry out their ministry, so Paul makes the claim that he too possesses it: "And they (the apostles) glorified God in me." (Gal. 1:24). These two claims combined imply an implied claim to prophethood, whereas if he had only made the latter claim, one might simply say that he was making a claim to be equal to the apostles as the New Testament portrays them. Further evidence of this implied claim to prophethood is provided in the following claim: "In the day when God shall judge the secrets of men by Jesus Christ according to *my gospel*." (Rom. 2:16). Not the gospel of Jesus, but a different message that he claims to have received from God. Indeed, in Paul, Jesus' prophecy was partially fulfilled.

and he will execute vengeance against those who shall say that I am more than man. Verily I say to you that the moon shall minister sleep to him in his boyhood, and when he shall be grown up he shall take her in his hands. Let the world beware of casting him out because he shall slay the idolaters, for many more were slain by Moses,[127] the servant of God, and Joshua, who spared not the cities which they burnt, and slew the children; for to an old wound one applieth fire.

'He shall come with truth more clear than that of all the prophets, and shall reprove him who useth the world amiss. The towers of the city of our father shall greet one another for joy: and so when idolatry shall be seen to fall to the ground and confess me a man like other men, verily I say unto you the messenger of God shall be come.'

73.

'Verily I say unto you, that if Satan shall try whether ye be friends of God - because no one assaileth his own cities, - if Satan should have his will over you he would suffer you to glide at your own pleasure; but because he knoweth that ye be enemies to him he will do every violence to make you perish. But fear not ye, for he will be aginst you as a dog that is chained, because God hath heard my prayer.'

John answered: 'O master, not only for us, but for them that shall believe the gospel, tell us how the ancient tempter layeth wait for man.'

Jesus answered: 'In four ways tempteth that wicked one. The first is when he tempteth by himself, with thoughts. The second is when he tempteth with words and deeds by means of his servants; the third is when he tempteth with false doctrine; the fourth is when he tempteth with false visions. Now how cautious ought men to be, and all the more according as he hath in his favour the flesh of man, which loveth sin as he who hath fever loveth water. Verily I say unto you, that if a man fear God he shall have victory over all, as saith David his prophet:[128] "God shall give his angels charge over thee, who shall keep thy ways, so that the devil shall not cause thee to stumble. A thousand shall fall on thy left hand, and ten thousand on thy right hand, so that they shall not come nigh thee."

'Furthermore, our God with great love promised to us by the same David[129] to keep us, saying: "I give unto thee understanding,

---

[127] *slain by Moses.* Ex. 32:1-28.
[128] *as saith David his prophet.* Ps. 91:11, 12, 7.
[129] *the same David.* Ps. 32:8.

which shall teach thee; and in thy ways wherein thou shalt walk I will cause Mine eye to rest upon thee."

'But what shall I say? He hath said by Isaiah:[130] "Can a mother forget the child of her womb? But I say unto thee, that when he forget, I will not forget thee."

'Tell me, then, who shall fear Satan, having for guard the angels and for protection the living God? Nevertheless, it is necessary, as saith the prophet Solomon,[131] that "Thou, my son, that art come to fear the Lord, prepare thy soul for temptations." Verily I say unto you, that a man ought to do as the banker who examineth money, examining his thoughts, that he sin not against God his creator.'

74.

'There have been and are in the world men who hold not thought for sin; who are in the greatest error. Tell me, how sinned Satan? It is certain that he sinned in the thought that he was more worthy than man. Solomon sinned in thinking to invite to a feast all the creatures of God, whereupon a fish corrected him by eating all that he had prepared. Wherefore, not without cause, saith David our father,[132] that "to ascend in one's heart setteth one in the valley of tears." And wherefore doth God cry by Isaiah[133] his prophet, saying: "Take away your evil thoughts from mine eyes?" And to what purpose saith Solomon:[134] "With all thy keeping, keep thine heart?" As God liveth, in whose presence standeth my soul, all is said against the evil thoughts wherewith sin is committed, for without thinking it is not possible to sin. Now tell me, when the husbandman planteth the vineyard doth he set the plants deep? Assuredly yea. Even so doth Satan, who in planting sin doth not stop at the eye or the ear, but passeth into the heart, which is God's dwelling. As he spake by Moses[135] his servant, saying: "I will dwell in them, in order that they may walk in my law."

'Now tell me, if Herod the king should give you a house to keep in which he desired to dwell, would ye suffer Pilate, his enemy, to enter there or to place his goods therein? Assuredly no. Then how much less ought ye to suffer Satan to enter into your heart, or to place his thoughts therein; seeing that our God hath given you your heart

---

[130] *He hath said by Isaiah.* Isa. 49:15.

[131] *as saith the prophet Solomon.* This saying of Solomon, found its way into Ecclesiasticus, 2:1.

[132] *saith David our father.* Ps. 84:5,6.

[133] *by Isaiah.* Isa. 1:16.

[134] *saith Solomon.* Prov. 4:23.

[135] *As he spake by Moses.* Lev. 26:11, 12.

to keep, which is his dwelling. Observe, therefore, that the banker considereth the money, whether the image of Caesar is right, whether the silver is good or false, and whether it is of due weight: wherefore he turneth it over much in his hand. Ah, mad world! How prudent thou art in thy business, so that in the last day thou wilt reprove and judge the servants of God of negligence and carelessness, for without doubt thy servants are more prudent than the servants of God. Tell me, now, who is he who examineth a thought as the banker a silver coin? Assuredly no one.'

75.

Then said James: 'O master, how is the examination of a thought like unto (that of) a coin'?

Jesus answered: 'The good silver in the thought is piety, because every impious thought cometh of the devil. The right image is the example of the holy ones and prophets,[136] which we ought to follow; and the weight of the thought is the love of God by which all ought to be done. Whereupon the enemy will bring there impious thoughts against your neighbor, (thoughts) conformed to the world, to corrupt the flesh; (thoughts) of earthly love to corrupt the love of God.'[137]

Bartholomew answered: 'O master, what ought we to do to think little, in order that we may not fall into temptation?'

Jesus answered: 'Two things are necessary for you. The first is to exercise yourselves much, and the second is to talk little: for idleness is a sink wherein is gathered every unclean thought, and too much talking is a sponge which picketh up iniquities. It is, therefore, necessary not only your working should hold the body occupied, but also that the soul be occupied with prayer. For it needeth never to cease from prayer.

'I tell you for an example: There was a man who paid ill, wherefore none that knew him would go to till his fields. Whereupon he, like a wicked man, said: "I will go to the market-place to find idle ones who are doing nothing, and will therefore come to till my vines." This man went forth from his house, and found many strangers who were standing in idleness, and had no money. To them he spake, and

---

[136] *the holy ones and prophets.* "The terms 'holy one' and 'Just one,'" says Dr. Schonfield, "belong to the language of the Essene sects, some of whom followed a nazirite way of life, refraining from meat and intoxicants." (The Passover Plot, p.204). See chapters one and two, where Barnabas reports that both Mary and Joseph were told to keep Jesus from wine and strong drink.

[137] *corrupt the love of God.* The reference here is to materialism, the love of material wealth at the cost of one's own soul.

led them to his vineyard. But verily none that knew him and had work for his hands went thither.

'He is Satan, that one who payeth ill; for he giveth labour and man receiveth for it the eternal fires in his service. Wherefore he hath gone forth from paradise, and goeth in search of labourers. Assuredly he setteth to his labours those who stand in idleness whosoever they be, but much more those who know him not. It is not in any wise enough for any one to know evil in order to escape it, but it behoveth to work at good[138] in order to overcome it.'

76.

'I tell you for an example. There was a man who had three vineyards, which he let out to three husbandmen. Because the first knew not how to cultivate the vineyard the vineyard brought forth only leaves. The second taught the third how the vines ought to be cultivated; and he most excellently hearkened to his words; and he cultivated his, as he told him, insomuch that the vineyard of the third bore much. But the second left his vineyard uncultivated, spending his time solely in talking. When the time was come for paying the rent to the lord of the vineyard, the first said: "Lord, I know not how thy vineyard ought to be cultivated: therefore I have not received any fruit this year."

'The lord answered: 'O fool, dost thou dwell alone in the world, that thou hast not asked counsel of my second vinedresser, who knoweth well how to cultivate the land? Certain it is that thou shalt pay me."

'And having said this he condemned him to work in prison until he should pay his lord; who moved with pity at his simplicity liberated him, saying: "Begone, for I will not that thou work longer at my vineyard; it is enough for thee that I give thee thy debt."

'The second came, to whom the lord said: "Welcome, my vinedresser! Where are the fruits that thou owest me? Assuredly, since thou knowest well how to prune the vines, the vineyard that I let out to thee must needs have borne much fruit."

'The second answered: "O lord, thy vineyard is backward because I have not pruned the wood nor worked up the soil; but the vineyard hath not borne fruit, so I cannot pay thee."

---

[138]*it behoveth to work at good.* Consider the words attributed to James the Just, Jesus' brother: "Faith, if it hath not works, is dead, being alone. Yea, a man may say, Thou hast faith, and I have works; show me thy faith without thy works, and I will show thee my faith by my works. Thou believest that there is one God; thou doest well. The [demons] also believe, and tremble. But wilt thou know, O vain man, that faith without works is dead?" (Jas. 2:17-20).

'Whereupon the lord called the third and with wonder said: "Thou saidst to me that this man, to whom I let out the second vineyard, taught thee perfectly to cultivate the vineyard which I let out to thee. How then can it be that the vineyard I let out to him should not have borne fruit, seeing it is all one soil?"

"The third answered: "Lord, the vines are not cultivated by talking only, but he needs must sweat a shirt every day who willeth to make it bring forth its fruit. And how shall thy vineyard of thy vinedresser bear fruit, O lord, if he doth naught but waste the time in talking? Sure it is, O lord, that if he had put into practice his own words, (while) I who cannot talk so much have given thee the rent for two years, he would have given thee the rent of the vineyard for five years."

'The lord was wroth, and said with scorn to the vinedresser: "And so thou hast wrought a great work in not cutting away the wood and levelling the vineyard, wherefore there is owing to thee a great reward!" And having called his servants he had him beaten without any mercy. And then he put him into prison under the keeping of a cruel servant who beat him every day, and never was willing to set him free for prayers of his friends.'

77.

'Verily I say unto you, that on the day of judgment many shall say to God: "Lord, we have preached and taught by thy law." Against them even the stones shall cry out, saying: "When ye preached to others, with your own tongue ye condemned yourselves, O workers of iniquity."

'As God liveth,' said Jesus, 'he who knoweth the truth and worketh the contrary shall be punished with such grievous penalty that Satan shall almost have compassion on him. Tell me, now, hath our God given us the law for knowing or for working? Verily I say unto you, that all knowledge hath for end that wisdom which worketh all it knoweth.

'Tell me, if one were sitting at table and with his eyes beheld delicate meats, but with his hands should choose unclean things and eat those, would not he be mad?'

'Yea, assuredly,' said the disciples.

Then said Jesus: 'O mad beyond all madmen art thou, O man, that with thine understanding knowest heaven, and with thine hands choosest earth; with thine understanding knowest God, and with thine affection desirest the world; with thine understanding knowest the delights of paradise, and with thy works choosest the miseries of hell. Brave soldier, that leaveth the sword and carrieth the scabbard to fight! Now, know ye not that he who walketh by night desireth light, not only to see the light, but rather to see the good road, in order that he may pass safely to the inn? O miserable world, to be a thousand times despised and abhorred! Since our God by his holy prophets hath ever willed to grant it to know the way to go to his country and his rest: but thou, wicked one, not only willest not to go, but, which is worse, hast despised the light! True is the proverb of the camel, that it liketh not clear water to drink, because it desireth not to see its own ugly face. So doth the ungodly who worketh ill; for he hateth the light lest his evil works should be known. But he who receiveth wisdom, and not only worketh not well, but, which is worse, employeth it for evil, is like to him who should use the gifts as instruments to slay the giver.'

78.

'Verily I say unto you, that God had not compassion on the fall of Satan, but yet (had compassion) on the fall of Adam. And let this suffice you to know the unhappy condition of him who knoweth good and doeth evil.'

Then said Andrew: 'O master, it is a good thing to leave learning aside, so as not to fall into such condition.'

Jesus answered: 'If the world is good without the sun, man without eyes, and the soul without understanding, then is it good not to know. Verily I say unto you, that bread is not so good for the temporal life as is learning for the eternal life. Know ye not that it is a precept of God to learn? For thus saith God: "Ask of thine elders, and they shall teach thee."[139] And of the law saith God: "See that my precept be before thine eyes, and when thou sittest down, and when thou walkest, and at all times meditate thereon."[140] Whether, then, it is good not to learn, ye may now know. Oh, unhappy he who despiseth wisdom, for he is sure to lose eternal life.'

James answered: 'O master, we know that Job learned not from a master, nor Abraham; nevertheless they became holy ones and prophets.'

Jesus answered: 'Verily I say unto you, that he who is of the bridegroom's house needeth not to be invited to the marriage, because he dwelleth in the house where the marriage is held; but they that are far from the house. Now know ye not that the prophets of God are in the house of God's grace and mercy, and so have the law

---

[139] *they shall teach thee.* Deut. 32:7.
[140] *at all times meditate thereon.* Deut. 6:7,8 & 11:18,19.

of God manifest in them: as David our father[141] saith on this matter: "The law of his God is in his heart; therefore his path shall not be digged up." Verily I say unto you that our God in creating man not only created him righteous, but inserted in his heart a light[142] that should show to him that it is fitting to serve God. Wherefore, even if this light be darkened after sin, yet is it not extinguished. For every nation hath this desire to serve God, though they have lost God and serve false and lying gods. Accordingly it is necessary that a man be taught of the prophets of God, for they have clear the light to teach the way to go to paradise, our country, by serving God well: just as it is necessary that he who hath his eyes diseased should be guided and helped.'

79.

James answered: 'And how shall the prophets teach us if they are dead; and how shall he be taught who hath not knowledge of the prophets?'

Jesus answered: 'Their doctrine is written down, so that it ought to be studied, for (the writing) is to thee for a prophet. Verily, verily, I say unto thee that he who despiseth the prophecy despiseth not only the prophet, but despiseth also God who hath sent the prophet. But concerning such as know not the prophet, as are the nations,[143] I tell you that if there shall live in those regions any man who liveth as his heart shall show him, not doing to others that which he would not receive from others, and giving to his neighbor that which he would receive from others, such a man shall not be forsaken of the mercy of God. Wherefore at death, if not sooner, God will show him and give him his law with mercy. Perchance ye think that God hath given the law for love of the law? Assuredly this is not true, but rather hath God given his law in order that man might work good for love of God. And so if God shall find a man who for love of him worketh good, shall he perchance despise him? Nay, surely, but rather will he love him more than those to whom he hath given the law. I tell you for an example: There was a man who had great

---

[141] *David our father.* Ps. 37:31.

[142] *inserted in his heart a light.* Once again we see the Essene connection with Jesus and the Nazarenes, for the thought expressed here is Essene. Repeatedly in the Essene Book of Hymns, says Professor Gaster, thanks are given to God for 'illumining the face' of his servant or for shining His light into His servant's heart. The acquisition of that light, however, was not attributed by the Essenes to any spontaneous or sudden act of grace. Rather they deemed it to be the result of man's own voluntary exercise of the divinely instilled power of discernment, which God had placed in every creature at the moment He created it. (The Dead Sea Scriptures, p. 7).

[143] *As are the nations.* The Gentiles.

possessions; and in his territory he had desert land that only bore unfruitful things. And so, as he was walking out one day through such desert land, he found among such unfruitful plants a plant that had delicate fruits. Whereupon this man said: "Now how doth this plant here bear these so delicate fruits? Assuredly I will not that it be cut down and put on the fire with the rest." And having called his servants he made them dig it up and set it in his garden. Even so, I tell you, that our God shall preserve from the flames of hell those who work righteousness[144] wheresoever they be.'

80.

'Tell me, where dwelt Job[145] but in Uz among idolaters? And at the time of the flood, how writeth Moses? Tell me, He saith: "Noah truly found grace[146] before God." Our father Abraham had a father without faith, for he made and worshipped false idols. Lot[147] abode among the most wicked men on earth. Daniel as a child,[148] with Ananias, Azarias, and Misael, were taken captive by Nebuchadnezzar in such wise that they were but two years old when they were taken; and they were nurtured among the multitude of idolatrous servants. As God liveth, even as the fire burneth dry things and converteth them into fire, making no difference[149] between olive and cypress and palm: even so our God hath mercy on every one that worketh righteously, making no difference between Jew, Scythian, Greek, or Ishmaelite. But let not thine heart stop there. O James, because where God hath sent the prophet it is necessary entirely to deny thine own judgment and to follow the prophet, and not to say: "Why saith he thus?: "Why doth he thus forbid and command?" But say: "Thus God willeth. Thus God commandeth." Now what said God to Moses when Israel despised Moses? "They have not despised thee, but they have despised me."

---

144 *those who work righteousness.* Whoever believes that there is no god but God, and is righteous according to his or her level of understanding will assuredly receive of God's grace and mercy. Therefore, no one, and no group of people have a monopoly on God.

145 *where dwelt Job.* Job 1:1.

146 *Noah truly found grace.* Gen. 6:8.

147 *Lot.* Gen.13:13.

148 *Daniel as a child.* Dan.1:6.

149 *making no difference.* The wisdom expressed here by the Prophet Jesus, was characteristic of the Galileans. For we are told: "They were eminent for patriotism and courage, as were their ancestors, with great respect for law and order. They were less bigoted than the Jews of Judea." (Peloubet's Bible Dictionary, art: Galileans; p.207).

'Verily I say unto you, that man ought to spend all the time of his life not in learning how to speak or to read, but in learning how to work well. Now tell me, who is that servant of Herod who would not study to please him by serving him with all diligence? Woe unto the world that studieth only to please a body that is clay and dung, and studieth not but forgetteth the service of God who hath made all things; who is blessed for evermore.'

81.

'Tell me, would it have been a great sin of the priests if when they were carrying the ark of the testimony of God they had let it fall to the ground?'

The disciples trembled hearing this, for they knew that God slew Uzzah[150] for having wrongly touched the ark of God. And they said: 'Most grievous would be such a sin.'

Then said Jesus: 'As God liveth, it is a greater sin to forget the word of God.[151] Wherewith he made all things, whereby he offereth thee eternal life.'

And having said this Jesus made prayer; and after his prayer he said: 'Tomorrow we needs must pass into Samaria, for so hath said unto me the holy angel of God.'[152]

Early on the morning of a certain day, Jesus arrived near to the well which Jacob made and gave to Joseph his son. Whereupon Jesus, being wearied with the journey, sent his disciples to the city to buy food. And so he sat himself down by the well, upon the stone of the well. And, lo, a woman of Samaria cometh to the well to draw water.

Jesus saith unto the woman, 'Give me to drink,; The woman answered; 'Now, art thou not ashamed[153] that thou, being an Hebrew, askest drink of me which am a Samaritan woman?'

Jesus answered: 'O woman, if thou knewest who he is that asketh thee for a drink, perchance thou wouldest have asked of him for drink.'

The woman answered: 'Now how shouldest thou give me to drink, seeing thou hast no vessel to draw the water, nor rope, and the well is deep?'

Jesus answered: 'O woman, whoso drinketh of the water of this well, thirst cometh to him again, but whosoever drinketh of the water

---

[150] *Uzzah.* II Sam. 6:6-7; in accordance with Num. 4:15.

[151] *the word of God.* Ps. 33:6.

[152] *the holy angel of God.* Gabriel, who by God's command repeatedly assisted other prophets.

[153] *art thou not ashamed.* The woman's reply here, is in jest to ridicule the haughty attitude of the Jews toward the Samaritans.

that I give hath thirst no more; but to them that have thirst give they to drink, insomuch that they come to eternal life.'

Then said the woman: 'O Lord, give me of this thy water.'

Jesus answered: 'Go call thy husband, and to both of you I will give to drink.'

Said the woman: 'I have no husband.'

Jesus answered: 'Well hast thou said the truth, for thou hast had five husbands, and he whom thou now hast is not thy husband.

The woman was confounded hearing this, and said: 'Lord, hereby perceive I that thou art a prophet; therefore tell me, I pray: the Hebrews make prayer on mount Sion in the temple built by Solomon in Jerusalem, and say that there and nowhere else (men) find grace and mercy of God. And our people worship on these mountains, and say that only on the mountains of Samaria ought worship to be made. Who are the true worshipers?'

82.

Then Jesus gave a sigh and wept, saying: 'Woe to thee, Judaea,[154] for thou gloriest, saying: "the temple of the Lord, the temple of the Lord," and livest as though there were no God; given over wholly to the pleasures and gains of the world; for this woman in the day of judgement shall condemn thee to hell; for this woman seeketh to know how to find grace and mercy before God.'

And turning to the woman he said: 'O woman, ye Samaritans worship that which ye know not,[155] but we Hebrews worship that which we know. Verily, I say unto thee, that God is spirit and truth, and so in spirit and in truth must he be worshipped. For the promise of God was made in Jerusalem, in the temple of Solomon, and not elsewhere. But believe me, a time will come that God will give his mercy in another city, and in every place it will be possible to worship him in truth. And God in every place will have accepted true prayer with mercy.'

The woman answered; 'We look for the Messiah; when he cometh he will teach us.'

---

[154] Woe to thee Judea. Jer. 7:4.

[155] which ye know not. At the final captivity of Israel by Shalmanser, the cities were at least partially depopulated in 722 B.C., and remained in that state until the king of Assyria brought people in from Babylon, Cuthah, Ava, Hamath and Sepharvaim (II Ki. 17:24;). They were troubled by predators, which had probably multiplied considerably before their arrival. On their explaining their plight to the king of Assyria, he, believing that they had offended the god of the land, despatched one of the captive Israelite priests to instruct them in the faith. As a result they adopted the faith, but adulterated it with elements of their idolatry. (II Kings 17:41).

Jesus answered: 'Knowest thou, woman, that the Messiah must come?'

She answered: 'Yea, Lord.'

Then Jesus rejoiced, and said: 'So far as I see, O woman, thou art faithful: know therefore that in the faith of the Messiah shall be saved every one that is elect of God; therefore it is necessary that thou know the coming of the Messiah.'

Said the woman: 'O Lord, perchance thou art the Messiah.'[156]

Jesus answered: 'I am indeed sent to the house of Israel as a prophet of salvation; but after me shall come the messiah, sent of God to all the world; for whom God hath made the world. And then through all the world will God be worshipped, and mercy received, insomuch that the year of jubilee, which now cometh every hundred years, shall by the Messiah be reduced to every year in every place.'

Then the woman left her waterpot and ran to the city to announce all that she had heard from Jesus.

83.

Whilst the woman was talking with Jesus came his disciples, and marvelled that Jesus was speaking so with a woman. Yet no one said unto him: 'Why speakest thou thus with a Samaritan woman?'

Whereupon, when the woman was departed, they said: 'Master, come and eat.'

---

[156] *perchance thou art the Messiah.* "According to the [Essene Book known as] *Commentary on Habakkuk*," says Professor Dupont-Sommer, "the [Essene] Teacher of Righteousness was 'the Priest whom God placed in [the House of Judah] to explain all the words of his servants the Prophets' (II, 8-9). 'God,' the author writes (VIII, 4-5), 'made known' to him 'all the Mysteries of the words of His servants the Prophets.' Similarly, in the *Hymns* he is called 'an interpreter of Knowledge concerning the marvelous Mysteries' (II, 13); he was 'the foundation of Truth and understanding' (II, 10), the man by whose mouth 'God established the teaching' and *within* whose heart 'He'set understanding, that he might open the fountain of knowledge to all the understanding' (II, 17-18)." (The Essene Writings From Qumran, pp. 360-61) Now consider the fact that this is precisely what we are told of Jesus in chapter ten of this gospel. Thus he is identified as the last Essene Teacher of Righteousness who is identified as one of the two messiahs that were expected by the Essenes. In fact, in his reply here to the Samaritan, his words may be taken as an identification of himself as the expected Essene Teacher of Righteousness: "I am indeed sent to the house of Israel as a prophet of salvation." For as Professor Dupont-Sommer says of the Teacher of Righteousness: "This 'interpreter' [of the Law] versed in all the Mysteries of Knowledge was the great Doctor [Rabbi] of Essene Gnosis, the Hierophant [commentator of the sacred Mysteries] par excellence. But he was also the Prophet, in the biblical sense of the word" (Ibid. 361). The Essene connection is ever there in this authentic gospel.

Jesus answered,: 'I must eat other food.'

Then said the disciples one to another: 'Perchance some wayfarer hath spoken with Jesus and hath gone to find him food.' And they questioned him who writeth this, saying: 'Hath there been any one here, O Barnabas, who might have brought food to the master?'

Then answered he who writeth: 'There hath not been here any other than the woman whom ye saw, who brought this empty vessel to fill it with water.' Then the disciples stood amazed, awaiting the issue of the words of Jesus. Whereupon Jesus said: 'Ye know not that the true food is to do the will of God; because it is not bread[157] that sustaineth man and giveth him life, but rather the word of God, by his will. And so for this reason the holy angels eat not, but live nourished only by the will of God. And thus we, Moses and Elijah[158] and yet another, have been forty days and forty nights without any food.'

And lifting up his eyes, Jesus said: 'How far off is the harvest?'

The disciples answered: 'Three months.'

Jesus said: 'Look now, how the mountain is white with corn; verily I say unto you, that to-day there is a great harvest to be reaped.' And then he pointed to the multitude who had come to see him. For the woman having entered into the city had moved all the city, saying: 'O men, come and see a new prophet sent of God to the house of Israel': and she recounted to them all that she had heard from Jesus. When they were come thither they besought Jesus to abide with them; and he entered into the city and abode there two days, healing all the sick, and teaching concerning the kingdom of God.

Then said the citizens to the woman: 'We believe more in his words and miracles than we do in what thou saidst; for he is indeed a holy one of God, a prophet sent for the salvation of those that shall believe on him.'

After the prayer of midnight the disciples came near unto Jesus, and he said to them: 'This night shall be in the time of the Messiah, messenger of God, the jubilee every year [159] that now cometh every

---

[157] *it is not bread*, Deut. 8:3.

[158] *Moses and Elijah*. Exod. 24:18; I Ki.19:8.

[159] *the Jubilee every year.* In accordance with the laws governing the Sabbatical year (see Introduction) the Jubilee was a time in which the landowner shared whatever his land produced on its own with all members of his community both man and beast. It was also a time in which all slaves of Israelite ancestry were freed. Thus what Jesus is referring to here, is that the advent of the Prophet Muhammad would mark the beginning of a greater emphasis on the abolishment of slavery and the universal brotherhood of man. This attitude toward mankind expressed by Jesus,

hundred years. Therefore I will not that we sleep, but let us make prayer, bowing our head a hundred times, doing reverence to our God, mighty and merciful, who is blessed for evermore, and therefore each time let us say: "I confess thee our God alone, that hast not had beginning, nor shalt ever have end; for by thy mercy gavest thou to all things their beginning, and by thy justice thou shalt give to all an end: that hast no likeness among men, because in thine infinite goodness thou art not subject to motion nor to any accident. Have mercy on us, for thou hast created us, and we are the works of thy hand."'

84.

Having made the prayer, Jesus said: 'Let us give thanks to God because he hath given to us this night great mercy; for that he hath made to come back the time that needs must pass in this night, in that we have made prayer[160] in union with the messenger of God. And I have heard his voice.'

The disciples rejoiced greatly at hearing this, and said: 'Master, teach us some precepts this night.'

Then said Jesus: 'Have ye ever seen dung mixed with balsam?'

They answered: 'Nay, Lord, for no one is so mad as to do this thing.'

'Now I tell you that there be in the world greater madmen,' said Jesus, 'because with the service of God they mingle the service of the world. So much so that many of blameless life have been deceived of Satan, and while praying have mingled with their prayer worldly business, whereupon they have become at that time abominable in the sight of God. Tell me, when ye wash yourselves[161] for prayer, do

characterizes that of the Esssenes, for Philo says: "Least of all were any slaves found among them (the Essenes); for they saw in slavery a violation of nature, which made all men free brethren one of the other." (*The Meaning of the Dead Sea Scrolls*, p. 138.)

[160] *have made prayer.* William Smith in his Bible Dictionary, points out, as does Peloubet's Bible Dictionary, concerning the manner of prayer (adoration) performed by the Israelites: "The acts and postures by which the Hebrews expressed adoration bear a great similarity to those still in use among Oriental [Eastern] nations [particularly the Muslims]. To rise up and suddenly prostrate the body was the most simple method; but generally speaking the prostration was conducted in a more formal manner, the person falling upon the knee and then gradually inclining the body until the forehead touched the ground. Such prostration was usual in the worship of Jehovah {Yahweh}". (Gen. 17:3; Ps.95:6).

[161] *when ye wash yourselves.* "Purification," says William Smith, "in its legal and technical sense, is applied to the ritual observances whereas an Israelite was formally absolved from the taint of uncleanness. The essence of purification, in all cases, consisted in the use of water, whether by way of ablution or aspersion." (Smith's Bible Dictionary, art: Purification, p. 557).

ye take care that no unclean thing touch you? Yea, assuredly. But what do ye when ye are making prayer? Ye wash your soul from sins through the mercy of God. Would ye be willing then, while ye are making prayer, to speak of worldly things? Take care not to do so, for every worldly word becometh dung of the devil upon the soul of him that speaketh.'

Then trembled the disciples, because he spake with vehemence of spirit; and they said: 'O master, what shall we do if when we are making prayer a friend shall come to speak to us?'

Jesus answered: 'Suffer him to wait, and finish the prayer.'

Said Bartholomew: 'But what if he shall be offended and go his way, when he see that we speak not with him?'

Jesus answered: 'If he shall be offended, believe me he will not be a friend of yours nor a believer, but rather an unbeliever and a companion of Satan. Tell me, if ye went to speak with a stable boy of Herod,[162] and found his speaking into Herod's ears, would ye be offended if he made you to wait?' No, assuredly; but ye would be comforted at seeing your friend in favour with the king. Is this true?' said Jesus.

The disciples answered: 'It is most true.'

Then said Jesus: 'Verily I say unto you, that every one when he prayeth speaketh with God. Is it then right that ye should leave speaking with God in order to speak with man? Is it right that your friend should for this cause be offended, because ye have more reverence for God than for him? Believe me that if he shall be offended when ye make him wait, he is a good servant of the devil. For this desireth the devil, that God should be forsaken for man. As God liveth, in every good work he that feareth God ought to separate himself[163] from the works of the world, so as not to corrupt the good work.'

85.

'When a man worketh ill or talketh ill, if one go to correct him, and hinder such work, what doth such an one?' said Jesus.

The disciples answered: 'He doth well, because he serveth God,

---

[162] *Herod.* Herod Antipas (4 B.C. - A.D.40).

[163] *separate himself.* Again we have evidence of the Essene, Nazarene connection via thought and doctrine. For what Jesus says here of separating one's self, is descriptive of the Essenes: "At first they [the Essenes]," says Philo, "lived in villages and avoided cities, in order to escape the contagion of evils rife therein. They pursued agriculture and other peaceful arts; but accumulated not gold nor silver, nor owned mines. No maker of warlike weapons, no huckster or trader by land or sea, was to be found among them." (The Meaning of the Dead Sea Scrolls, p.138).

who always seeketh to hinder evil, even as the sun that always seeketh to chase away the darkness.'

Said Jesus: 'And I tell you on the contrary that when one worketh well or speaketh well, whosoever seeketh to hinder him under pretext of aught that is not better, he serveth that devil, nay, he even becometh his companion. For the devil attendeth to nought else but to hinder every good thing.

'But what shall I say unto you now? I will say unto you as said Solomon the prophet,[164] holy one, and friend of God: 'Of a thousand whom ye know, one be your friend.'

Then said Matthew: 'Then shall we not be able to love any one.'

Jesus answered: 'Verily I say unto you, that it is not lawful for you to hate anything save only sin: insomuch that ye cannot hate even Satan as creature of God, but rather as enemy of God. Know ye wherefore? I will tell you; because he is a creature of God, and all that God hath created is good and perfect. Accordingly, whoso hateth the creature hateth also the creator. But the friend is a singular thing, that is not easily found, but is easily lost. For the friend will not suffer contradiction against him whom he supremely loveth. Beware, be ye cautious, and choose not for friend one who loveth not him whom ye love. Know ye what friend meaneth? Friend meaneth naught but physician of the soul. And so, just as one rarely findeth a good physician who knoweth the sickness and understandeth to apply the medicines thereto, so also are friends rare who know the faults and understand how to guide unto good. But herein is an evil, that there are many who have friends that feign not to see the faults of their friend; others excuse them; others defend them under earthly pretext; and, what is worse, there are friends who invite and aid their friend to err, whose end shall be like unto their villainy. Beware that ye receive not such men for friends, for that in truth they are enemies and slayers of the soul.

86.

Let thy friend be such that, even as he willeth to correct thee, so he may receive correction; and even as he willeth that thou shouldest leave all things for love of God, even so again it may content him that thou forsake him for the service of God.

'But tell me, if a man know not how to love God how shall he know how to love himself; and how shall he know how to love others, not knowing how to love himself? Assuredly this is impossible. Therefore when thou choose thee one for friend (for verily he is

---

[164] *Solomon the prophet* Prov. 18:24.

supremely poor who hath no friend at all), see that thou consider first, not his fine lineage, nor his fine family, not his fine house, not his fine clothing, nor his fine person, not yet his fine words, for thou shalt be easily deceived. But look how he feareth God, how he despiseth earthly things, how he loveth good works, and above all how he hateth his own flesh,[165] and so shalt thou easily find the true friend; if he above all things shall fear God, and shall despise the vanities of the world; if he shall be always occupied in good works, and shall hate his own body as a cruel enemy. Nor yet shalt thou love such a friend in such wise that thy love stay in him, for (so) shalt thou be an idolater. But love him as a gift that God hath given thee, for so shall God adorn (him) with greater favour. Verily I say unto you, that he who hath found a true friend hath found one of the delights of paradise; nay, such is the key of paradise.'

Thaddaeus answered: 'But if perchance a man shall have a friend who is not such as thou hast said, O master? What ought he to do? Ought he to forsake him?'

Jesus answered: 'He ought to do as the mariner doth with the ship, who saileth it so long as he perceiveth it to be profitable, but when he seeth it to be a loss forsaketh it. So shalt thou do with thy friend that is worse than thou; in those things wherein he is an offence to thee, leave him if thou wouldst not be left of the mercy of God.'

87.

'Woe unto the world because of offences. It needs must be that the offence come, because all the world lieth in wickedness. But yet woe to that man through whom the offence cometh. It were better for the man if he should have a millstone about his neck and should be sunk in the depths of the sea than that he should offend his neighbor. If thine eye be an offence to thee, pluck it out; for it is better that thou go with one eye only into paradise than with both of them into hell. If thy hand or thy foot offend thee, do likewise, for it is better that thou go into the kingdom of heaven with one foot or with one hand, than with two hands and two feet go into hell.'

Said Simon, called Peter: 'Lord, how must I do this? Certain it is that in a short time I shall be dismembered.'

Jesus answered: 'O Peter, put off fleshly prudence and straightway thou shalt find the truth. For he that teacheth thee is

---

[165] *hateth his own flesh.* The weaknesses of the flesh which lead men astray when allowed to prevail over the spiritual needs of man; when a balance is not maintained between the positive needs of the flesh and the spiritual needs of the soul.

thine eye, and he that helpeth thee to work is thy foot, and he that ministereth aught unto thee is thine hand. Wherefore when such are to thee an occasion of sin leave them; for it is better for thee to go into paradise ignorant, with few works, and poor, than to go into hell wise, with great works, and rich. Everything that may hinder thee from serving God, cast it from thee as a man casteth away everything that hindereth his sight.'

And having said this, Jesus called Peter close to him, and said unto him: 'if thy brother shall sin against thee, go and correct him. If he amend, rejoice, for thou hast gained thy brother; but if he shall not amend go and call afresh two witnesses and correct him afresh; and if he shall not amend, go and tell it to the church;[166] and if he shall not then amend, count him for an unbeliever, and therefore thou shalt not dwell under the same roof whereunder he dwelleth, thou shalt not eat at the same table whereat he sitteth, and thou shalt not speak with him; insomuch that if thou know where he setteth his foot in walking thou shalt not set they foot there.'

88.

'But beware that thou hold not thyself for better; rather shalt thou say thus: "Peter, Peter, if God helped thee not with his grace thou wouldst be worse than he."'

Peter answered: 'How must I correct him?'

Jesus answered: 'In the way that thou thyself wouldst fain be corrected. And as thou wouldst fain be borne with, so bear with others. Believe me, Peter for verily I say unto thee that every time thou shalt correct thy brother with mercy thou shalt receive mercy of God, and thy words shall bear some fruit; but if thou shalt do it with rigour, thou shalt be rigorously punished by the justice of God, and shalt bear no fruit. Tell me, Peter: Those earthen pots wherein the poor cook their food - do they wash them, perchance, with stones and iron hammers? Nay, assuredly; but rather with hot water. Vessels are broken in pieces with iron, things of wood are burned with fire; but man is amended with mercy. Wherefore, when thou shalt correct thy brother thou shalt say to thyself: "If God help me not, I shall do to-morrow worse than all that he hath done today."'

Peter answered: 'How many times must I forgive my brother, O master?'

Jesus answered: 'As many times as thou wouldst fain be forgiven by him.'

---

[166] *the church.* The word Synagogue is more properly rendered 'congregation,' rather than 'church.'

Said Peter: 'Seven times a day?'

Jesus answered: 'Not only seven, but seventy times seven thou shalt forgive him every day; for he that forgiveth, to him shall it be forgiven, and he that condemneth shall be condemned.'

Then said he who writeth this: 'Woe unto princes! for they shall go to hell.'

Jesus reproved him, saying: 'Thou art become foolish, O Barnabas, in that thou hast spoken thus. Verily I say unto thee, that the bath is not so necessary for the body, the bit for the horse, and the tiller for the ship, as the prince is necessary for the state. And for what cause did God give Moses, Joshua, Samuel, David, and Solomon, and so many others who passed judgement? To such hath God given the sword for the extirpation of iniquity.'

Then said he who writeth this: 'Now, how ought judgement to be given, condemning and pardoning?'

Jesus answered: 'Not every one is a judge: for to the judge alone it appertaineth to condemn others, O Barnabas. And the judge ought to condemn the guilty, even as the father commandeth a putrified member to be cut off from his son in order that the whole body may not become putrified.'

89.

Said Peter: 'How long must I wait for my brother to repent?'

Jesus answered: 'So long as thou wouldst be waited for.'

Peter answered: 'Not every one will understand this; wherefore speak to us more plainly.'

Jesus answered: 'Wait for thy brother as long as God waiteth for him.'

'Neither will they understand this,' said Peter.

Jesus answered: 'Wait for him so long as he hath time to repent.'

Then was Peter sad, and the others also, because they understood not the meaning. Whereupon Jesus answered: 'If ye had sound understanding, and knew that ye yourselves were sinners, ye would not think ever to cut off your heart from mercy to the sinner. And so I tell you plainly, that the sinner ought to be waited for that he may repent, so long as he hath a soul beneath his teeth to breathe. For so doth our God wait for him, the mighty and merciful. God said not: "In that hour that the sinner shall fast, do alms, make prayer, and go on pilgrimage, I will forgive him." Wherefore this have many accomplished, and are damned eternally. But he said:[167] "In that

---

[167] *But he said.* Exek. 18:27.

hour that the sinner shall bewail his sins, I for my part will not remember any more his iniquities." Do ye understand?' said Jesus.

The disciples answered: 'Part we understand, and part not.'

Said Jesus: 'Which is the part that ye understood not?'

They answered: 'That many who have made prayer with fastings are damned.'

Then said Jesus: 'Verily I say unto you, that the hypocrites and the Gentiles make more prayers, more alms, and more fasts than do the friends of God. But because they have not faith, they are not able to repent for love of God, and so they are damned.'

Then said John: 'Teach us, for love of God, of the faith.' Jesus answered: 'It is time that we say the prayer of the dawn.' Whereupon they arose, and having washed themselves made prayer to our God, who is blessed for evermore.

90.

When the prayer was done, his disciples again drew near to Jesus, and he opened his mouth and said: 'Draw near, John, for to-day will I speak unto thee of all that thou hast asked. Faith is a seal[168] whereby God sealeth his elect: which seal he gave to his messenger, at whose hands every one that is elect hath received faith. For even as God is one, so is the faith one. Wherefore God, having created before all things his messenger, gave to him before aught else the faith which is as it were a likeness of God and of all that God hath done and said. And so the faithful by faith seeth all things,[169] better than one seeth with his eyes; because the eyes can err; nay they do almost always err; but faith erreth never, for it hath for foundation God and his word. Believe me that by faith are saved all the elect of God. And it is certain that without faith it is impossible for any one to please God. Wherefore Satan seeketh not to bring to naught fasting and prayer, alms and pilgrimages, nay rather he inciteth unbelievers thereto, for he taketh pleasure in seeing man work without receiving pay. But he taketh pains with all diligence to bring

---

[168] *Faith is a seal.* One who is pleased with God as his Lord; monotheism (not trinitarianism) as his religion; acknowledges the prophets of God; hates the hatred of him who hates God; and does unto others as he wants others to do unto himself, bears the seal of the elect of God.

[169] *by faith seeth all things.* Not blind faith, but faith as a product of intuition tempered by logic and reason, for it was by such faith that Abraham perceived that there is no god but God. The religion of God being demonstrated by the application of observation, logic and reason, thus one "1", being the numerical symbol of God's indivisibility, multiplied and divided by itself, still equals one, "1". While three, "3" divided into one,"1", (3 persons divided into one godhead) is illogical.

faith to nought, wherefore faith ought especially to be guarded with diligence, and the safest course will be to abandon the "Wherefore," seeing that the "Wherefore" drove men out of Paradise and changed Satan from a most beautiful angel into a horrible devil.'

Then said John: 'Now, how shall we abandon the "Wherefore" seeing that it is the gate of knowledge?'

Jesus answered: 'Nay, rather the "Wherefore" is the gate of hell.'

Thereupon John kept silence, when Jesus added: 'When thou knowest that God hath said a thing, who art thou, O man, that thou shouldst say, forsooth, "Wherefore hath thou so said, O God: wherefore hast thou so done?" Shall the earthen vessel, perchance say to its maker: "Wherefore hast thou made me to hold water and not to contain balsam?" Verily I say unto you, it is necessary against every temptation to strengthen yourself with this word, saying "God hath so said"; "So hath God done"; "God so willeth'; for so doing thou shalt live safely.'

91.

At this time there was a great disturbance throughout Judea for the sake of Jesus; for that the Roman soldiery, through the operation of Satan, stirred up the Hebrews, saying that Jesus was God come to visit them. Whereupon so great sedition arose, that nigh upon the Forty days[170] all Judea was in arms, insomuch that the son was found against the father, and the brother against the brother, for that some said that Jesus was God come to the world; others said: 'Nay, but he is a son of God'; and others said: 'Nay for God hath no human similitude, and therefore begetteth not sons; but Jesus of Nazareth is a prophet of God.'

And this arose by reason of the great miracles which Jesus did.

Thereupon, to quiet the people, it was necessary that the high-priest should ride in procession, clothed in his priestly robes, with the holy name of God, the teta gramaton (sic), on his forehead. And in like manner rode the governor Pilate and Herod.

Whereupon, in Mizpeh assembled three armies, each one of two hundred thousand men that bare sword. Herod spake to them, but they were not quieted. Then spake the governor and the high-priest, saying: 'Brethren, this war is aroused by the work of Satan, for Jesus is alive, and to him ought we to resort, and ask him that he give testimony of himself, and then believe in him, according to his word.'

So at this they were quieted, every one; and having laid down

---

[170]*Forty days.* See note to chap. 92.

their arms they all embraced one another, saying one to the other: 'Forgive me, brother!'

On that day, accordingly, every one laid this in his heart, to believe Jesus, according as he shall say. And by the governor and the high-priest were offered rewards to him who should come to announce where Jesus was to be found.

92.

At this time we with Jesus, by the word of the holy angel, were gone to Mount Sinai. And there Jesus with his disciples kept the Forty days.[171] When this was past, Jesus drew nigh to the river Jordan, to go to Jerusalem. And he was seen by one of them who believed Jesus to be God.[172] Whereupon, with greatest gladness crying ever 'Our God cometh!' having reached the city he moved the whole city saying: 'Our God cometh, O Jerusalem; prepare thee to receive him!' And he testified that he had seen Jesus near to Jordan.

Then went out from the city every one, small and great, to see Jesus, insomuch that the city was left empty, for the women bare their children in their arms, and insomuch that they forgat to take food to eat.

When they perceived this, the governor and the high- priest rode forth and sent a messenger to Herod, who in like manner rode forth to find Jesus, in order that the sedition of the people might be quieted. Whereupon for two days they sought him in the wilderness near to Jordan, and the third day they found him, near the hour of midday, when he with his disciples was purifying himself for prayer, according to the book of Moses.

Jesus marvelled greatly, seeing the multitude which covered the ground with people, and said to his disciples: 'Perchance Satan hath raised sedition in Judaea. May it please God to take away from Satan the dominion which he hath over sinners.'

And when he had said this, the crowd drew nigh, and when they knew him they began to cry out: 'Welcome to thee, O our God!' and they began to do him reverence, as unto God. Whereupon Jesus gave a great groan and said; 'Get ye from before me, O madmen, for I fear

---

[171] *Forty days.* The Nazarenes - at least under Jesus' leadership - in accordance with the great emphasis placed upon the forty-year wanderings of the Israelites in the wilderness by the Essenes in particular, and the nation as a whole, commemorated this event with a forty day observance at Mount Sinai, where the Law, by Moses had been received.(See *The Dead Sea Scrolls, The Gospel of Barnabas, and The New Testament*, pp.4-5).

[172] *who believed Jesus to be God.* See the note to chp.70; and *The Dead Sea Scrolls, The Gospel of Barnabas, and The New Testament*, pp. 27-48.

lest the earth should open and devour me with you for your abominable words!' Whereupon the people were filled with terror and began to weep.

93.

Then Jesus, having lifted his hand in token of silence, said: 'Verily ye have erred greatly, O Israelites, in calling me, a man, your God. And I fear that God may for this give heavy plague upon the holy city, handing it over in servitude to strangers. O a thousand times accursed Satan, that hath moved you to this!'

And having said this, Jesus smote his face with both his hands, whereupon arose such a noise of weeping that none could hear what Jesus was saying. Whereupon once more he lifted up his hand in token of silence, and the people being quieted from their weeping, he spake once more: 'I confess before heaven, and I call to witness everything that dwelleth upon the earth, that I am a stranger to all that ye have said: seeing that I am man, born of mortal woman,[173] subject to the judgement of God, suffering the miseries of eating and sleeping, of cold and heat, like other men. Wherefore when God shall come to judge, my words like a sword shall pierce each one (of them) that believe me to be more than man.'

And having said this, Jesus saw a great multitude of horsemen, whereby he perceived that there were coming the governor with Herod and the high-priest.

Then said Jesus: 'Perchance they also are become mad.'

When the governor arrived there, with Herod and the priest, every one dismounted, and they made a circle round about Jesus, insomuch that the soldiery could not keep back the people that were desirous to hear Jesus speaking with the priest.

Jesus drew near to the priest with reverence, but he was wishful to bow himself down and worship Jesus, when Jesus cried out:

---

[173] *born of mortal woman.* Those who hold the belief that because of the manner of his generation within his mother's womb without the agency of a husband, Jesus was more than man, have inherited the error of their forefathers, who knew not in their day that certain creatures in nature reproduce without the agency of the male of the specie. Even rabbits, a specie that multiplies by way of the two parents, have demonstrated an ability under laboratory conditions, to reproduce without the agency of a father. Yet in this day and age, it would be most difficult to find an intelligent person who would declare the offspring of these various creatures as being gods. Indeed, if man can bring about reproduction without a male in rabbits, how much more is Almighty God able to bring about reproduction in woman without the agency of a husband. (See *Biology, The Unity And Diversity Of Life,* 2nd ed.,p. 322).

'Beware of that which thou doest, priest of the living God! Sin not against our God!'

The priest answered: 'Now is Judaea so greatly moved over thy signs and thy teaching that they cry out that thou art God; wherefore, constrained by the people, I am come hither with the Roman governor and king Herod. We pray thee therefore from our heart, that thou wilt be content to remove the sedition which is arisen on thy account. For some say thou art God, some say thou art son of God, and some say thou art a prophet.'

Jesus answered: 'And thou, O high-priest of God, wherefore hast thou not quieted this sedition? Art thou also, perchance, gone out of thy mind? Have the prophecies, with the law of God, so passed into oblivion, O wretched Judaea, deceived of Satan!'

94.

And having said this, Jesus said again: 'I confess before heaven, and call to witness everything that dwelleth upon the earth, that I am a stranger to all that men have said of me, to wit, that I am more than man. For I am a man, born of a woman, subject to the judgement of God; that live here like as other men, subject to the common miseries. As God liveth, in whose presence my soul standeth, thou hast greatly sinned, O priest, in saying what thou hast said. May it please God that there come not upon the holy city great vengeance for this sin.'

Then said the priest: 'May God pardon us, and do thou pray for us.'

Then said the governor and Herod: 'Sir, it is impossible that man should do that which thou doest; wherefore we understand not that which thou sayest.'

Jesus answered: 'That which ye say is true, for God worketh good in man, even as Satan worketh evil. For man is like a shop, wherein whoso entereth with his consent worketh and selleth therein. But tell me, O governor, and thou O king, ye say this because ye are strangers to our law; for if ye read the testament and covenant of our God ye would see that Moses with a rod made the water turn into blood, the dust into fleas, the dew into tempest, and the light into darkness. He made the frogs and mice to come into Egypt, which covered the ground, he slew the first-born, and opened the sea, wherein he drowned Pharaoh. Of these things I have wrought none. And of Moses, every one confesseth that he is a dead man at this present. Joshua made the sun to stand still,[174] and opened the Jordan,

---

[174] *stand still.* Josh. 10:12-14.

which I have not yet done. And of Joshua every one confesseth that he is a dead man at this present. Elijah[175] made fire to come visibly down from heaven, and rain, which I have not done. And of Elijah every one confesseth that he is a man. And (in like manner) very many other prophets, holy men, friends of God, who in the power of God have wrought things which cannot be grasped by the minds of those who know not our God, almighty and merciful, who is blessed for evermore.'

95.

Accordingly the governor and the priest and the king prayed Jesus that in order to quiet the people he should mount up into a lofty place and speak to the people. Then went up Jesus on to one of the twelve stones which Joshua made the twelve tribes take up from the midst of Jordan, when all Israel passed over there dry shod;[176] and he said with a loud voice; 'Let our priest go up into a high place whence he may confirm my words.' Thereupon the priest went up thither; to whom Jesus said distinctly, so that everyone might hear; 'It is written in the testament[177] and covenant of the living God that our God hath no beginning, neither shall he ever have an end.'

The priest answered: 'Even so is it written therein.'

Jesus said: 'It is written there that our God by his word alone hath created all things.'[178]

'Even so it is,' said the priest.

Jesus said: 'It is written there that God is invisible and hidden from the mind of man, seeing he is incorporeal and uncomposed, without variableness.'

'So it is, truly,' said the priest.

Jesus said: 'It is written there how that the heaven of heavens cannot contain him,[179] seeing that our God is infinite.'

'So said Solomon the prophet.' said the priest. 'O Jesus.'

Said Jesus: 'It is written there that God hath no need, forasmuch as he eateth not, sleepeth not, and suffereth not from any deficiency.'

'So is it,' said the priest.

Said Jesus: 'It is written there that our God is everywhere, and

---

175 *Elijah.* I Ki. 18:38-39; 18:41.
176 *dry shod.* Josh. 4:8
177 *in the testament.* Ps. 90:2
178 *created all things.* Ps. 33:6
179 *cannot contain him.* I Ki. 8:27

that there is not any other god but he, who striketh down and maketh whole, and doeth all that pleaseth him.'[180]

'So is it written.' replied the priest.

Then Jesus, having lifted up his hands, said: 'Lord our God, this is my faith wherewith I shall come to thy judgement; in testimony against every one that shall believe the contrary. And turning himself towards the people, he said: 'Repent, for from all that of which the priest hath said that it is written in the book of Moses, the covenant of God for ever, ye may perceive your sin; for that I am a visible man and a morsel of clay that walketh upon the earth, mortal as are other men. And I have had a beginning, and shall have an end, and (am) such that I cannot create a fly over again.'

Thereupon the people raised their voices weeping, and said: 'We have sinned, Lord our God, against thee; have mercy upon us.' And they prayed Jesus, every one, that he would pray for the safety of the holy city, that our God in his anger should not give it over to be trodden down of the nations. Thereupon Jesus, having lifted up his hands, prayed for the holy city and for the people of God, every one crying: 'So be it.' 'Amen.'

96.

When the prayer was ended, the priest said with a loud voice: 'Stay, Jesus, for we need to know who thou art, for the quieting of our nation.'

Jesus answered: 'I am Jesus, son of Mary, of the seed of David, a man that is mortal and feareth God, and I seek that to God be given honour and glory.'

The priest answered: 'In the book of Moses it is written that our God must send us the Messiah, who shall come to announce to us that which God willeth, and shall bring to the world the mercy of God. Therefore I pray thee tell us the truth, art thou the Messiah of God whom we expect?'

Jesus answered: 'It is true that God hath so promised, but indeed I am not he, for he is made before me, and shall come after me.'

The priest answered: 'By thy words and signs at any rate we believe thee to be a prophet and an holy one of God, wherefore I pray thee in the name of all Judaea and Israel that thou for love of God shouldst tell us in what wise the Messiah will come.'

Jesus answered: 'As God liveth, in whose presence my soul standeth, I am not the Messiah whom all the tribes of the earth

---

[180] *all that pleaseth him.* Deut. 32:39

expect, even as God promised to our father Abraham, saying: "In thy seed will I bless all the tribes of the earth."[181] But when God shall take me away from the world, Satan will raise again this accursed sedition, by making the impious believe that I am God and son of God, whence my words and my doctrine shall be contaminated, insomuch that scarcely shall there remain thirty faithful ones; whereupon God will have mercy upon the world, and will send his messenger for whom he hath made all things; who shall come from the south[182] with power, and shall destroy the idols with the idolaters; who shall take away the dominion[183] from Satan which he hath over men. He shall bring with him the mercy of God for salvation of them that shall believe in him, and blessed is he who shall believe his words.

97.

'Unworthy though I am to untie his hosen, I have received grace and mercy from God to see him.' Then answered the priest, with the governor and the king, saying: 'Distress not thyself, O Jesus, holy one of God, because in our time shall not this sedition be any more seeing that we will write to the sacred Roman senate in such wise that by imperial decree none shall any more call thee God or son of God.'

Then said Jesus; 'with your words I am not consoled, because where ye hope for light darkness shall come;[184] but my consolation is in the coming of the messenger, who shall destroy every false opinion of me, and his faith shall spread and shall take hold of the whole world, for so hath God promised to Abraham our father. And that which giveth me consolation is that his faith shall have no end, but shall be kept inviolate by God.'

The priest answered: 'After the coming of the messenger of God shall other prophets come?'

---

[181] *In thy seed.* Gen. 22:18; as already demonstrated in chapter 43, and commentary, this promise was made in Ishmael.

[182] *who shall come from the south.* The Hejaz.

[183] *who shall take away the dominion from Satan.* "For thus saith the Lord of hosts: Yet once, it is a little while, and I will shake the heavens, and the earth, and the sea, and the dry land; and I will shake all nations, and the desire of all nations shall come; and I will fill this house [the Temple of the Lord] with glory, saith the Lord of hosts. The silver is mine, and the gold is mine, saith the Lord of hosts. The glory of this latter house shall be greater than of the former, saith the Lord of hosts; and in this place will I give peace, saith the Lord of hosts." (Haggi 2:6-9).

[184] *where ye hope for light darkness shall come.* This statement is a prophecy concerning the rise of the Gentile Church after 70 A. D., in Rome as the chief agency through which the false doctrine of divinity ascribed to Jesus would be propagated.

Jesus answered: 'There shall not come after him true prophets sent by God but there shall come a great number of false prophets, whereat I sorrow. For Satan shall raise them up by the just judgement of God, and they shall hide themselves under the pretext of my gospel.[185]

Herod answered: 'How is it a just judgement of God that such impious men should come?'

Jesus answered: 'It is just that he who will not believe in the truth to his salvation should believe in a lie to his damnation.[186] Wherefore I say unto you, that the world hath ever despised the true prophets and loved the false, as can be seen in the time of Michaiah and Jeremiah. For every like loveth his like.'

Then said the priest: 'How shall the Messiah be called, and what sign shall reveal his coming?'

Jesus answered: 'The name of the Messiah is admirable, for God himself gave him the name when he had created his soul, and placed it in a celestial splendour. God Said: 'Wait Mohammed; for thy sake I will to create paradise, the world, and a great multitude of creatures, whereof I make thee a present, insomuch that whoso shall bless thee shall be blessed, and whoso shall curse thee shall be

[185] *they shall hide themselves under the pretext of my gospel.* Consider how Jesus' prophetic warning to his apostles can only apply to the Christians. And the following words attributed to him in the Grecian gospel supposedly written by Matthew: "Beware of false prophets, who come to you in sheep's clothing, but inwardly they are ravening wolves. Ye shall know them by their fruits. Do men gather grapes of thorns, or figs of thistles? Even so, every good tree bringeth forth good fruit. A good tree cannot bring forth evil fruit, neither can a corrupt tree bring forth good fruit. Every tree that bringeth not forth good fruit is hewn down, and cast into the fire. Wherefore, by their fruits ye shall know them." (Matt. 7:15-20)

Under the pretext of abiding by Jesus' gospel, the Christians have stolen America, enslaved the African, exterminated tens of thousands of Muslims and Jews during the Inquisition, and the list of demonic behavior goes on and on.

[186] *to his damnation.* In the preface to his work: *Race, Science and Humanity,* Ashley Montagu, relates: "When I was younger I naively believed that racists were simply wrongheaded people who had fallen into easy error. I now know better. I now know that racists are often viciously unscrupulous persons who will, literally, stop at nothing to further their sick ideas. Because they are sick they are dangerous, for they carry infection with them wherever they go." What is said here of the mentality of the racist is also applicable to he who rejects the truth that leads to salvation. They believe the way they do because they choose to. Indeed, those who bear the mark of Satan, are given up to a reprobate mind. Further evidence of the connection is provided by the following report going as far back as 1967: "The Christian religion bids its followers to 'love thy neighbor as thyself,' but social science research has long since shown that churchgoers, as a group, are more prejudiced against strangers-Jews, (so called) Negroes, hippies (non-conformists), etc. - than people who don't go to church." (*Sociology, The Human Science,* pp.398-99).

accursed. When I shall send thee into the world I shall send thee as my messenger of salvation, and thy word shall be true, insomuch that heaven and earth shall fail, but thy faith shall never fail.'' Mohammed is his blessed name.'

Then the crowd lifted up their voices, saying: 'O God, send us thy messenger: O Mohammed, come quickly for the salvation of the world!'

98.

And having said this, the multitude departed with the priest and the governor with Herod, having great disputations concerning Jesus and concerning his doctrine. Whereupon the priest prayed the governor to write unto Rome to the senate the whole matter; which thing the governor did; wherefore the senate had compassion on Israel,[187] and decreed that on pain of death none should call Jesus the Nazarene, prophet of the Jews, either God or son of God. Which decree was posted up in the temple, engraved upon copper.[188]

When the greater part of the crowd had departed, there remained about five thousand men, without women and children; who being wearied by the journey, having been two days without bread, for that through longing to see Jesus they had forgotten to bring any, whereupon they ate raw herbs - therefore they were not able to depart like the others.

Then Jesus, when he perceived this, had pity on them, and said to Philip: 'Where shall we find bread for them that they perish not of hunger?'

Philip answered: 'Lord, two hundred pieces of gold could not buy so much bread that each one should taste a little.' Then said Andrew: 'There is here a child which hath five loaves and two fishes, but what will it be among so many?'

Jesus answered: 'Make the multitude sit down.' And they sat down upon the grass by fifties and by forties. Thereupon said Jesus:

---

[187] *the senate had compassion on Israel.* In light of the tolerant attitude of the Romans in religious matters, particularly for the sake of preventing disturbances in potentially troublesome provinces like Palestine, one should not be surprised at the possibility of what is suggested here. As to whether the Senate literally took up the matter, or merely left it up to the governor's superior in Syria, one can only guess.

[188] *engraved upon copper.* This may very well have been carried off with other Temple treasures when Jerusalem fell in 70 A. D., or not permitted to stay long in the temple by the Nazarenes. They may have placed it somewhere else, and would have, if time permitted, taken it with them when they fled to Pella. (See *The Dead Sea Scrolls, The Gospel of Barnabas, and The New Testament*, pp.96-99).

'In the name of God!' And he took the bread, and prayed to God and then brake the bread, which he gave to the disciples, and the disciples gave it to the multitude; and so did they with the fishes. Every one ate and every one was satisfied. Then said Jesus: 'Gather up that which is over. So the disciples gathered fragments, and filled twelve baskets. Thereupon every one put his hand to his eyes, saying: 'Am I awake, or do I dream?' And they remained, every one, for the space of an hour, as it were beside themselves by reason of the great miracle.

Afterwards Jesus, when he had given thanks to God, dismissed them, but there were seventy-two men that willed not to leave him; wherefore Jesus, perceiving their faith, chose them for disciples.

99.

Jesus, having withdrawn into a hollow part of the desert in Tiro[189] near to Jordan, called together the seventy-two with the twelve, and, when he had seated himself upon a stone, made them to sit near him. And he opened his mouth with a sigh and said: This day have we seen a great wickedness in Judaea and in Israel, and such an one that my heart yet trembleth within my breast for fear of God. Verily I say unto you, that God is jealous for his honour, and loveth Israel as a lover. Ye know that when a youth loveth a lady, and she love not him, but another, he is moved to indignation and slayeth his rival. Even so, I tell you, doth God; for, when Israel hath loved anything by reason whereof he forgetteth God, God hath brought such thing to nought. Now what thing is more dear to God here on earth than the priesthood and the holy temple? Nevertheless, in the time of Jeremiah the prophet,[190] when the people had forgotten God, and boasted only of the temple, for that there was none like it in all the world, God raised up his wrath by Nebuchadnezzar,[191] king of Babylon, and with an army caused him to take the holy city and burn it with the sacred temple, insomuch that the sacred things which the prophets of God trembled to touch were trodden under[192] foot of infidels full of wickedness.

Abraham loved his son Ishmael a little more that was right, wherefore God commanded, in order to kill that evil love out of the

---

[189] *Tiro.* The text here is obscure, and thus it is not clear as to what place is being referred to here.

[190] *in the time of Jeremiah.* Jer. 7:4.

[191] *by Nebuchadnezzar.* Jer. 39:1-10; 52:1-30.

[192] *trodden under.* Lam. 1:1-10.

heart of Abraham, that he should slay his son; which he would have done had the knife cut.

David loved Absalom vehemently, and therefore God brought it to pass that the son rebelled against his father and was suspended by his hair and slain by Joab.[193] O fearful judgement of God that Absalom loved his hair above all things, and this was turned into a rope to hang him withal!

Innocent Job[194] come near to loving over much his seven sons and three daughters, when God gave him into the hand of Satan, who not only deprived him of his sons and his riches in one day, but smote him also with grievous sickness, insomuch that for seven years following worms came out of his flesh.

Our father Jacob[195] loved Joseph more than his other sons, wherefore God caused him to be sold, and caused Jacob to be deceived by these same sons, insomuch that he believed that the beasts had devoured his son, and so abode ten years mourning.

100.

As God liveth, brethren, I fear lest God be angered against me. Therefore ye needs must go through Judaea and Israel, preaching to the twelve tribes of Israel the truth, that they may be undeceived.'

The disciples answered with fear, weeping: 'We will do whatsoever thou shalt bid us.'

Then said Jesus; 'Let us for three days make prayer and fast and from henceforth every evening when the first star shall appear,[196] when prayer is made to God, let us make prayer three times, asking Him three times for mercy; because the sin of Israel is three times more grievous than other sins.'

'So be it.' answered the disciples.

When the third day was ended, on the morning of the fourth day, Jesus called together all the disciples and apostles and said to them: 'Suffice it that there abide with me Barnabas and John: do ye others go through all the region of Samaria and Judaea and Israel, preaching penitence; because the axe is laid nigh unto the tree to cut it down.[197] And make prayer over the sick, because God hath given me authority over every sickness.

---

[193] *slain by Joab.* II Sam. 18:9-14.

[194] *Job.* Job. 1:2, 2:8.

[195] *Our father Jacob.* Gen. 37.

[196] *first star shall appear.* For the times of prayer observed by the Nazarenes, see *The Dead Sea Scrolls, The Gospel of Barnabas, and The New Testament,* pp. 8-9.

[197] *to cut it down.* 'The fig tree,' symbolizes Israel, whose fruit was, and had been for some time, evil fruit.

Then said he who writeth: 'O Master, if thy disciples be asked of the manner in which they ought to show penitence, what shall they answer?'

Jesus answered: 'when a man loseth a purse doth he turn back only his eye, to see it? or his hand, to take it? or his tongue, to ask? No, assuredly, but he turneth back his whole body and employeth every power of his soul to find it. Is this true?'

Then answered he who writeth: It is most true.

101.

Then said Jesus: 'Penitence is a reversing of the evil life; for every sense must be turned round to the contrary of that which it wrought while sinning. For instead of delight must be put mourning; for laughter, activity; for lust, chastity let story-telling be turned into prayer and avarice into almsgiving.

Then answered he who writeth: 'But if they be asked, how we ought to mourn, how we ought to weep, how we ought to fast, how we ought to show activity, how we ought to remain chaste, how we ought to make prayer and do alms: what answer shall they give? And how shall they do penance aright if they know not how to repent?'

Jesus answered: 'Well hast thou asked, O Barnabas, and I wish to answer all fully if it be pleasing to God. So today I will speak to thee of penitence generally, and that which I say to one I say unto all,

'Know then that penitence more than anything must be done for pure love of God; otherwise it will be vain to repent. For I will speak unto you by a similitude.

'Every building, if its foundation be removed, falleth into ruin: is this true?'

'It is true,' answered the disciples.

Then said Jesus: 'The foundation of our salvation is God,[198] without whom salvation is not. When man hath sinned, he hath lost the foundation of his salvation; so it is necessary to begin from the foundation.

Tell me, if your slaves had offended you, and ye knew that they did not grieve at having offended you, but grieved at having lost their reward, would ye forgive them? Certainly not. Even so I tell you that God will do to those who repent for having lost paradise. Satan, the

---

[198] *foundation of our salvation is God.* "Look unto me, and be saved, all the ends of the earth; for I am God, and there is none else. I have sworn by myself, the word is gone out of my mouth in righteousness, and shall not return, that unto me every knee shall bow, every tongue shall swear." (Isa. 45:22-23).

enemy of all good, hath great remorse for having lost paradise and gained hell. But yet will he never find mercy, and know ye why? Because he hath no love of God; nay he hateth his Creator.'

102.

'Verily I say unto you, that every animal after its own nature, if it lose that which it desireth, mourneth for the lost good. Accordingly, the sinner who will be truly penitent must have great desire to punish in himself that which he hath wrought in opposition to his Creator; in such wise that when he prayeth he dare not to crave of God paradise, or that he free him from hell, but in confusion of mind, prostate before God, he saith in his prayer: "Behold the guilty one, O Lord, who hath offended thee without any cause at the very time when he ought to have been serving thee. Wherefore here he seeketh that what he hath done may be punished by thy hand, and not by the hand of Satan, thine enemy; in order that the ungodly may not rejoice over thy creatures. Chastise, punish as it pleaseth thee, O Lord, for thou wilt never give me so much torment as this wicked one deserveth."

'Whereupon the sinner, holding to this manner (of penitence), will find the more mercy with God in proportion as he craveth justice.'

'Assuredly, an abominable sacrilege is laughter of the sinner; insomuch that this world is rightly called by our father David a vale of tears.'[199]

'There was a king who adopted as son one of his slaves, whom he made lord of all that he possessed. Now it chanced that by the deceit of a wicked man the wretched one fell under the displeasure of the king, so that he suffered great miseries, not only in his substance, but in being despised, and being deprived of all that he won each day by working. Think ye that such a man would laugh for any time?'

'No, assuredly,' answered the disciples, for if the king should have known it he would have caused him to be slain, seeing him laugh at the king's displeasure. But it is probable that he would weep day and night.'

Then Jesus wept saying: 'Woe to the world, for it is sure of eternal torment. Oh wretched mankind, for that God hath chosen thee as a son, granting thee paradise, whereupon thou, O wretched one, by the operation of Satan didst fall under the displeasure of God, and wast cast out of paradise and condemned to the unclean world, where thou receivest all things with toil, and every good work is

---

[199]*a vale of tears.* Ps. 84:6.

taken from thee by continual sinning. And the world simply laugheth, and, what is worse, he that is the greatest sinner laugheth more than the rest. It will be, therefore, as ye have said: that God will give the sentence of eternal death upon the sinner who laugheth at his sins and weepeth not therefor.'

103.

'The weeping of the sinner ought to be as that of a father who weepeth over his son nigh to death. Oh madness of man, that weepest over the body from which the soul is departed, and weepest not over the soul from which, through sin, is departed the mercy of God!

Tell me, if the mariner, when his ship hath been wrecked by a storm, could by weeping recover all that he had lost, what would he do? It is certain that he would weep bitterly. But I say unto you verily, that in every thing wherein a man weepeth he sinneth, save only when he weepeth for his sin. For every misery that cometh to man cometh to him from God for his salvation,[200] so that he ought to rejoice thereat. But sin cometh from the devil for the damnation of man, and at that man is not sad. Assuredly here ye can perceive that man seeketh loss and not profit.'

Said Bartholomew; 'Lord, what shall he do who cannot weep for that his heart is a stranger to weeping? Jesus answered: 'Not all those who shed tears weep, O Bartholomew. As God liveth, there are found men from whose eyes no tear hath ever fallen, and they have wept more than a thousand of those who shed tears. The weeping of a sinner is a consumption of earthly affection by vehemence of sorrow. Insomuch that just as the sunshine preserveth from putrefaction what is placed uppermost, even so this consumption preserveth the soul from sin. If God should grant tears to the true penitent as many as the sea hath waters he would desire far more and so this desire consumeth that little drop that he fain would shed, as a blazing furnace consumeth a drop of water. But they who readily burst into weeping are like the horse that goeth the faster the more lightly he is laden.'

---

[200] *for his salvation*. Man brings affliction upon himself, whether as an individual, a family, or a people. But affliction is a mercy from God in response to sin. For affliction is chastisement, as a loving parent chastises a child to make him or her a better person. In affliction man humbles himself and turns to God, unless he or she has a reprobate mind. In such a case the chastisement is still just, for everyone is given the opportunity to improve themselves, the choice of their response is their own. Through the experience of life it becomes apparent that most times, until man reaches the higher levels of maturity he will turn aside from God in varying degrees when the misery is no more.

104.

'Verily there are men who have both the inward affection and the outward tears. But he who is thus, will be a Jeremiah.[201] In weeping, God measureth more the sorrow than the tears.'

Then said John: 'O master, how doth man lose in weeping over things other than sin?'

Jesus answered: 'If Herod should give thee a mantle to keep for him, and afterwards should take it away from thee, wouldest thou have reason to weep?'

'No,' said John. Then said Jesus: 'Now hath man less reason to weep when he loseth aught, or hath not that which he would; for all cometh from the hand of God. Accordingly, shall not God have power to dispose at his pleasure of his own things, O foolish man? For thou hast of thine own, sin alone; and for that oughest thou to weep, and not for aught else.'

Said Matthew: 'O master, thou hast confessed before all Judaea that God hath no similitude like man,[202] and now thou hast said that man receiveth from the hand of God; accordingly, since God hath hands he hath a similitude with man.'

Jesus answered: 'Thou art in error, O Matthew, and many have so erred, not knowing the sense of the words. For man ought to consider not the outward (form) of the words, but the sense; seeing that human speech is as it were an interpreter between us and God. Now know ye not, that when God willed to speak to our fathers on mount Sinai, our fathers cried out: "Speak thou to us, O Moses, and let not God speak to us, lest we die?"[203] And what said God by Isaiah the prophet,[204] but that, so far as the heaven is distant from the earth, even so are the ways of God distant from the ways of men, and the thoughts of God from the thoughts of men?

105.

'God is so immeasurable that I tremble to describe him. But it is necessary that I make unto you a proposition. I tell you, then, that the heavens are nine and that they are distant from one another even as the first heaven is distant from the earth, which is distant from the earth five hundred years' journey. Wherefore the earth is distant

---

[201] *will be a Jeremiah.* Lam. 1:12.

[202] *God hath no similitude like man.* In Numbers 23:19, we are told that God is not man, and again in Hosea 11:9, and again as stated here by Jesus, who reminding his people of this truth, for the ignorance of the Gentiles was in the land.

[203] *lest we die.* Ex. 20:19.

[204] *Isaiah the prophet.* Isa. 55:9.

from the highest heaven four thousand and five hundred years' journey. I tell you, accordingly, that the earth is in proportion to the first heaven as the point of a needle, and the first heaven in like manner is in proportion to the second as a point, and similarly all the heavens are inferior each one to the next. But all the size of the earth with that of all the heavens is in proportion to paradise as a point, nay, as a grain of sand. Is this greatness immeasurable?'[205]

The disciples answered: 'Yea, surely.'

Then said Jesus: 'As God liveth, in whose presence my soul standeth, the universe before God is small as a grain of sand, and God is as many times greater (than it) as it would take grains of sand to fill all the heavens and paradise, and more. Now consider ye if God hath any proportion with man, who is a little piece of clay that standeth upon the earth. Beware, then, that ye take the sense and not the bare words, if ye wish to have eternal life.' The disciples answered: 'God alone can know himself, and truly it is as said Isaiah the prophet;[206] "He is hidden from human senses."' Jesus answered: 'So is it true; wherefore, when we are in paradise we shall know God, as here one knoweth the sea from a drop of salt water.' 'Returning to my discourse, I tell you that for sin alone one ought to weep, because by sinning man forsaketh his Creator. But how shall he weep who attendeth at revellings and feasts? He will weep even as ice will give fire! Ye needs must turn revellings into fasts[207] if ye will have lordship over your senses, because even so hath our God lordship.' Said Thaddaeus: 'So then, God hath sense over which to have lordship.' Jesus answered: 'Go ye back to saying, "God hath this," "God is such"? Tell me, hath man sense?'

---

[205] *Is this greatness immeasurable?* Fully in accordance with his role as Rabbi (a teacher of the Israelites), the ancient tradition of 500 years distance between each heaven that Jesus uses here as a metaphor, eventually found its way into the Jerusalem Talmud. (Ber. ix).

[206] *Isaiah the prophet.* Isa. 45:15.

[207] *turn revellings into fasts.* Two main schools of philosophy arose towards the end of the fourth century, which continued till the end of the Roman Empire in the West. The Epicurean, founded by Epicurus (341-270 B.C.) and the Stoic founded by Zeno (340-270 B.C.). In contradiction to the teachings of Epicurus, who taught that pleasure (complete mental tranquility) was attained through virtue, those calling themselves Epicureans of a later period before the birth of Jesus, taught that mere sensual gratification (the gluttonous satisfaction of the senses), especially in matters of food and drink (revellings-feasting) was the means of man's pleasure. It is this impious doctrine that Jesus is condemning. Which is why he emphasizes fasting, though it is not merely fasting from food and drink that he suggests. It is not total abstinence on an ongoing basis that he speaks of, but rather the manner by which one may gain mastery over his weaknesses.

'Yes,' answered the disciples.

Said Jesus: 'Can a man be found who hath life in him, yet in him sense worketh not?'

'No,' said the disciples.

'Ye deceive yourselves,' said Jesus. 'for he that is blind, deaf, dumb, and mutilated - where is his sense? And when a man is in a swoon?'

Then were the disciples perplexed; when Jesus said: 'Three things there are that make up man: that is, the soul and the sense and the flesh, each one of itself separate. Our God created the soul and the body as ye have heard, but ye have not yet heard how he created the sense. Therefore to-morrow, if God please. I will tell you all.'

And having said this Jesus gave thanks to God, and prayed for the salvation of our people, every one of us saying:'Amen.'

106.

When he had finished the prayer of dawn, Jesus sat down under a palm tree, and thither his disciples drew nigh to him. Then said Jesus: As God liveth, in whose presence standeth my soul, many are deceived concerning our life. For so closely are the soul and the sense joined together, that the more part[208] of men affirm the soul and the sense to be one and the same thing, dividing it by operation and not by essence, calling it the sensitive, vegetative, and intellectual soul.[209] But verily I say to you, the soul is one, which thinketh and

---

[208] *the more part.* The major part.

[209] *the sensative, vegetative, and intellectual soul.* Aristotle (384-322 B.C.) believed, that in nature we find a series of souls, beginning with plant souls and moving upwards to the human soul. Plant souls, said he, are concerned with eating and digesting food, and with the growth of the body as well as reproduction. He further believed that man's soul was like the plant soul, in that it governs the life functions while resembling the animal soul, in that by means of it man is able to receive sense impressions and deal with them. It is by means of the sense, according to him, that man comes into contact with and knows the world outside his body. However, man's soul is higher, in that it has the ability to think in terms of concepts, is able to think about the inner things. Thus his soul has the power of reason. Because Aristotle believed that the world could be understood only as a combination of ideal (form) and material (matter), he divided reason into creative reason (form) and passive reason (matter). Creative reason (form), said he, existed before either the body or soul were created. And that passive reason (material part of the soul) is connected with the body and will be destroyed, while creative reason being uninfluenced by the body, being immaterial, will continue to live on after the body dies. Thus, in Aristotle's philosophical system, form (creative reason) is a spark of the divine, a part of divinity, which comes into man's soul from without and is not influenced by the material side of the soul.

liveth. O foolish one, where will they find the intellectual soul without life? Assuredly, never. But life without senses will readily be found, as is seen in the unconscious when the sense leaveth him.

Thaddaeus answered: 'O master, when the sense leaveth the life, a man hath not life.'

Jesus answered: 'This is not true, because man is deprived of life when the soul departeth: because the soul returneth not any more to the body, save by miracle. But sense departeth by reason of fear that it receiveth, or by reason of great sorrow that the soul hath. For the sense hath God created for pleasure, and by that alone it liveth, even as the body liveth by food and the soul liveth by knowledge and love. This sense is now rebellious against the soul, through indignation that it hath at being deprived of the pleasure of paradise through sin. Wherefore there is the greatest need to nourish it with spiritual pleasure for him who willeth not that it should live of carnal pleasure. Understand ye? Verily I say unto you, that God having created it condemned it to hell and to intolerable snow and ice; because it said that it was God; but when he deprived it of nourishment, taking away its food from it, it confessed that it was a slave of God and the work of his hands. And now tell me, how doth sense work in the ungodly? Assuredly, it is as God in them: seeing that they follow sense, forsaking reason and the law of God. Whereupon they become abominable, and work not any good.'

107.

'And so the first thing that followeth sorrow for sin is fasting. For he that seeth that a certain food maketh him sick, for that he feareth death, after sorrowing that he hath eaten it, forsaketh it, so as not to make himself sick. So ought the sinner to do. Perceiving that pleasure hath made him to sin against God his creator by following sense in these good things of the world, let him sorrow at having done so, because it depriveth him of God, his life, and giveth him the eternal death of hell. But because man while living hath need to take these good things of the world, fasting is needful here. So let him proceed to mortify sense and to know God for his lord. And when he seeth the sense abhor fastings, let him put before it the condition of hell, where no pleasure at all but infinite sorrow is

---

The Stoics held that man is both soul and body, and that man's soul is a spark from the divine fire controlled by a governing part located in the heart. According to them like a blank tablet, sense impressions are written upon the tablet, such is the source of man's knowledge.

From such elements of speculative thought was formulated the erroneous philosophy Jesus attacks in these chapters:105, 106 & 107.

received: let him put before it the delights of paradise, that are so great that a grain of one of the delights of paradise is greater than all those of the world. For so will it easily be quieted: for that it is better to be content with little in order to receive much, than to be unbridled in little and be deprived of all and abide in torment.

'Ye ought to remember the rich feaster[210] in order to fast well. For he, wishing here on earth to fare deliciously every day, was deprived eternally of a single drop of water; while Lazarus, being content with crumbs here on earth, shall live eternally in full abundance of the delights of paradise.

'But let the penitent be cautious; for that Satan seeketh to annul every good work, and more in the penitent than in others, for that the penitent hath rebelled against him, and from being his faithful slave hath turned into a rebellious foe. Whereupon Satan will seek to cause that he shall not fast in any wise, under pretext of sickness, and when this shall not avail he will invite him to an extreme fast, in order that he may fall sick and afterwards live deliciously. And if he succeed not in this, he will seek to make him set his fast simply upon bodily food, in order that he may be like unto himself, who never eateth but always sinneth.

'As God liveth, it is abominable to deprive the body of food and fill the soul with pride, despising them that fast not, and holding oneself better than they. Tell me, will the sick man boast of the diet that is imposed on him by the physician, and call them mad who are not put on diet? Assuredly not. But he will sorrow for the sickness by reason of which he needs must be put upon diet. Even so I say unto you, that the penitent ought not to boast in his fast, and despise them that fast not; but he ought to sorrow for the sin by reason whereof he fasteth. Nor should the penitent that fasteth procure delicate food, but he should content himself with coarse food. Now will a man give delicate food to the dog that biteth and to the horse that kicketh? No, surely, but rather the contrary. And let this suffice you concerning fasting.

108.

'Hearken, then to what I shall say to you concerning watching. For just as there are two kinds of sleeping, viz., that of the body and that of the soul, even so must ye be careful in watching that while the body watcheth the soul sleep not. For this would be a most grievous error. Tell me, in parable: there is a man who whilst walking striketh himself against a rock, and in order to avoid striking it the

---

[210] *the rich feaster.* See chapter 24.

more with his foot, he striketh with his head - what is the state of such a man?'

'Miserable,' answered the disciples, 'for such a man is frenzied.'

Then said Jesus: 'Well have ye answered, for verily I say to you that he who watcheth with the body and sleepeth with the soul is frenzied. As the spiritual infirmity is more grievous than the corporeal, even so is it more difficult to cure. Wherefore, shall such a wretched one boast of not sleeping with the body, which is the foot of the life, while he perceiveth not his misery that he sleepeth with the soul, which is the head of the life? The sleep of the soul is forgetfulness of God and of his fearful judgement. The soul, then, that watcheth is that which in everything and in every place perceiveth God,[211] and in everything and through everything and above everything giveth thanks to his majesty, knowing that always at every moment it receiveth grace and mercy from God. Wherefore in fear of his majesty there always resoundeth in its ear that angelic utterance - "Creatures, come to judgement, for your Creator willeth to judge you." For it abideth habitually ever in the service of God. Tell me, whether do ye desire the more: to see by the light of a star or by the light of the sun?'

Andrew answered: 'By the light of the sun; for by the light of the star we cannot see the neighboring mountains, and by the light of the sun we see the tiniest grain of sand. Wherefore we walk with fear by the light of the star, but by the light of the sun we go securely.'

109.

Jesus answered: 'Even so I tell you that ye ought to watch with the soul by the sun of justice (which is) our God, and not to boast

---

[211] *perceiveth God.* Man sees by virtue of reflected light, and hears by virtue of disturbance of the air, but just as there are colors of the spectrum that man does not see with the eye, and sounds that are too low and too high for his range of hearing, so there are limitations to his other physical senses: smell, taste, and touch. And limitations to his technology, and thus the perception of his instruments and machines. Indeed, the unseen exists because it is beyond man's perception. Who can describe the color, height, width, depth, and shape of the emotions? Who has ever seen what they look like? What is their texture? Are they hot or cold to the touch? What are their fragrances? Other than the manifestations of their presence, how do we know they exist? We have never actually seen them, nor smelled them, or heard them come or go. Nor have we touched them, nor tasted them. What we perceive of them in others is the effects of their existence, and presence, and often if one is skillful in hiding the results of their presence from us, we will not be aware of them, or which one is really present. So it is with God, we perceive the effects of His existence and presence through His handiwork, and at least some of us through a higher sense.

yourselves of the watchings of the body. It is most true, therefore, that bodily sleep is to be avoided as much as is possible, but (to avoid it) altogether is impossible, the sense and the flesh being weighed down with food and the mind with business. Wherefore let him that will sleep little avoid too much business and much food.

'As God liveth, in whose presence standeth my soul, it is lawful to sleep somewhat every night, but it is never lawful to forget God and his fearful judgement: and the sleep of the soul is such oblivion.'

Then answered he who writeth: 'O master, how can we always have God in memory? Assuredly, it seemeth to us impossible.'

Said Jesus, with a sigh: 'This is the greatest misery that man can suffer, O Barnabas. For man cannot here upon earth have God his creator always in memory; saving them that are holy, for they always have God in memory, because they have in them the light of the grace of God, so that they cannot forget God. But tell me, have ye seen them that work quarried stones, how by their constant practice they have so learned to strike that they speak with others and all the time are striking the iron tool that worketh the stone without looking at the iron, and yet they do not strike their hands? Now do ye likewise. Desire to be holy if ye wish to overcome entirely this misery of forgetfulness. Sure it is that water cleaveth the hardest rocks with a single drop striking there for a long period.

'Do ye know why ye have not overcome this misery? Because ye have not perceived that it is sin. I tell you then that it is an error, when a prince giveth thee a present, O man, that thou shouldst shut thine eyes and turn thy back upon him. Even so do they err who forget God, for at all times man receiveth from God gifts and mercy.'

110.

'Now tell me, doth our God at all times grant you (his) bounty? Yea, assuredly; for unceasingly he ministereth to you the breath whereby ye live. Verily, verily, I say unto you, every time that your body receiveth breath your heart ought to say: "God be thanked!"'

Then said John: 'It is most true what thou sayest, O master; teach us therefore the way to attain to this blessed condition.'

Jesus answered: 'Verily I say to you, one cannot attain to such condition by human powers, but rather by the mercy of God our Lord. It is true indeed that man ought to desire the good in order that God may give it him. Tell me, when ye are at table do ye take those meats which ye would not so much as look at? No, assuredly. Even so I say unto you that ye shall not receive that which ye will not desire. God is able, if ye desire holiness, to make you holy in less time than the twinkling of an eye, but in order that man may be sensible of the gift and the giver our God willeth that we should wait and ask.

'Have ye seen them that practise shooting at a mark? Assuredly they shoot many times in vain. Howbeit, they never wish to shoot in vain, but are always in hope to hit the mark. Now do ye this, ye who ever desire to have our God in remembrance, and when ye forget, mourn; for God shall give you grace to attain to all that I have said.

'Fasting and spiritual watching are so united one with the other that, if one break the watch, straightway the fast is broken. For in sinning a man breaketh the fast of the soul, and forgetteth God. So is it that watching and fasting as regardeth the soul are always necessary for us and for all men. For to none is it lawful to sin. But the fasting of the body and its watchings, believe me, they are not possible at all times, nor for all persons. For there are sick and aged folk, women with child, men that are put upon diet, children, and others that are of weak complexion. For indeed everyone, even as he clotheth himself according to his proper measure, so should choose this (manner of) fasting. For just as the garments of a child are not suitable for a man of thirty years, even so the watchings and fastings of one are not suitable for another.'

111.

'But beware that Satan will use all his strength (to) bring it to pass that ye (shall) watch during the night, and afterward be sleeping when by commandment of God ye ought to be praying and listening to the word of God.

'Tell me, would it please you if a friend of yours should eat the meat and give you the bones?'

Peter answered: 'No, master, for such an one ought not to be called friend, but a mocker.'

Jesus answered with a sigh: 'Thou hast well said the truth, O Peter, for verily every one that watcheth with the body more than is necessary, sleeping, or having his head weighed down with slumber when he should be praying or listening to the words of God, such a wretch mocketh God his creator, and so is guilty of such a sin. Moreover, he is a robber, seeing that he stealeth the time that he ought to give to God, and spendeth it then, and as much as, pleaseth him.

'In a vessel of the best wine a man gave his enemies to drink so long as the wine was at its best, but when the wine came down to the dregs he gave to his lord to drink. What, think ye, will the master do to his servant when he shall know all, and the servant be before him? Assuredly, he will beat him and slay him in righteous indignation according to the laws of the world. And now what shall God do to the man that spendeth the best of his time in business, and the worst in prayer and study of the law? Woe to the wicked, because with this and with greater sin is its heart weighed down! Accordingly, when I said unto you that laughter should be turned into weeping, feasts into fasting, and sleep into watching, I compassed in three words all that ye have heard - that here on earth one ought always to weep, and that weeping should be from the heart, because God our creator is offended; that ye ought to fast in order to have lordship over the sense, and to watch in order not to sin; and that bodily weeping and bodily fasting and watching should be taken according to the constitution of each one.'

112.

Having said this, Jesus said: 'Ye needs must seek of the fruits of the field the wherewithal to sustain our life, for it is now eight days that we have eaten no bread. Wherefore I will pray to our God, and will await you with Barnabas.'

So all the disciples and apostles departed by fours and by sixes and went their way according to the word of Jesus. There remained with Jesus he who writeth; whereupon Jesus, weeping, said: 'O Barnabas, it is necessary that I should reveal to thee great secrets, which, after that I shall be departed from the world, thou shalt reveal to it.'

Then answered he that writeth, weeping, and said: 'Suffer me to weep, O master, and other men also, for that we are sinners. And thou, that art an holy one and prophet of God, it is not fitting for thee to weep so much.'

Jesus answered: 'Believe me, Barnabas, that I cannot weep as much as I ought. For if men had not called me God, I should have seen God here as he will be seen in paradise, and should have been safe not to fear the day of judgement. But God knoweth that I am innocent, because never have I harboured thought to be held more than a poor slave.[212] Nay, I tell thee that if I had not been called God I should have been carried into paradise when I shall depart from the world, whereas now I shall not go thither[213] until the judgement.

---

[212] *poor slave*. A poor and humble servant of God.

[213] *I shall not go thither.* Here we have a prophetic reference to that belief held in common by Muslims and Christians: that Jesus will return in the last days. As for the Christians, consider the words attributed to Jesus in the so-called New Testament: "Many will say to me in that day, Lord, Lord, have we not prophesied in thy name? And in thy name done many wonderful works? And then will I profess unto them, I never knew you; depart from me, ye that work iniquity." (Matt.7:22-23). Indeed, there

Now thou seest if I have cause to weep. Know, O Barnabas, that for this I must have great persecution, and shall be sold by one of my disciples for thirty pieces of money. Whereupon I am sure that he who shall sell me shall be slain in my name,[214] for that God shall take me up from the earth,[215] and shall change the appearance of the traitor so that every one shall believe him to be me; nevertheless, when he dieth an evil death, I shall abide in that dishonor[216] for a long time in the world. But when Mohammed shall come, the sacred messenger of God, that infamy shall be taken away. And this shall God do because I have confessed the truth of the Messiah; who shall give me this reward, that I shall be known to be alive and to be a stranger to that death of infamy.'

Then answered he that writeth: 'O master, tell me who is that wretch, for I fain would choke him to death.'

'Hold thy peace,' answered Jesus, ' for so God willeth,[217] and he cannot do otherwise; but see thou that when my mother is afflicted at such an event thou tell her the truth, in order that she may be comforted.'

Then answered he who writeth: 'All this will I do, O master, if God please.'

---

can be no doubt that since it is the Christians who do these things in Jesus' name, that it is they that are being addressed here.

[214] *shall be slain in my name.* Jesus' statement here: "I am sure that he who shall sell me [betray me for thirty pieces of money] shall be slain in my name," refers to God's justice referred to in chapter 97: "It is just that he who will not believe in the truth to his salvation should believe in a lie to his damnation." For the truth is, that God is not man, nor the son of man, and therefore no man is, or has ever been, nor will ever be, the son of God. (Num. 23:19.) But those who seek after unrighteousness will proclaim the slain man made to look like Jesus, was Jesus, and falsely declare that Jesus was the Son of God, slain as a human sacrifice to God for the sins of man. In this manner they will falsely portray God as being a savage deity like those of the pagans of old, while misrepresenting the facts concerning Jesus who is innocent of all this. And this evil was done by the agency of the Nicolaitans at the instigation of Satan, by God's permissive will, because of the waywardness of their own souls. (See Romans, 1:24-32; for the consequences of such evil, and compare it to the sorry state of affairs today).

[215] *God shall take me up form the earth.* "And Enoch walked with God, and he was not; for God took him [up]." (Gen. 5:22.) See also, II Kings 2:9-11; in which passage we are told: "And it came to pass, as they [Elijah and Elisha] went on, and talked, that, behold, there appeared a chariot of fire, and horses of fire, and separated them, and Elijah went up by a whirlwind into heaven." And in God's message revealed to Muhammad: "And because of their saying: 'We slew the Messiah Jesus, son of Mary, God's messenger.' They slew him not, nor crucified him, but it appeared so unto them; and behold! those who disagree concerning it are in doubt thereof; they have no knowledge thereof save pursuit of a conjecture; they slew him not for certain. But God took him up unto Himself. God is ever Mighty, Wise." (4:157-158).

[216] *I shall abide in that dishonor.* The false notion promoted by the Nicolaitans, that

113.

When the disciples were come they brought pine-cones, and by the will of God they found a good quantity of dates. So after the midday prayer they ate with Jesus. Whereupon the apostles and disciples, seeing him that writeth of sad countenance, feared that Jesus needs must quickly depart from the world. Whereupon Jesus consoled them, saying: 'Fear not, for my hour is not yet come that I should depart from you. I shall abide with you still for a little while. Therefore must I teach you now, in order that ye may go, as I have said, through all Israel to preach penitence; in order that God may have mercy upon the sin of Israel. Let every one therefore beware of sloth, and much more he that doeth penance; because every tree that beareth not good fruit shall be cut down and cast in the fire.

'There was a citizen who had a vineyard, and in the midst thereof had a garden, which had a fine fig-tree; whereon for three years when the owner came he found no fruit, and seeing every other tree bare fruit there he said to his vinedresser; "Cut down this bad tree, for it cumbereth the ground."

'The vinedresser answered: "Not so, my Lord, for it is a beautiful tree."

'"Hold they peace," said the owner, "for I care not for useless beauties. Thou shouldest know that the palm and the balsam are nobler than the fig. But I had planted in the courtyard of my house a plant of palm and one of balsam, which I had surrounded with costly walls, but when these bare no fruit, but leaves which heaped themselves up and putrefied the ground in front of the house, I caused them both to be removed. And how shall I pardon a fig-tree far from the house, which cumbreth my garden and my vineyard where every other tree beareth fruit? Assuredly I will not suffer it any longer."

'Then said the vinedresser: "Lord, the soil is too rich. Wait, therefore, one year more, for I will prune the fig-plant's branches, and take away from it the richness of the soil, putting in poor soil with stones, and so shall it bear fruit."

'The owner answered: "Now go and do so; for I will wait, and the fig-plant shall bear fruit." Understand ye this parable?'

Jesus a prophet of God was slain upon a tree, or a cross, being the symbol of a tree, has brought dishonor to his honorable name. (See Deut. 21:22-23).

[217] *for so God willeth.* That those who insist on believing a lie, after having been exposed to the truth, shall be condemned by that lie to hell. For such is the consequences of their waywardness. Christianity is not the continuation of the Abrahamic religion, but the continuation of the Greco-Roman tradition. And they (the Greeks and the Romans) were not adherents of the Abrahamic religion.

The disciples answered: 'No, Lord; therefor explain it to us.'

114.

Jesus answered: 'Verily I say unto you, the owner is God, and the vinedresser is his law. God, then, had in paradise the palm and the balsam; for Satan is the palm and the first man the balsam. Them did he cast out because they bare not fruit of good works, but uttered ungodly words that were the condemnation of many angels and many men. Now that God hath man in the world, in the midst of his creatures that serve God, all of them, according to his precept; and man, I say, bearing no fruit, God would cut him down and commit him to hell, seeing he pardoned not the angel and the first man, punishing the angel eternally, and the man for a time. Whereupon the law of God saith that man hath too much good in this life, and so it is necessary that he should suffer tribulation and be deprived of earthly goods, in order that he may do good works. Therefore our God waiteth for man to be penitent. Verily I say unto you, that our God hath condemned man to work so that, as said Job,[218] the friend and prophet of God: "As the bird is born to fly and the fish to swim, even so is man born to work."

'So also David[219] our father, a prophet of God, saith: "Eating the labours of our hands we shall be blessed, and it shall be well with us."

'Wherefore let every one work, according to his quality. Now tell me, if David our father and Solomon his son worked with their hands, what ought the sinner to do?'

Said John: 'Master, to work is a fitting thing, but this ought the poor to do.'

Jesus answered: 'Yea, for they cannot do otherwise. But knowest thou not that good, to be good, must be free from necessity? Thus the sun and the other planets are strengthened by the precepts of God so that they cannot do otherwise, wherefore they shall have no merit. Tell me, when God gave the precept to work, he said not: "A poor man shall live of the sweat of his face"? And Job did not say that: "As a bird is born to fly, so a poor man is born to work?" But God said to man: "In the sweat of thy countenance shalt thou eat bread," and Job that "Man is born to work." Therefore (only) he who is not man is free from this precept. Assuredly for no other reason are all things costly, but that there are a great multitude of idle folk: if these were to labour, some attending the ground and some at

---

[218] *as said Job.* Job 5:7.
[219] *So, also David.* Ps. 128:2.

fishing the water, there would be the greatest plenty in the world. And of the lack thereof it will be necessary to render an account in the dreadful day of judgement.'

115.

'Let man say somewhat to me. What hath he brought into the world, by reason of which he would live in idleness? Certain it is that he was born naked, and incapable of anything. Hence, of all that he has found, he is not the owner, but the dispenser. And he will have to render an account thereof in that dreadful day. The abominable lust, that maketh man like the brute beasts, ought greatly to be feared; for the enemy is of one's own household,[220] so that it is not possible to go into any place whither thine enemy may not come. Ah, how many have perished through lust! Through lust came the deluge,[221] insomuch that the world perished before the mercy of God and so that there were saved only Noah and eighty-three[222] human persons.

'For lust God overwhelmed three wicked cities[223] whence escaped only Lot and his two children.

'For lust the tribe of Benjamin[224] was all but extinguished. And I tell you verily that if I should narrate to you how many have perished through lust, the space of five days would not suffice.'

James answered: 'O Master, what signifieth lust?'

Jesus answered: 'Lust is an unbridled desire of love, which, not being directed by reason, bursts the bounds of man's intellect and affections; so that the man, not knowing himself, loveth that which he ought to hate. Believe me, when a man loveth a thing, not because God hath given him such thing, but as its owner, he is a fornicator; for that the soul, which ought to abide in union with God its creator, he hath united with the creature. And so God lamenteth by Isaiah the prophet, saying: "Thou hast committed fornication with many lovers; nevertheless, return unto me and I will receive thee."

---

[220] *enemy is of one's own household.* Often those who choose the path of sin, are born and raised in the same households of those who seek after righteousness.

[221] *the deluge.* Genesis, chapters 6, 7 & 8.

[222] *eighty-three.* In its present form, Gen. 6:18, mentions only eight.

[223] *overwhelmed three wicked cities.* For their idolatry and accompanying practice of homosexuality. (Gen. 19:1-29). Thus William Smith points out concerning the term Sodomites: "This word does not denote the inhabitants of Sodom; but it is employed in the A.V. of the Old Testament for those who practiced as a religious rite the abominable and unnatural vice from which the inhabitants of Sodom and Gomorrah have derived their lasting infamy." (*Smith's Bible Dictionary, art: Sodomites*, p.655).

[224] *tribe of Benjamin.* Judges, 19, 20.

'As God liveth in whose presence my soul standeth, if there were not internal lust within the heart of man, he would not fall into the external; for if the root be removed the tree dieth speedily.

'Let a man content himself therefore with the wife whom his creator hath given him, and let him forget every other woman.'

Andrew answered: 'How shall a man forget the women if he live in the city where there are so many of them?'

Jesus replied: 'O Andrew, certain it is he who liveth in the city, it will do him harm; seeing that the city is a sponge that draweth in every iniquity.

116.

'It behoveth a man to live in the city, even as the soldier liveth when he hath enemies around the fortress, defending himself against every assault and always fearing treachery on the part of the citizens. Even so, I say, let him repell every outward enticement of sin, and fear the sense, because it hath a supreme desire for things impure. But how shall he defend himself if he bridle not the eye, which is the origin of every carnal sin? As God liveth in whose presence my soul standeth, he who hath not bodily eyes is secure not to receive punishment save only to the third degree, while he that hath eyes receiveth it to the seventh degree.

'In the time of the prophet Elijah it came to pass that Elijah seeing a blind man weeping, a man of good life, asked him, saying: "Why weepest thou, O brother?" The blind man answered: "I weep because I cannot see Elijah the prophet, the holy one of God."[225]

'Then Elijah rebuked him, saying: "Cease from weeping, O man, for in weeping thou sinnest."

'The blind man answered: "Now tell me, is it a sin to see a holy prophet of God, that raiseth the dead and maketh the fire to come down from heaven?"

'Elijah answered: "Thou speakest not the truth, for Elijah is not able to do anything of all that thou sayest, because he is a man as thou art. For all the men in the world cannot make one fly to be born."

'Said the blind man: "Thou sayest this, O man, because Elijah must have rebuked thee for some sin of thine, wherefore thou hatest him."

'Elijah answered: "May it please God that thou be speaking the truth; because, O brother, if I should hate Elijah I should love God, and the more I should hate Elijah the more I should love God."

---

[225] *holy one of God.* Here again, as in other places in this gospel we have evidence of the Essene connection, this time this title is applied to Elijah.

'Hereupon was the blind man greatly angered, and said: "As God liveth, thou art an impious fellow! Can God then be loved while one hateth the prophets of God? Begone forthwith, for I will not listen to thee any longer!"

'Elijah answered: "Brother, now mayest thou see with thine intellect how evil is bodily seeing. For thou desirest sight to see Elijah, and hatest Elijah with thy soul."

'The blind man answered: "Now begone! For thou art the devil, that wouldst make me sin against the holy one of God."

'Then Elijah gave a sigh, and said with tears: "Thou hast spoken the truth, O brother, for my flesh, which thou desirest to see, separateth thee from God."

'Said the blind man: "I do not wish to see thee; nay, if I had my eyes, I would close them so as not to see thee?"

'Then said Elijah: Know, brother, that I am Elijah!"

'The blind man answered: "Thou speakest not the truth."

'Then said the disciples of Elijah: "Brother, he verily is the prophet of God, Elijah."

'"Let him tell me," said the blind man, "if he be the prophet, of what seed I am, and how I became blind?"

117.

'Elijah answered: "Thou art of the tribe of Levi; and because thou, in entering the temple of God, lookedst lewdly upon a woman, thou being near the sanctuary, our God took away thy sight."

'Then the blind man weeping said: "Pardon me, O holy prophet of God, for I have sinned in speaking with thee; for if I had seen thee I should not have sinned."

'Elijah answered: "May our God pardon thee, O brother because as regardeth me I know that thou hast told me the truth, seeing that the more I hate myself the more I love God, and if thou sawest me thou wouldst still thy desire, which is not pleasing to God. For Elijah is not your creator, but God; whence, so far as concerneth thee, I am the devil," said Elijah weeping, "because I turn thee aside from thy creator. Weep then, O brother, because thou hast not that light which would make thee see the true from the false, for if thou hadst had that thou wouldst not have despised my doctrine. Wherefore I say unto thee, that many desire to see me and come from far to see me, who despise my words. Wherefore it were better for them, for their salvation, that they had no eyes, seeing that everyone that findeth pleasure in the creature, be he who he may, and seeketh not to find pleasure in God, hath made an idol in his heart, and forsaken God."'

Then said Jesus, sighing: 'Have ye understood all that Elijah said?''

The disciples answered: 'In sooth, we have understood, and we are beside ourselves at the knowledge that here on earth there are very few that are not idolaters.'

118.

Then said Jesus: 'Ye speak the truth, for now was Israel desirous to establish the idolatry that they have in their hearts, in holding me for God; many of whom have now despised my teaching, saying that I could make myself lord of all Judaea, if I confessed myself to be God, and that I am mad to wish to live in poverty among desert places, and not abide continually among princes in delicate living. Oh hapless man, that prizest the light that is common to flies and ants and despisest the light that is common only to angels and prophets and holy friends of God![226]

'If, then, the eye shall not be guarded, O Andrew, I tell thee that it is impossible not to fall headlong into lust. Wherefore Jeremiah the prophet,[227] weeping vehemently, said truly: "Mine eye is a thief that robbeth my soul." For therefore did David[228] our father pray with greatest longing to God our lord that he would turn away his eyes in order that he might not behold vanity. For truly everything which hath an end is vain. Tell me, then, if one had two pence to buy bread, would he spend it to buy smoke? Assuredly not, seeing that smoke doth hurt to the eyes and giveth no sustenance to the body. Even so then let man do, for with the outward sight of his eyes and the inward sight of his mind he should seek to know God his creator and the good-pleasure of his will, and should not make the creature his end, which causeth him to lose the creator.

119.

'For verily every time that a man beholdeth a thing and forgetteth God who hath made it for man, he hath sinned. For if a friend of thine should give thee somewhat to keep in memory of him, and thou

---

[226] *holy friend of God.* In light of The Dead Sea Scrolls, not only is this title in conformity with Essene terminology, but this whole passage identifies Jesus and his disciples with the Essene movement in general. For the lifestyle, 'living in poverty in desert places,' characterizes the lifestyle of many who were Essenes. The reference to the light despised by the wayward amongst men, is Essenic terminology for the enlightenment that comes to everyone from God. Some receive it, others reject it, preferring a wayward life.

[227] *Jeremiah.* Lam 3:51.

[228] *David.* Ps. 119:37.

shouldest sell it and forget thy friend, thou hast offended against thy friend. Even so doth man; for when he beholdeth the creature and hath not in memory the creator, who for love of man hath created it, he sinneth against God his creator by ingratitude.

'He therefore who shall behold women and shall forget God who for the good of man created woman, he will love her and desire her. And to such degree will this lust of his break forth, that he will love everything like unto the thing loved: so that hence cometh that sin of which it is a shame to have memory. If, then, man shall put a bridle upon his eyes, he shall be lord of the sense, which cannot desire that which is not presented to it. For so shall the flesh be subject to the spirit. Because as the ship cannot move without wind, so the flesh without the sense cannot sin.

'That thereafter it would be necessary for the penitent to turn story-telling into prayer, reason itself showeth, even if it were not also a precept of God. For in every idle word man sinneth,[229] and our God blotteth out sin by reason of prayer. For that prayer is the advocate of the soul; prayer is the medicine of the soul; prayer is the defense of the heart; prayer is the weapon of faith, prayer is the bridle of sense; prayer is the salt of the flesh that suffereth it not to be corrupted by sin. I tell you that prayer is the hands of our life, whereby the man that prayeth shall defend himself in the day of judgement: for he shall keep his soul from sin here on earth, and shall preserve his heart that it be not touched by evil desires; offending Satan because he shall keep his sense within the law of God, and his flesh shall walk in righteousness, receiving from God all that he shall ask.

'As God liveth in whose presence we are, a man without prayer [230] can no more be a man of good works than a dumb man can plead

---

[229] *in every idle word man sinneth.* It has been said symbolically, that perhaps God gave man two eyes, two ears, and one tongue, because it is better that he should observe and listen at least twice as much as he speaks. It has also been said, that a jar full of coins rattles less than a jar with few coins. Thus we learn that the foolish do much talking, while the wise speak little. And when the wise do speak, they have something beneficial to say. The foolish on the other hand, gossip, and love gossip and foolish conversation; the wise love learning, and share that learning with others. Unfortunately, by individual choice, the fools are many, while the wise are few.

[230] *a man without prayer.* Consider I Kings 19:11-13. In verses 11 & 12, we are told: "And after the earthquake a fire; but the Lord was not in the fire. And after the fire a *still small voice.* And it was so, when Elijah heard it, that he wrapped his face in his mantle, and went out, and stood in the [entrance] of the cave. And, behold, there came a voice unto him, and said, what doest thou here Elijah?"

How shall one hear that still small voice of God He sometimes uses, except in silence, quiet prayer, and in meditation?

his cause to a blind one; than fistula can be healed without unguent; a man defend himself without movement; or attack another without weapons, sail without rudder, or preserve dead flesh without salt. For verily he who hath no hand cannot receive. If man could change dung into gold and clay into sugar, what would he do?'

Then Jesus being silent, the disciples answered: 'No one would exercise himself in any way other than in making gold and sugar.'

Then said Jesus: 'Now why doth not man change foolish story-telling into prayer? Is time, perchance, given him by God that he may offend God? For what prince would give a city to his subject in order that the latter might make war upon him? As God liveth, if man knew after what manner the soul is transformed by vain talking he would sooner bite off his tongue with his teeth than talk. O wretched world! for to-day men do not assemble together for prayer, but in the porches of the temple and in the very temple itself Satan hath there the sacrifice of vain talk, and that which is worse - of things which I cannot talk of without shame.

120.

'The fruit of vain talking is this, that it weakeneth the intellect in such wise that it is not ready to receive the truth; even as a horse accustomed to carry but one ounce of cotton flock cannot carry an hundred pounds of stone.

'But what is worse is the man who spendeth his time in jests. When he is fain to pray, Satan will put into his memory those same jests, insomuch that when he ought to weep over his sins to provoke God to mercy and to win forgiveness for his sins, by laughing he provoketh God to anger; who will chastise him, and cast him out.

'Woe, therefore, to them that jest and talk vainly! But if our God hath in abomination them that jest and talk vainly, how evil he hold them that murmur and slander their neighbour, and in what plight will they be who deal with sinning as with a business supremely necessary? Oh impure world, I cannot conceive how grievously thou wilt be punished by God! He, then, who would do penance, he, I say, must give out his words at the price of gold.'

His disciples answered: 'Now who will buy a man's words at the price of gold? Assuredly no one. And how shall he do penance? It is certain that he will become covetous!'

Jesus answered: 'Ye have your heart so heavy that I am not able to lift it up. Hence in every word it is necessary that I should tell you the meaning. But give thanks to God, who hath given you grace to know the mysteries of God. I do not say that the penitent should sell his talking, but I say that when he talketh he should think that he is casting forth gold. For indeed, so doing, even as gold is spent on necessary things, so he will talk only when it is necessary to talk. And just as no one spendeth gold on a thing which shall cause hurt to his body, so let him not talk of a thing that may cause hurt to his soul.

121.

'When the governor hath arrested a prisoner whom he examineth while the notary writeth down (the case), tell me, how doth such a man talk?'

The disciples answered: 'He talketh with fear and to the point, so as not to give suspicion of himself, and he is careful not to say anything that may displease the governor, but seeketh to speak somewhat whereby he may be set free.'

Then answered Jesus: 'This ought the penitent to do, then, in order not to lose his soul. For that God hath given two angels to every man for notaries, the one writing the good, the other the evil that the man doth. If then a man would receive mercy let him measure his talking more than gold is measured.

122.

'As for avarice, that must be changed into almsgiving. Verily I say unto you, that even as the plummet hath for its end the centre, so the avaricious hath hell for his end, for it is impossible for the avaricious to possess any good in paradise. Know ye wherefore? for I will tell you. As God liveth, in whose presence my soul standeth, the avaricious, even though he be silent with his tongue, by his works saith: "There is no other God than I." Inasmuch as all that he hath he is fain to spend at his own pleasure, not regarding his beginning or his end, that he is born naked, and dying leaveth all.[231]

'Now tell me: if Herod should give you a garden to keep, and ye were fain to bear yourselves as owners, not sending any fruit to Herod, and when Herod sent for fruit ye drove away his messengers, tell me, would ye be making yourselves kings over that garden? Assuredly yea. Now I tell you that even so the avaricious man maketh himself god over his riches which God hath given him.

'Avarice is a thirst of the sense, which having lost God through sin because it liveth by pleasure, and being unable to delight itself in God, who is hidden from it, surroundeth itself with temporal things which it holdeth as its good; and it groweth the stronger the more it seeth itself deprived of God.

---

[231] *leaveth all.* Job. 1:21.

'And so the conversion of the sinner is from God, who giveth the grace to repent. As said our father David:[232] "This change cometh from the right hand of God."

'It is necessary that I should tell you of what sort man is, if ye would know how penitence ought to be done. And so to-day let us render thanks to God, who hath given us the grace to communicate His will by my word.'

Whereupon he lifted up his hands and prayed,[233] saying: 'Lord God almighty and merciful, who in mercy hath created us, giving us the rank of men, thy servants, with the faith of thy true messenger, we thank thee for all thy benefits and would fain adore thee only all the days of our life, bewailing our sins, praying and giving alms, fasting and studying thy word, instructing those that are ignorant of thy will, suffering from the world for love of thee, and giving up our life unto the death to serve thee. Do thou, O Lord, save us from Satan, from the flesh and from the world, even as thou savedst thine elect for love of thine own self and for love of thy messenger for whom thou didst create us, and for love of all thy holy ones and prophets.'

The disciples ever answered: 'So be it,' 'So be it, Lord,' 'So be it, O our merciful God.'

123.

When it was day, Friday morning, early, Jesus, after the prayer, assembled his disciples and said to them: 'Let us sit down; for even as on this day God created man of the clay of the earth; even so will I tell you what a thing is man, if God please.'

When all were seated, Jesus said again: 'Our God, to shew to

---

[232] *David.* Ps. 77:10.

[233] *and prayed.* Carefully compare this prayer uttered by Jesus, with the following descriptive statement made by Eusebius around 300 A.D.: "Even in our own day, there are still men whose only guide is God; men who live by the true reason of nature, not only themselves free, but filling their neighbors with a spirit of freedom. They are not very numerous indeed. But that is not strange. For the highest nobility is ever rare; and then these men have turned aside from the vulgar herd to devote themselves to a contemplation of nature's verities. They pray, if it were possible, that they may reform our fallen lives; but if they cannot, owing to the tide of evils and wrongs which surges up in cities, they flee away, lest they too be swept off their feet by the force of its current. And we, if we had a true zeal for self-improvement, would have to track them to their places of retreat, and halting as suppliants before them, would beseech them to come to us and tame our life, grown too fierce and wild; preaching, instead of war and slavery and untold ills, their gospel of peace and freedom, and all the fullness of other blessings." (*The Meaning of the dead Sea Scrolls*, p. 139.) Indeed, the similarity between Jesus' prayer and this description implies that the people he is describing were Nazarenes.

his creatures his goodness and mercy and his omnipotence, with his liberality and justice, made a composition of four things contrary the one to the other, and united them in one final object, which is man - and this is earth, air, water, and fire -[234] in order that each one might temper its opposite. And he made of these four things a vessel, which is man's body, of flesh, bones, blood, marrow, and skin, with nerves and veins, and with all his inward parts; wherein God placed the soul and the sense, as two hands of this life: giving for lodgement to the sense every part of the body, for it diffused itself there like oil. And to the soul gave he for lodgement the heart, where, united with the sense, it should rule the whole life.

'God, having thus created man, put into him a light which is called reason, which was to unite the flesh, the sense, and the soul in a single end - to work for the service of God.

'Whereupon, he placing this work in paradise, and the reason being seduced of the sense by the operation of Satan, the flesh lost its rest, the sense lost the delight whereby it liveth, and the soul lost its beauty.

'Man having come to such a plight, the sense, which findeth not repose in labour, but seeketh delight, not being curbed by reason, followeth the light which the eyes show it; whence, the eyes not being able to see aught but vanity, it deceiveth itself, and so, choosing earthly things, sinneth.

'Thus it is necessary that by the mercy of God man's reason be enlightened afresh, to know good from evil and (to distinguish) the true delight: knowing which, the sinner is converted to penitence. Wherefore I say unto you verily, that if God our Lord enlighten not the heart of man,[235] the reasonings of men are of no avail.'

John answered: 'Then to what end serveth the speech of men?'

Jesus replied: 'Man as man availeth naught to convert man to penitence: but man as a means which God useth converteth man; so that seeing God worketh by a secret fashion in man for man's

---

[234] *earth, air, water and fire.* The Babylonians and the Egyptians speculated that water, air and earth were elements of which the earth was composed. To these, the Greek philosopher, Anaximander, (c. 611-547 B.C.) added a fourth, that of fire, and taught in his philosophical system, that these four elements were ever in opposition to one another: wet to dry, etc. There can be no doubt that here again in this passage, Jesus is teaching in the manner of one who is an Essene. For as Philo points out: "Abstract philosophy and logic they eschewed except so far as it could subserve ethical truth and practice. Natural philosophy they only studied so far as it teaches that there is a God who made and watches over all things. Moral philosophy or ethic was their chief preoccupation, and their conduct was regulated by their national (Mosaic) laws." (*The Meaning of the Dead Sea Scrolls*, p. 138).

[235] *if God our Lord enlighten not the heart.* See the note to chapter 78.

salvation, one ought to listen to every man, in order that among all may be received him in whom God speaketh to us.'

James answered: 'O Master, if perchance there shall come a false prophet and lying teacher pretending to instruct us, what ought we to do?

124.

Jesus answered in parable: 'A man goeth to fish with a net, and therein he catcheth many fishes, but those that are bad he throweth away.

'A man went forth to sow, but only the grain that falleth on good ground beareth seed.

'Even so ought ye to do, listening to all and receiving only the truth, seeing that the truth alone beareth fruit unto eternal life.'

Then answered Andrew: 'Now how shall the truth be known?'

Jesus answered: 'Everything that conformeth to the book of Moses, that receive ye for true; seeing that God is one, the truth is one; whence it followeth that the doctrine is one and the meaning of the doctrine is one; and therefore the faith is one. Verily I say unto you that if the truth had not been erased from the book of Moses, God would not have given to David our father the second. And if the book of David had not been contaminated, God would not have committed the Gospel to me; seeing that the Lord our God is unchangeable, and hath spoken but one message to all men.[236] Wherefore, when the messenger of God shall come, he shall come to cleanse away all wherewith the ungodly have contaminated my book.'

Then answered he who writeth: 'O Master, what shall a man do when the law shall be found contaminated and the false prophet shall speak?'

Jesus answered: 'Great is thy question, O Barnabas: wherefore I tell thee that in such a time few are saved, seeing that men do not consider their end, which is God. As God liveth in whose presence my soul standeth, every doctrine that shall turn man aside from his end, which is God, is most evil doctrine. Wherefore there are three things that thou shalt consider in doctrine - namely, love towards God, pity towards one's neighbour, and hatred towards thyself, who hast offended God, and offendest him every day. Wherefore every doctrine that is contrary to these three heads do thou avoid, because it is most evil.

---

[236] *one message to all men.* There is but one path to salvation: obedience to God. Every true prophet taught his people to be in submission to God.

125.

'I will return now to avarice: and I tell you that when the sense would fain acquire a thing or tenaciously keep it, reason must say: "Such a thing will have its end." It is certain that if it will have an end it is madness to love it. Wherefore it behoves one to love and to keep that which will not have an end.

'Let avarice then be changed into alms, distributing rightly what a man hath acquired wrongly.

'And let him see to it that what the right hand shall give the left hand shall not know'. Because the hypocrites when they do alms desire to be seen and praised of the world. But verily they are vain, seeing that for whom a man worketh from him doth he receive his wages. If, then, a man would receive anything of God, it behoveth him to serve God.

'And see that when ye do alms, ye consider that ye are giving to God all that (ye give) for love of God. Wherefore be not slow to give, and give of the best of that which ye have, for love of God.

'Tell me, desire you to receive of God anything that is bad? Certainly not, O dust and ashes! Then how have ye faith in you if ye shall give anything bad for love of God?

'It were better to give nothing than to give a bad thing; for in not giving ye shall have some excuse according to the world: but in giving a worthless thing, and keeping the best for yourselves, what shall be the excuse?

'And this is all that I have to say to you concerning penitence.'

Barnabas answered: 'How long ought penitence to last?'

Jesus replied: 'As long as a man is in a state of sin he ought always to repent and do penance for it. Wherefore as human life always sinneth, so ought it always to do penance; unless ye would make more account of your shoes than of your soul, since every time that your shoes are burst ye mend them.'

126.

Jesus having called together his disciples, sent them forth by two and two through the region of Israel, saying: 'Go and preach even as ye have heard.'

Then they bowed themselves and he laid his hand upon their heads, saying: 'In the name of God, give health to the sick, cast out the demons, and undeceive Israel concerning me, telling them that which I said before the high priest.'

They departed therefore, all of them save him who writeth, with James and John; and they went through all Judaea, preaching penitence even as Jesus had told them, healing every sort of sickness, insomuch that in Israel were confirmed the words of Jesus that God is one and Jesus is prophet of God, when they saw such a multitude do that which Jesus did concerning the healing of the sick.

But the sons of the devil found another way to persecute Jesus, and these were the priests and the scribes. Whereupon they began to say that Jesus aspired to the monarchy over Israel. But they feared the common people, wherefore they plotted against Jesus secretly.

Having passed throughout Judaea the disciples returned to Jesus, who received them as a father receiveth his sons, saying: 'Tell me, how hath wrought the Lord our God? Surely I have seen Satan fall under your feet and ye trample upon him even as the vinedresser treadeth the grapes!'

The disciples answered: 'O Master, we have healed numberless sick persons, and cast out many demons which tormented men.'

Said Jesus: 'God forgive you, O brethren, because ye have sinned in saying "We have healed." seeing it is God that hath done all.'

Then said they: 'We have talked foolishly; wherefore, teach us how to speak.'

Jesus answered: 'In every good work say "God hath wrought" and in every bad one say "I have sinned."'

'So will we do,' said the disciples to him.

Then said Jesus: 'Now what saith Israel, having seen God do by the hands of so many men that which God hath done by my hands?'

The disciples answered: 'They say that there is one God alone and that thou art God's prophet.'

Jesus answered with joyful countenance: 'Blessed be the holy name of God, who hath not despised the desire of me his servant!' And when he had said this they retired to rest.

127.

Jesus departed from the desert and entered into Jerusalem; whereupon all the people ran to the temple to see him. So after the reading of the psalms Jesus mounted up on the pinnacle where the scribe used to mount, and, having beckoned for silence with his hand, he said: 'Blessed be the holy name of God, O brethren, who hath created us of the clay of the earth, and not of flaming spirit. For when we sin we find mercy before God, which Satan will never find, because through his pride he is incorrigible, saying that he is always noble, for that he is flaming spirit.

'Have ye heard, brethren, that which our father David saith[237]

---

[237] *David saith.* Ps. 103: 14-17.

of our God, that he remembereth that we are dust and that our spirit goeth and returneth not again, wherefore he hath had mercy upon us? Blessed are they that know these words, for they will not sin against their Lord eternally, seeing that after the sin they repent, wherefore their sin abideth not. Woe unto them that extol themselves, for they shall be humbled to the burning coals of hell. Tell me, brethren, what is the cause for self-exaltation? Is there, perchance, any good here upon earth? No, assuredly, for as saith Solomon,[238] the prophet of God: "Everything that is under the sun is vanity."[239] But if the things of the world do not give us cause; "To extol ourselves in our heart, much less doth our life give us cause;" for it is burdened with many miseries, since all the creatures inferior to man fight against us. O, how many have been slain by the burning heat of summer; how many have been slain by the frost and cold of winter; how many have been slain by lightning and by hail: how many have been drowned in the sea by the fury of winds; how many have died of pestilence, of famine, or because they have been devoured of wild beasts, bitten of serpents, choked by food! O hapless man, who extolleth himself having so much to weigh him down, being laid wait for by all the creatures in every place! But what shall I say of the flesh and the sense that desire only iniquity; of the world, that offereth nought but sin; of the wicked, who, serving Satan, persecute whosoever would live according to the law of God? Certain it is, brethren, that if man, as saith our father David,[240] with his eyes should consider eternity, he would not sin.

'To extol oneself in one's heart is but to lock up the pity and mercy of God, that he pardon not. For our father David[241] saith that our God remembereth that we are but dust and that our spirit goeth and returneth not again. Whoso extolleth himself, then, denieth that he is dust, and hence, not knowing his need, he asketh not help, and so angereth God his helper. As God liveth in whose presence my soul standeth, God would pardon Satan if Satan should know his own misery, and ask mercy of his Creator, who is blessed for evermore.'

128.

'Accordingly, brethren, I, a man, dust and clay, that walk upon the earth, say unto you: Do penance and know your sins. I say,

---

[238] *as saith Solomon.* Eccl. 1:2.

[239] *is vanity.* Vanity refers to the emptiness in the final phase of this earthly life when one is apart from God.

[240] *our father David.* This Psalm is now lost, and does not appear in Psalsms in its present form.

[241] *David saith.* Ps. 103:14-15.

brethren, that Satan, by means of the Roman soldiery, deceived you when ye said that I was God. Wherefore, beware that ye believe them not, seeing they are fallen under the curse of God, serving the false and lying gods; even as our father David invoketh a curse[242] upon them, saying: "The gods of the nations are silver and gold, the work of their hands; that have eyes and see not, have ears and hear not, have noses and smell not, have a mouth and eat not, have a tongue and speak not, have hands and touch not, have feet and walk not." Wherefore said David our father, praying our living God, "Like unto them be they that make them and they trust in them."

'O pride unheard-of, this pride of man, who being created by God out of earth forgetteth his condition and would fain make God at his own pleasure![243] Wherein he silently mocketh God, as though he should say: "There is no use in serving God." For so do their works show.[244] To this did Satan desire to reduce you, O brethren, in making you believe me to be God; because, I not being able to create a fly, and being passable and mortal, I can give you nothing of use, seeing that

---

[242] *David invoketh a curse.* Ps. 115: 4-8.

[243] *would fain make God at his own pleasure.* The same is also ironically reported in Romans: "Professing themselves to be wise, they (the Gentiles) became fools. *And changed the glory of the incorruptible God into an image made like corruptible man, and birds, and four-footed beasts, and creeping things.* Wherefore, God also gave them up to uncleanness through the lusts of their own hearts, to dishonor their own bodies between themselves, who [exchanged] the truth of God for a lie, and worshipped and served the creature more than the Creator, who is blessed forever. Amen. For this cause God gave them up unto vile affections; for even their women did (exchange) the natural use for that which is against nature; and likewise also the men, leaving the natural use of the woman, burned in their lust one toward another, men with men working that which is unseemly, and receiving in themselves that recompense of their error which was [fitting]." (Romans 1:22-27.) This description of the ancient pagans, is also very descriptive of western Christendom.

[244] *their works show.* The consequences of atheism and idolatry are further described in Romans by one who was guilty of preaching idolatry. "And even as they [the Gentiles] did not like to retain God in their knowledge," says he, "God gave them over to a reprobate mind, to do those things which are not [seemly], being filled with all unrighteousness, fornication, wickedness, covetousness, maliciousness; full of envy, murder, [strife], deceit, malignity; whisperers, backbiters, haters of God, [insolent] proud boasters, inventors of evil things, disobedient to parents; without understanding, covenant breakers, without natural affection, implacable, unmerciful; who, knowing the judgement of God, that they who commit such things are worthy of death, not only do the same but have pleasure in them that do them." (Romans 1:28-32).

"To this," said Jesus, "did Satan desire to reduce you, O brethren, in making you believe me to be God." Indeed, the description in Romans fits the Christian world like a glove, and those who though they profess not to be Christians, nevertheless, follow in their footsteps.

I myself have need of everything. How, then, could I help you in all things, as it is proper to God to do?

'Shall we, then, who have for our God the great God who hath created the universe with his word, mock at the Gentiles and their gods?

There were two men who came up here into the temple to pray: the one was a Pharisee and the other a publican. The Pharisee drew nigh to the sanctuary, and praying with his face uplifted said: "I give thee thanks, O Lord my God, because I am not as other men, sinners, who do every wickedness, and particularly as this publican; for I fast twice in the week and give tithes of all I possess."

'The publican remained afar off, bowed down to the earth, and beating his breast he said with bent head: "Lord, I am not worthy to look upon the heaven nor upon thy sanctuary, for I have sinned much; have mercy upon me!"

'Verily I say unto you, the publican went down from the temple in better case than the Pharisee, for that our God justified him, forgiving him all his sin. But the Pharisee went down in worse case than the publican, because our God rejected him, having his works in abomination.

129.

'Shall the axe, perchance, boast itself[245] at having cut down the forest where a man hath made a garden? Nay, assuredly, for the man hath done all, yea and (made) the axe, with his hands.

'And thou, O man, shalt thou boast thyself of having done aught that is good, seeing our God created thee of clay and worketh in thee all good that is wrought?'

'And wherefore despisest thou thy neighbour? Knowest thou not that if God had not preserved thee from Satan thou wouldst be worse than Satan?

Now knowest thou not that one single sin changed the fairest angel into the most repulsive demon? And that the most perfect man that hath come into the world, which was Adam, it changed into a wretched being, subjecting him to what we suffer, together with all his offspring? What decree, then, hast thou, in virtue whereof thou mayest live at thine own pleasure without any fear: Woe unto thee, O clay, for because thou hast exalted thyself above God who created thee thou shalt be abased beneath the feet of Satan who layeth wait for thee.'

And having said this, Jesus prayed, lifting up his hands to the

---

[245] *boast itself.* Isa. 10:15.

Lord, and the people said: 'So be it! So be it!' When he had finished his prayer he descended from the pinnacle. Whereupon there were brought unto him many sick folk whom he made whole, and he departed from the temple. Thereupon Simon, a leper whom Jesus had cleansed, invited him to eat bread.

The priests and scribes, who hated Jesus, reported to the Roman soldiers that which Jesus had said against their gods. For indeed they were seeking how to kill him, but found it not, because they feared the people.

Jesus, having entered the house of Simon, sat down to the table. And while he was eating, behold a woman named Mary, a public sinner, entered into the house, and flung herself upon the ground behind Jesus' feet, and washed them with her tears, anointed them with precious ointment, and wiped them with the hairs of her head.

Simon was scandalized, with all that sat at meat, and they said in their hearts: 'If this man were a prophet he would know who and of what sort is this woman, and would not suffer her to touch him.'

Then said Jesus: 'Simon, I have a thing to say to thee.'

Simon answered: 'Speak, O Master, for I desire thy word.'

130.

Jesus said: 'There was a man who had two debtors. The one owed to his creditor fifty pence, the other five hundred. Whereupon, when neither of them had wherewithal to pay, the owner, moved with compassion, forgave the debt to each. Which of them would love his creditor most?'

Simon answered: 'He to whom was forgiven the greater debt.'

Said Jesus: 'Thou hast well said' I say unto thee, therefore, behold this woman and thyself; for ye were both debtors to God, the one for leprosy of the body, the other for leprosy of the soul, which is sin.

'God our Lord, moved with compassion through my prayers, hath willed to heal thy body and her soul. Thou, therefore, lovest me little, because thou hast received little as a gift. And so, when I entered thy house thou didst not kiss me nor anoint my head. But this woman, lo! Straightway on entering thy house she placed herself at my feet, which she hath washed with her tears and anointed with precious ointment. Wherefore verily I say unto thee, many sins are forgiven her, because she hath loved much.' And turning to the woman he said: 'Go thy way in peace, for the Lord our God hath pardoned thy sins; but see thou sin no more. Thy faith hath saved thee.'

131.

His disciples drew nigh unto Jesus after the nightly prayer, and said: 'O Master, how must we do to escape pride?'

Jesus answered: 'Have ye seen a poor man invited to a prince's house to eat bread?'

John answered: 'I have eaten bread in Herod's house. For before I knew thee I went to fish, and used to sell the fish to the family of Herod. Whereupon, one day when he was feasting, I having brought thither a fine fish, he made me stay and eat there.'

Then said Jesus: 'Now how didst thou eat bread with infidels? God pardon thee, O John! But tell me, how didst thou bear thyself at the board? Didst thou seek to have the most honourable place? Didst thou ask for the most delicate food? Didst thou speak when thou wast not questioned at the table? Didst thou account thyself more worthy than the others to sit at table?'

John answered: 'As God liveth, I did not dare to lift up my eyes, seeing myself, a poor fisherman, ill-clad, sitting among the king's barons. Whereupon, when the king gave me a little piece of flesh, methought that the world had fallen upon my head, for the greatness of the favour that the king did unto me. And verily I say that, if the king had been of our Law, I should have been fain to serve him all the days of my life.'

Jesus cried out: 'Hold thy peace, John, for I fear lest God should cast us into the abyss, even like Abiram,[246] for our pride!'

The disciples trembled with fear at the words of Jesus; when he said again: 'Let us fear God, that he cast us not into the abyss for our pride.

'O brethren, have ye heard of John what is done in the house of a prince? Woe to the man that come into the world, for as they live in pride they shall die in contempt and shall go into confusion.

'For this world is a house where God feasteth men, wherein have eaten all the holy ones and prophets of God. And verily I say to you, everything that a man receiveth, he receiveth it from God. Wherefore man ought to bear himself with deepest humility; knowing his own vileness and the greatness of God, with the great bounty wherewith he nourisheth us. Therefore it is not lawful for man to say: "Ah, why is this done and this said in the world?: but rather to account himself, as in truth he is, unworthy to stand in the world at God's board. As God liveth, in whose presence my soul standeth, there is nothing so

---

[246] *Abiram.* Num. 16.

small received there in the world from the hand of God, but that in return man ought to spend his life for love of God.

'As God liveth, thou sinnedst not, O John, in eating with Herod, for it was of God's disposition thou didst so, in order that thou mightest be our teacher and (the teacher) of every one that feareth God. So do, said Jesus to disciples, 'that ye may live in the world as John lived in the house of Herod when he ate bread with him, for so shall ye be in truth free from all pride.'

132.

Jesus walking along the sea of Galilee was surrounded by a great multitude of folk, wherefore he sent into a little boat which lay a little off from the shore by itself, and anchored so near the land that the voice of Jesus might be heard. Whereupon they all drew nigh to the sea, and sitting down awaited his word. He then opened his mouth and said: 'Behold, the sower went out to sow, whereupon as he sowed some of the seed fell upon the road, and this was trodden under foot of men and eaten up of birds; some fell upon the stones, whereupon when it sprang up, because it had no moisture, it was burnt up by the sun; some fell in the hedges, whereupon when it grew up the thorns chocked the seed; and some fell on good ground, whereupon it bare fruit, even to thirty, sixty, and an hundredfold.'

Again Jesus said: 'Behold, the father of a family sowed good seed in his field: whereupon, as the servants of the good man slept, the enemy of the man their master came and sowed tares over the good seed. Whereupon, when the corn[247] sprang up, there was seen sprung up among the corn a great quantity of tares. The servants came to their master and said: "O sir, didst thou not sow good seed in thy field? Wherefore then is there sprung up therein a great quantity of tares?" The master answered: "Good seed did I sow, but while men slept the enemy of man came and sowed tares over the corn."

'Said the servants: "Wilt thou that we go and pull up the tares from among the corn?"

'The master answered: "Do not so, for ye would pull up the corn therewith; but wait till the time of harvest cometh. For then shall ye go and pull up the tares from among the corn and cast them into the fire to be burned, but the corn ye shall put into my granary."'

Again Jesus said: 'There went forth many men to sell figs. But when they arrived at the market-place, behold, men sought not good

---

[247] *the corn*, That is to say, the grain, for the term corn is frequently used for grain and not for maize.

figs but fair leaves. Therefore the men were not able to sell their figs. And seeing this, an evil citizen said: "Surely I may become rich." Whereupon he called together his two sons and (said): "Go ye and gather a great quantity of leaves with bad figs." And these they sold for their weight in gold, for the men were mightily pleased with leaves. Whereupon the men, eating the figs, became sick with a grievous sickness.'

Again Jesus said: 'Behold a citizen hath a fountain, from which all the neighbouring citizens take water to wash off their uncleanness; but the citizen suffereth his own clothes to putrefy.'

Again Jesus said: 'There went forth two men to sell apples. The one chose to sell the peel of the apple for its weight in gold, caring nought for the substance of the apples. The other desired to give the apples away, receiving only a little bread for his journey. But men bought the peel of the apples for its weight in gold, caring nought for him who was fain to give them, nay even despising him.'

And thus on that day Jesus spake to the crowd in parables. Then having dismissed them, he went with his disciples to Nain, where he had raised to life the widow's son; who, with his mother, received him into his house and ministered unto him.

133.

His disciples drew nigh to Jesus and asked him, saying: 'O Master, tell us the meaning of the parables which thou spakest unto the people.

Jesus answered: 'The hour of prayer draweth nigh: wherefore when the evening prayer is ended I will tell you the meaning of the parables.'

When the prayer was ended, the disciples came near to Jesus and he said to them: 'The man who soweth seed upon the road, upon the stones, upon the thorns, upon the good ground, is he who teacheth the word of God, which falleth upon a great number of men.

'It falleth upon the road when it cometh to the ears of sailors and merchants, who by reason of the long journeys which they make, and the variety of nations with whom they have dealings, have the word of God removed from their memory by Satan. It falleth upon the stones when it cometh to the ears of courtiers, for by reason of the great anxiety these have to serve the body of a prince the word of God to doth not sink into them. Wherefore, albeit they have some memory thereof, as soon as they have any tribulation the word of God goeth out of their memory: for, seeing they serve not God, they cannot hope for help from God.

'It falleth among the thorns when it cometh to the ears of them that love their own life, whereupon, though the word of God grow upon them, when carnal desires grow up they choke the good seed of the word of God, for carnal comforts cause men to forsake the word of God. That which falleth on good ground is when the word of God cometh to the ears of him who feareth God, whereupon it bringeth forth fruit of eternal life. Verily I say unto you, that in every condition when man feareth God the word of God will bear fruit in him.

'Of that father of a family, I tell you verily that he is God our Lord; father of all things, for that he hath created all things. But he is not a father after the manner of nature, for that he is incapable of motion, without which generation is impossible. It is, then, our God, whose is this world; and the field where he soweth is mankind, and the seed is the word of God. So when the teachers are negligent in preaching the word of God, through being occupied in the business of the world, Satan soweth error in the heart of men, whence are come countless sects of wicked doctrine.

'The holy ones and prophets[248] cry: "O sir, gavest thou not, then, good doctrine to men? Wherefore, then, be there so many errors?"

'God answereth:[249] "I have given good doctrine to men, but while men have been given up to vanity Satan hath sowed errors to bring to naught my law."

'The holy ones say:[250] "O Sir, we will disperse these errors by destroying men."

'God answereth:[251] "Do not so, for the faithful are so closely

---

[248] *The Holy ones and prophets.* The Essenes and prophets. Because the Essenes held the belief that a righteous remnant was ever present throughout Israelite history to preserve the faith reaffirmed on Mt. Sinai, the title: "holy one of God," being one of the titles by which they were known, could be used by Jesus in this manner.

[249] *God answereth.* History bears witness to this answer given by God.

[250] *The holy ones say.* The words attributed here to the "holy ones" by Jesus, characterizes the attitude of the Essenes, for in their scroll: The War of the Sons of Light and the Sons of Darkness (also known as the Scroll of The War Rule), the theme is the final war against Gog and Magog, a theme that appears many times in the Hebrew Bible itself, particularly in Ezekiel, and Daniel. In the Essene document in which their battle plans are spelled out, the Essenes refer to themselves as the Sons of Light, and their enemies, Gog and Magog, and the Jews with them, as the Sons of Darkness. Other names such as Kittim, Moabites, etc., are also used to describe the enemy. So that these writings bear witness to the attitude attributed here to the Essenes (holy ones), "O Sir, we will disperse these errors by destroying men."

[251] *God answereth.* Although the Essenes held the above stated belief and attitude, they nevertheless abided by what is expressed here by God. That they should wait for the judgement. However, there did come forth from the Essene movement those who joined the Zealots, and it is these who along with the Galilean party known as Zealots are advised to wait until the Judgement. (*Jews, God and History*, p. 98.)

joined to the infidels by kinship that the faithful will be lost with the infidel. But wait until the judgment, for at that time shall the infidels be gathered by mine angels and shall be cast out with Satan into hell, while the good faithful ones shall come to my kingdom." Of a surety, many infidel fathers shall beget faithful sons, for whose sake God waiteth for the world to repent.

134.

"They that bear good figs[252] are the true teachers who preach good doctrine, but the world, which taketh pleasure in lies, seeketh from the teachers leaves of fine words and flattery.[253] The which seeing, Satan joineth himself with the flesh and the sense, and bringeth a large supply of leaves; that is, a quantity of earthly things,[254] in which he covereth up sin; the which receiving, man becometh sick and ready for eternal death.

'The citizen who hath the water and giveth his water to others to wash off their uncleanness, but suffereth his own garments to become putrefied, is the teacher who to others preacheth penitence and himself abideth still in sin.

'O wretched man, because not the angels but his own tongue writeth upon the air the punishment that is fitting for him!

'If one had the tongue of an elephant, and the rest of his body were as small as an ant, would not this thing be monstrous? Yea, of a surety. Now I say unto you, verily, that he is more monstrous who preacheth penitence to others, but himself repenteth not of his sins.

'Those two men that sell apples are - the one, he who preacheth for love of God, wherefore he flattereth none, but preacheth in truth, seeking only a poor man's livelihood. As God liveth, in whose presence my soul standeth, such a man is not received by the world,

---

[252] *They that bear good figs.* It is this statement that is most likely responsible for the following statement in Luke: "For every tree is known by its own fruit. For from thorns men do not gather figs, nor from a bramble bush gather they grapes. A good man, out of the good treasure of his heart, bringeth forth that which is good; and an evil man, out of the evil treasure of his heart, bringeth forth that which is evil; for of the abundance of the heart his mouth speaketh." (Luke 6:44-45).

[253] *leaves of fine words and flattery.* To cover up the true nature of their lies, and the stench of their evil.

[254] *a quantity of earthly things.* The world will tend to judge the disciples of Satan, not by their evil, but being blinded, they will erroneously judge them to be worthy by virtue of their material gain and technological achievements, ignoring the fact that these gains and achievements were brought about through the exploitation of others. So that the thief is glorified by the victim; the ignorant by those who have been ignorized by them; the rapist by the raped; and the murderer by the slain. Such is the sorry state of affairs.

but rather despised. But he who selleth the peel for its weight in gold, and giveth the apple away, he it is who preacheth to please men: and, so flattering the world, he ruineth the soul that followeth his flattery. Ah! how many have perished for this cause!;

Then answered he who writeth and said: 'How should one listen to the word of God; and how should one know him that preacheth for love of God?'

Jesus answered: 'He that preacheth should be listened to as though God were speaking, when he preacheth good doctrine; because God is speaking through his mouth. But he that reproveth not sins, having respect of persons, flattering particular men, should be avoided as an horrible serpent, for in truth he poisoneth the human heart.'

'Understand ye? Verily I say unto you, even as a wounded man hath no need of fine bandages to bind up his wounds, but rather of a good ointment, so also hath a sinner no need of fine words, but rather of good reproofs, in order that he may cease to sin.'

135.

Then said Peter: 'O Master, tell us how the lost shall be tormented, and how long they shall be in hell, in order that man may flee from sin.

Jesus answered: 'O Peter, it is a great thing that thou hast asked, nevertheless, if God please, I will answer thee. Know ye, therefore, that hell is one, yet hath seven centres[255] one below another. Hence, even as sin is of seven kinds, for as seven gates of hell hath Satan generated it: so are there seven punishments therein.

'For the pound, that is the loftiest in heart, shall be plunged into the lowest centre, passing through all the centres above it, and

---

[255] *hell is one, yet hath seven centers.* Because of serious deficiencies in their scholarship, Lonsdale and Laura Ragg, erroneously thought that this chapter was further evidence that this authentic Gospel was not authentic. It was their opinion that the doctrine of hell having seven compartments, was the work of an imaginary 14th century forger drawing upon Dante Aligheri's *Divine Comedy*, written sometime after 1302 A.D. Had they researched rabbinic literature, they would have realized their mistake. For as Professor Sandmel points out by the age in which Jesus lived, an afterlife was acknowledged in the oral traditions expounded by the rabbis - and as we know, Jesus was referred to as a rabbi. He also points out, that according to tradition, God had created a place called Gehenna, "hell," in the sixth time period of creation. It is held to be so large as to be immeasurable and divided into seven compartments. Although there is fire there, hell is nevertheless dark. (*Judaism and Christian Beginnings*, pp. 200-201).

suffering in them all the pains that are therein. And as here he seeketh to be higher than God, in wishing to do after his own manner, contrary to that which God commandeth, and not wishing to recognize anyone above him: even so there shall he be put under the feet of Satan and his devils, who shall trample him down as the grapes are trampled when wine is made, and he shall be ever derided and scorned of devils.

'The envious, who here chafeth at the good of his neighbor and rejoiceth at his misfortune, shall go down to the sixth centre, and there shall be chafed by the fangs of a great number of infernal serpents.

'And it shall seem to him that all things in hell rejoice at his torment, and mourn that he be not gone down to the seventh centre. For although the damned are incapable of any joy, yet the justice of God shall cause that it shall so seem to the wretched envious man, as when one seemeth in a dream to be spurned by some one and feeleth torment thereby - even so shall be the object set before the wretched envious man. For where there is no gladness at all it shall seem to him that every one rejoiceth at his misfortune, and mourneth that he hath no worse.

'The covetous shall go down to the fifth centre, where he shall suffer extreme proverty, as the rich feaster suffered. And the demons, for greater torment, shall offer him that which he desireth, and when he shall have it in his hands other devils with violence shall snatch it from his hands with these words: "Remember that thou wouldest not give for love of God; so God willeth not that thou now receive."

'Oh unhappy man! Now shall he find himself in that condition when he shall remember past abundance and behold the penury of the present; and that with the goods that then he may not have he could have acquired eternal delights!

'To the fourth centre shall go the lustful, where they that have transformed the way given them by God shall be as corn that is cooked in the burning dung of the devil. And there shall they be embraced by horrible infernal serpents. And they that shall have sinned with harlots, all these acts of impurity shall be transformed for them into union with the infernal furies; which are demons like women, whose hair is serpents, whose eyes are flaming sulphur, whose mouth is poisonous, whose tongue is gull, whose body is all girt with barbed hooks like those wherewith they catch the silly fish, whose claws are those of gryphons, whose nails are razors, the nature of whose generative organs is fire. Now with these shall all the lustful enjoy the infernal embers which shall be their bed.

'To the third centre shall go down the slothful who will not work now. Here are built cities and immense palaces, which as soon as they are finished must needs be pulled down straightway, because a single stone is not placed aright. And these enormous stones are laid upon the shoulders of the slothful, who hath not his hands free to cool his body as he walketh and to ease the burden, seeing that sloth hath taken away the power of his arms, and his legs are fettered with infernal serpents.

'And, what is worse, behind him are the demons, who push him, and make him fall to earth many times beneath the weight; nor doth any help him to lift it up; nay, it being too much to lift, a double amount is laid upon him.

'To the second centre shall go down the gluttonous. Now here there is dearth of food, to such a degree that there shall be nought to eat but live scorpions and live serpents, which give such torment that it would be better never to have been born than to eat such food. There are offered to them indeed by the demons, in appearance, delicate meats; but for that they cannot put out a hand on the occasion when the meat appeareth to them. But what is worse, those very scorpions which he eateth that they may devour his belly, not being able to come forth speedily, rend the secret parts of the glutton. And when they are come forth foul and unclean, filthy as they are, they are eaten over again.

'The wrathful goeth down to the first centre, where he is insulted by all the devils and by as many of the damned as go down lower than he. They spurn him and smite him, making him lie down upon the road where they pass, planting their feet upon his throat. Yet is he not able to defend himself, for that he hath his hands and feet bound. And what is worse, he is not able to give vent to his wrath by insulting others, seeing that his tongue is fastened by a hook, like that which he useth who selleth flesh.

'In this accursed place shall there be a general punishment, common to all the centres, like the mixture of various grains to make a loaf. For fire, ice, thunderstorms, lightning, sulphur, heat, cold, wind, frenzy, terror, shall all be united by the justice of God, and in such wise that the cold shall not temper the heat nor the fire the ice, but each shall give torment to the wretched sinner.

136.

'In this accursed spot shall abide the infidels for evermore: insomuch that if the world were filled with grains of millet, and a single bird once in a hundred years should take away a single grain to empty the world - if when it should be empty the infidels were to go into paradise, they would rest delighted. But there is not this hope, because their torment cannot have an end, seeing that they were not willing for the love of God to put an end to their sin.[256]

'But the faithful shall have comfort, because their torment shall have an end.'

The disciples were affrighted, hearing this, and said: 'So then the faithful must go into hell?'[257]

Jesus answered: 'Every one, be he who he may, must go into hell. It is true, however, that the holy ones and prophets of God shall go there to behold, not suffering any punishment; and the righteous, only suffering fear. And what shall I say? I tell you that thither shall come (even) the messenger of God, to behold the justice of God. Thereupon hell shall tremble at his presence. And because he hath human flesh, all those that have human flesh and shall be under punishment, so long as the messenger of God shall abide to behold hell, so long shall they abide without punishment. But he shall abide there (only) so long as it taketh to shut and open the eyes.

'And this shall God do in order that every creature may know that he hath received benefit from the messenger of God.

'When he shall go there all the devils shall shriek, and seek to hide themselves beneath the burning embers, saying one to another: "Fly, fly, for here cometh Mohammed our enemy!" Hearing which, Satan shall smite himself upon the face with both his hands, and screaming shall say: "Thou art more noble than I, in my despite, and this is unjustly done!"

'As for the faithful, who are in seventy-two grades, those of the two last grades, who shall have had the faith without good works - the one being sad at good works, and the other delighting in evil - they shall abide in hell seventy thousand years.

'After those years shall the angel Gabriel come into hell, and shall hear them say: "O Mohammed, where are thy promises made

---

[256]*put an end to their sin.* Like Satan, they refuse to repent, thus hell will be the abode of both demons and wicked men.

[257]*faithful must go into hell.* Jesus' answer is Hebraic. As Professor Sandmel explains: "The righteous are to go into paradise, nevertheless a person can not be sure." He goes on to point out that there is a tradition that allocates to every man a prospective share in both heaven and hell; for the righteous, the share in hell is converted into a second share in paradise upon their death. And for the wicked their share in paradise is converted into a second share in hell. A stay in hell for moderate sinners purifies them after a period of time, but the very wicked, it is held, who both sin and lead others astray, shall remain there forever. (Ibid. 201-202). Indeed, had the Raggs taken a more objective approach in accordance with scientific inquiry, they would have ventured into Hebraic sources and not led so many astray concerning this authentic gospel.

to us, saying that those who have thy faith shall not abide in hell for evermore?''

'Then the angel of God shall return to paradise, and having approached with reverence the messenger of God shall narrate to him what he hath heard.

'Then shall his messenger speak to God and say: "Lord, my God, remember the promise made to me thy servant, concerning them that have received my faith, that they shall not abide for evermore in hell."

'God shall answer: "Ask what thou wilt, O my friend, for I will give thee all that thou askest."

137.

'Then shall the messenger of God say: "O Lord, there are of the faithful who have been in hell seventy thousand years. Where, O Lord, is thy mercy? I pray thee, Lord, to free them from those bitter punishments."

'Then shall God command the four favourite angels of God that they go to hell and take out every one that hath the faith of his messenger, and lead him into paradise. And this they shall do.

'And such shall be the advantage of the faith of God's messenger, that those that shall have believed in him, even though they have not done any good works, seeing they died in this faith, shall go into paradise after the punishment of which I have spoken.'

138.

When morning was come, early, all the men of the city, with the women and children, came to the house where Jesus was with his disciples, and besought him saying: 'Sir, have mercy upon us, because this year the worms have eaten the corn, and we shall not receive any bread this year in our land.'

Jesus answered: 'Oh what fear is yours! Know ye not that Elijah, the servant of God, whilst for three years the persecution of Ahab continued, saw not bread, nourishing himself only with herbs and wild fruits? David our father, the prophet of God, for two years ate wild fruits and herbs, being persecuted of Saul, insomuch that twice only did he eat bread.'

The men answered: 'Sir, they were prophets of God, nourished with spiritual delight, and therefore they endured well; but how shall these little ones fare?' and they showed him the multitude of their children. Then Jesus had compassion on their misery, and said: 'How long is it until harvest?' They answered? 'Twenty days.'

Then said Jesus: 'See that for these twenty days we give ourselves to fasting and prayer; for God will have mercy upon you. Verily I say unto you God hath caused this dearth because here began the madness of men[258] and the sin of Israel when they said that I was God, or Son of God.'

When they had fasted for nineteen days, on the morning of the twentieth day, they beheld the fields, and hills covered with ripe corn. Thereupon they ran to Jesus, and recounted all to him. And when he had heard it Jesus gave thanks to God, and said: 'Go, brethren, gather the bread which God hath given you.' The men gathered so much corn that they knew not where to store it; and this thing was cause of plenty in Israel.

The citizens took council to set up Jesus as their king; knowing which he fled from them. Wherefore the disciples strove fifteen days to find him.

139.

Jesus was found by him who writeth, and by James with John. And they, weeping, said: 'O Master, wherefore didst thou flee from us? We have sought thee mourning; yea, all the disciples seek thee weeping.' Jesus answered: 'I fled because I knew that a host of devils is preparing for me that which in a short time ye shall see. For, there shall rise against me the chief priests with the elders of the people, and shall wrest authority to kill me from the Roman governor, because they shall fear that I wish to usurp kingship over Israel. Moreover, I shall be sold and betrayed by one of my disciples, as Joseph was sold into Egypt.[259] But the just God shall make him fall, as saith the prophet David:[260] "He shall make him fall into the pit who spreadeth a snare for his neighbour." For God shall save me from their hands, and shall take me out of the world.'

The three disciples were afraid; but Jesus comforted them saying: 'Be not afraid, for none of you shall betray me.' Whereat they received somewhat of consolation.

The day following there came, two by two, thirty-six of Jesus' disciples; and he abode in Damascus[261] awaiting the others. And they

---

[258] *here began the madness.* The reference here must be to Nain. See, chapters 47 & 48.

[259] *Joseph was sold into Egypt.* Genesis 37:28.

[260] *the prophet David.* Ps. 9:15; 57:6.

[261] *he abode in Damascus.* Damascus played an important part in the esoteric terminology of the Essenes, for its name was used by them as a symbolic reference to their community at Qumran, near the Dead Sea. And for the city of Damascus itself. And here in the *Gospel According To Barnabas* we are being told that Jesus took flight

mourned every one, for that they knew that Jesus must depart from the world. Wherefore he opened his mouth and said: 'Unhappy of a surety is he who walketh without knowing whither he goeth; but more unhappy is he who is able and knoweth how to reach a good hostelry, yet desireth and willeth to abide on the miry road, in the rain, and in peril of robbers. Tell me, brethren, is this world our native country? Surely not, seeing that the first man was cast out into the world as to exile; and therein he suffereth the punishment of his error. Shall there perchance be found an exile who aspireth not to return to his own rich country when he findeth himself in poverty? Assuredly reason denieth it, but experience proveth it, because the lovers of the world will not think upon death; nay, when one speaketh to them thereof, they will not hearken to his speech.

140.

'Believe ye, O men, that I am come into the world with a privilege which no man hath had, nor will even the messenger of God have it; seeing that our God created not man to set him in the world, but rather to place him in paradise.

'Sure it is that he who hath no hope to receive aught of the Romans, because they are of a law that is foreign to him, is not willing to leave his own country with all that he hath, never to return, and go to live in Rome. And much less would he do so when he found himself to have offended Caesar. Even so I tell you verily, and Solomon,[262] God's prophet, crieth with me; "O death, how bitter is the remembrance of thee to them that have rest in their riches!" I say not this because I have to die now: seeing that I am sure that I shall live even nigh to the end of the world.

'But I will speak to you of this in order that ye may learn to die.

'As God liveth, everything that is done amiss, even once,

---

from Nain and journeyed unto Damascus, and that it took 15 days for the apostles to find him. Here we have once again, evidence in conjunction with other evidence, of a connection between the Essenes and Nazarenes. For in the *Damascus Document* of the Essenes, found amongst the rest of the Dead Sea Scrolls, we are told how 'the Penitents of Israel (Essenes)' left Judea to dwell in Damascus. "This indication of locality," says Dr. Schonfield," should be taken much more seriously and literally. Those who followed the restored Mosaism [teachings of Moses] did not all gravitate towards Qumran." *(Passover Plot,* p. 31). Here in the city of Damascus, Essenes and Nazarenes, would find others of their persuasion with which to fellowship with. And in fact, one of Jesus' disciples, a man named Ananias, is mentioned in Acts as having lived in Damascus. (Acts 9:10; 22:12.) And let us not forget, that we are told in Acts, that Paul when persecuting the Nazarenes, went unto Damascus in search of them.

[262] *and Solomon.* Ecclesiasticus 41:1.

showeth that to work a thing well it is necessary to exercise oneself therein.

'Have ye seen the soldiers, how in time of peace they exercise themselves with one another as if they were at war? But how shall that man die a good death, who hath not learned to die well?

'"Precious is the death of the holy in the sight of the Lord," said the prophet David.[263] Know ye wherefore? I will tell you: it is because, even as all rare things are precious, so the death of them that die well, being rare, is precious in the sight of God our creator.

'Of a surety, whenever a man beginneth aught, not only is he fain to finish the same, but he taketh pains that his design may have a good conclusion.

'O miserable man, that prizeth his hosen more than himself, for when he cutteth the cloth he measureth it carefully before he cutteth it; and when it is cut he seweth it with care. But his life - which is born to die, insomuch that he alone dieth not who is not born - wherefore will not men measure their life by death?

'Have ye seen them that build, how for every stone that they lay they have the foundation in view, measuring if it be straight, that the wall fall not down? O wretched man! For with greatest ruin shall fall the building of his life, because he looketh not to the foundation of death!

141.

'Tell me: when a man is born, how is he born? Surely, he is born naked. And when he is laid dead beneath the ground, what advantage hath he? A mean linen cloth,[264] wherein he is wound: and this is the reward which the world giveth him.

---

[263] *said the prophet David.* Ps. 116:15.

[264] *A mean linen cloth.* Burial if at all possible, was to take place on the very day of death, in the ground or in a cave. "Such hasty burial," says Professor Sandmel, "prevented disgrace to the body." The body was washed, scented with spices (a bed of spices for those who could afford it), wrapped in white cloth, and placed in its place of rest. (*Judaism and Christian Beginnings*, p. 201) "The grave-clothes," says William Smith, "were probably of the fashion worn in life, but swathed and fastened with bandages, and the head covered separately." (*Smith's Bible Dictionary*, art. Burial Sepulchre). If indeed the burial clothes were in the fashion of those worn in life, then Jesus' reference here, to "a mean linen cloth" is possibly even further evidence of the connection between the Essenes and Nazarenes. For the Essenes of Qumran for instance, are known to have manufactured a grade of linen cloth coarser in texture than the finer grade produced in Egypt. (*The Dead Sea Scrolls*, pp. 85, 89ff., 123.) And according to Josephus, the Essenes wore white garments of simple manufacture. (*The Meaning of the Dead Sea Scrolls*, p. 140.)

'Now if the means in every work must needs be proportionate to the beginning and the end, in order that the work be brought to a good end, what end shall the man have who desireth earthly riches? He shall die, as saith David,[265] prophet of God: "The sinner shall die a most evil death."

'If a man sewing cloth should thread beams instead of thread in the needle, how would the work attain its end? Of a surety he would work in vain, and be despised of his neighbours. Now man seeth not that he is doing this continually when he gathereth earthly goods. For death is the needle, wherein the beams of earthly goods cannot be threaded. Nevertheless in his madness he striveth continually to make the work succeed; but in vain.

'And whoso believeth not this at my word, let him gaze upon the tombs, for there shall he find the truth. He who would fain become wise beyond all others in the fear of God, let him study the book of the tomb, for there shall he find the true doctrine for his salvation. For he will know to beware of the world, the flesh, and the sense, when he seeth that man's flesh is reserved to be food of worms.

'Tell me, if there were a road which was of such condition that walking in the midst thereof a man should go safely, but walking on the edges he would break his head; what would ye say if ye saw men opposing one another, and striving in emulation to get nearest to the edge and kill themselves? What amazement would be yours! Assuredly ye would say: "They are mad and frenzied, and if they are not frenzied they are desperate."'

'Even so is it true,' answered the disciples.

Then Jesus wept and said: 'Even so, verily, are the lovers of the world. For if they lived according to reason, which holdeth a middle place in man, they would follow the law of God, and would be saved from eternal death. But because they follow the flesh and the world they are frenzied, and cruel enemies of their own selves, striving to live more arrogantly and more lasciviously than one another.'

142.

Judas, the traitor, when he saw that Jesus was fled, lost the hope of becoming powerful in the world, for he carried Jesus' purse, wherein was kept all that was given him for love of God. He hoped that Jesus would become king of Israel, and so he himself would be a powerful man. Wherefore, having lost his hope, he said within himself: 'If this man were a prophet, he would know that I steal his money; and so he would lose patience and cast me out of his service,

---

[265] *as saith David.* Ps. 104:35.

knowing that I believe not in him. And if he were a wise man he would not flee from the honour that God willeth to give him. Wherefore it will be better that I make arrangement with the chief priests and with the scribes and Pharisees, and see how to give him up into their hands, for so shall I be able to obtain something good.' Whereupon, having made this resolution, he gave notice to the scribes and Pharisees how the matter had passed in Nain. And they took counsel with the high priest, saying: 'what shall we do if this man become king? Of a surety we shall fare badly; because he is fain to reform the worship of God after the ancient custom,[266] for he cannot away with our traditions. Now how shall we fare under the sovereignty of such a man? Surely we shall all perish with our children: for being cast out of our office we shall have to beg our bread.

'We now, praised be God, have a king and a governor that are alien to our law, who care not for our law, even as we care not for theirs. And so we are able to do whatsoever we list, for, even though we sin, our God is so merciful that He is appeased with sacrifice and fasting. But if this man become king he will not be appeased unless he shall see the worship of God according as Moses wrote: and what is worse, he saith that the Messiah shall not come of the seed of David (as one of his chief disciples hath told us), but saith that he shall come of the seed of Ishmael, and that the promise was made in Ishmael and not in Isaac.

'What then shall the fruit be if this man be suffered to live? Assuredly the Ishmaelites[267] shall come into repute with the

---

[266] *after the ancient custom.* An understanding of the significance of this statement made nearly 2000 years ago, only began to emerge in the 1960s. As Dr. Schonfield explains, there has been emerging ever clearer evidence that in Galilee an older and purer form of the Abrahamic religion had persisted down to the time of Jesus, defying Jewish attempts to destroy it. Such was their fear of it, a fear expressed in their statement: "he is fain to reform the worship of God after the ancient custom." As Dr. Schonfield points out: "To an extent we have to think of him [Jesus] in the context of that northern [purer form of the] faith which so strongly coloured and influenced those communities of 'the Saints' [Essenes = 'holy ones'] which were spread across this area [Galilee], etc." (*The Passover Plot*, p. 31).

[267] *the Ishmaelites.* The Ishmaelites through Moses as an agent for God, were given by God's permission, a share in the 'Promised Land.' (Num. 10:29-32). As stated in the commentary in the Soncino Chumash, p. 848; Moses' statement: "we will do thee good," (v. 32) was an assurance that the Ishmaelites were to share in the promised land. It has also been pointed out, in Smith's and Peloubet's Bible dictionaries, article: Rechabites, that they had all along been worshippers of God under the appellation: Jehovah. That in accordance with the Abrahamic covenant, they practiced circum-

Romans, and they shall give them our country in possession; and so shall Israel again be subjected to slavery as it was aforetime'. Wherefore, having heard the proposal, the high priest gave answer that he must needs treat with Herod and with the governor, 'because the people are so inclined towards him that without the soldiery we shall not be able to do anything; and may it please God that with the soldiery we may accomplish this business.'

Wherefore, having taken counsel among themselves, they plotted to seize him by night, when the governor and Herod should agree thereto.

143.

Then came all the disciples to Damascus, by the will of God. And on that day Judas the traitor, more than any other, made show of having suffered grief at Jesus' absence. Wherefore Jesus said: 'Let every one beware of him who without occasion laboureth to give thee tokens of love.'

And God took away our understanding, that we might not know to what end he said this.

After the coming of all the disciples, Jesus said: 'Let us return into Galilee, for thus hath the angel of God said unto me, that I needs must go thither.' Whereupon, one Sabbath morning Jesus came to Nazareth. When the citizens recognized Jesus, everyone desired to see him. Whereupon a publican, by name Zacchaeus, who was of small stature, not being able to see Jesus by reason of the great multitude, climbed to the top of a sycamore, and there waited for

cision. Therefore, the worship of Baal was no less offensive to them than it was to their cousins the Israelites. In the Book of Jeremiah, 35:2-19; we are shown that their rigid Nazarite life gained for them admission into the Temple of the Lord, into one of the chambers assigned to Levites and priests, within its precincts. And that their righteousness exceeded that of the Israelites, for which God gave them a special blessing (v. 19). The words in that verse: "Jehonadab, the son of Rechab, shall not want for a man to stand before me forever," says Smith, "are essentially liturgical. The Rechabites were solemnly adopted into the families of Israel, and were recognized as incorporated into the tribe of Levi." (Ibid).

Concerning them, Dr. Schonfield, says that they led a bedouin existence (to avoid going astray like the Israelites). And quotes Eisler, in stating that they earned a living as craftsmen, carpenters, and smiths. And that they may well have become before the time of Jesus, as much a sect as a clan, having a religious connection with other communities who had separated themselves from the wayward of Israel, and dwelt in camps in the wilderness which through northern Arabia linked Syria with Mesopotamia. "Such groups," says he, "were the 'holy ones of God' and the very term Essean-Essene which was applied to them appears to have come from the northern Aramaic word Chasya (Greek, Hosios) meaning Saint." (*The Passover Plot*, p. 202).

Jesus to pass that place when he went to the synagogue. Jesus then, having come to that place, lifted up his eyes and said: 'Come down, Zacchaeus, for to-day I will abide in thy house.'

The man came down and received him with gladness, making a splendid feast.

The Pharisees murmured, saying to Jesus' disciples: 'Wherefore is your master gone in to eat with publicans and sinners?'

Jesus answered: 'For what cause doth the physician (enter) into an house? Tell me, and I will tell you wherefore I am come in hither.'

They answered: 'To heal the sick.'

'Ye say the truth,' said Jesus, 'for the whole have no need of medicine, only the sick.'

144.

'As God liveth, in whose presence my soul standeth, God sendeth his prophets and servants into the world in order that sinners may repent; and he sendeth not for the sake of the righteous, because they have no need of repentance, even as he that is clean hath no need of the bath. But verily I say unto you, if ye were true Pharisees[268] ye would be glad that I should have gone in to sinners for their salvation.

'Tell me, know ye your origin, and wherefore the world began to receive Pharisees? Surely I will tell you, seeing that ye know it not. Wherefore hearken to my words.

'Enoch, a friend of God, who walked with God[269] in truth, making no account of the world, was translated into paradise; and there he abideth until the judgment (for when the end of the world draweth nigh he shall return to the world with Elijah and one other). And so men, having knowledge of this, through desire of paradise, began to seek God their creator. For "Pharisee" strictly meaneth

---

[268] *if ye were true Pharisees.* It used to be customary to believe that Jesus was brought up in a religious atmosphere characterized by the Judaism of the second century A.D. derived from the Pharisees. This view as Dr. Schonfield points out, is no longer tenable. So that if the Gospel of Barnabas was a product of the 14th century as the Raggs mistakenly thought, it would probably have reflected that type of erroneous thinking. But because it is authentic, the picture given us as in this chapter, corresponds with the findings of modern scholarship. "In the spiritual sphere," says Schonfield, "the Pharisees were not nearly so well entrenched in Galilee as they were in Judea. They had a following in the north because of their piety and because they represented themselves as the People's Party, but they had an uphill struggle to contend with the Galilean way of life." (*The Passover Plot,* p. 30). This is precisely what we are being shown here.

[269] *walked with God.* Gen. 5:24.

"seeketh God" in the language of Canaan, for there did this name begin by way of deriding good men, seeing that the Canaanites were given up to idolatry, which is the worship of human hands.

'Whereupon the Canaanites beholding those of our people that were separated from the world to serve God, in derision when they saw such an one, said "Pharisee!" that is, "He seeketh God"; as much as to say: "O mad fellow, thou hast no statues of idols and adorest the wind; wherefore look to thy fate and come and serve our gods."

'Verily I say unto you,' said Jesus, 'all the saints and prophets of God[270] have been Pharisees not in name, as you are, but in very deed. For in all their acts they sought God their creator, and for love of God they forsook cities and their own goods, selling these and giving to the poor for love of God.'

145.

'As God liveth, in the time of Elijah, friend and prophet of God, there were twelve mountains inhabited by seventeen thousand Pharisees; and so it was that in so great a number there was not found a single reprobate; but all were elect of God. But now, when Israel hath more than a hundred thousand Pharisees, may it please God that out of every thousand there be one elect!'

The Pharisees answered in indignation: 'So then we are all reprobate, and thou holdest our religion in reprobation!'

Jesus answered: 'I hold not in reprobation but in approbation the religion of true Pharisees, and for that I am ready to die. But come, let us see if ye be Pharisees. Elijah, the friend of God, at the prayer of his disciple Elisha, wrote a little book wherein he included all human wisdom with the law of God our Lord.'

The Pharisees were confounded when they heard the name of the book of Elijah, because they knew that, through their traditions no one observed such doctrine. Wherefore they were fain to depart under pretext of business to be done.

Then said Jesus: 'If ye were Pharisees ye would forsake all other business to attend to this; for the Pharisee seeketh God alone. Wherefore in confusion they tarried to listen to Jesus, who said again? '"Elijah, servant of God" (for so beginneth the little Book).

---

[270] *all the saints and prophets.* Whereas in earlier chapters we have repeatedly seen the expression: "holy ones and prophets" in reference to the Essenes and prophets, here Jesus refers to the Essenes in conjunction with the prophets once again. But this time he uses the northern aramaic term: "Chasya," (Essean-Essene), which translators have rendered "saints." Indeed, the evidence is ever mounting, demonstrating the authenticity of this Gospel account of Jesus' life and ministry.

"to all them that desire to walk with God their creator, writeth this. Whoso desireth to learn much, they (sic) fear God little, because he who feareth God is content to know only that which God willeth.[271]

'They that seek fair words seek not God, who doth naught but reprove our sins.

"They that desire to seek God, let them shut fast the doors and windows of their house, for the master suffereth not himself to be found outside his house, (in a place) where he is not loved. Guard therefore your senses and guard your heart, because God is not found outside of us, in this world wherein he is hated.

"They that wish to do good works, let them attend to their own selves, for it booteth not to gain the whole world and lose one's own soul.

"They that wish to teach others, let them live better than others, because nothing can be learned from him who knoweth less than ourselves. How, then, shall the sinner amend his life when he heareth one worse than he teaching him?

"They that seek God, let him (sic) flee the[272] conversation of men; because Moses being alone upon mount Sinai found him and spake with God, as doth a friend who speaketh with a friend.[273]

"They that seek God, once only in thirty days shall they come forth where be men of the world; for in one day can be done works for two years in respect of the business of him that seeketh God.

"When he walketh, let him not look save at his own feet.

"When he speaketh, let him not speak save that which is necessary.

"When they eat, let them rise from the table still hungry; thinking every day not to attain to the next; spending their time as one draweth his breath.

"Let one garment,[274] of the skin of beasts, suffice.

---

[271] *only that which God willeth.* Here Jesus alludes to the difference between those who love God as well as fear his chastisement (as a child dearly loves good parents, but also fears their chastisement for wrongdoing).

[272] *let him flee.* That is to say, let him flee the [vain] conversation of men.

[273] *speaketh with a friend.* Exod. 33:2.

[274] *"let one garment.* The attitude expressed throughout this chapter, is characteristic of that held by the Essenes, for Philo remarks concerning them: "At first they lived in villages and avoided cities, in order to escape the contagion of evils rife therein. They pursued agriculture and other peaceful arts." (*The Meaning of the Dead Sea Scrolls*, p. 138). On the same subject, Josephus adds: "Nor do they allow of the change of garments, or shoes [though they kept them clean], till they be first entirely torn to pieces or worn out by time." (Ibid. p. 140).

"Let the lump of earth sleep on the naked earth; for every night let two hours of sleep suffice.

"Let him hate no one save himself; condemn no one save himself.

"In prayer, let them stand in such fear as if they were at the judgment to come.

'Now do this in the service of God, with the law that God hath given you through Moses, for in such wise shall ye find God that in every time and placed ye shall feel that ye are in God and God in you."

'This is the little book of Elijah, O Pharisees, wherefore again I say unto you that if ye were Pharisees ye would have had joy that I am entered in here, because God hath mercy upon sinners.'

146.

Then said Zacchaeus: 'Sir, behold I will give, for love of God, fourfold all that I have received by usury.'

Then said Jesus: 'This day hath salvation come to this house. Verily, verily, many publicans, harlots, and sinners shall go into the kingdom of God, and they that account themselves righteous shall go into eternal flames.'

Hearing this, the Pharisees departed in indignation. Then said Jesus to them that were converted to repentance, and to his disciples: 'There was a father who had two sons, and the younger said: "Father, give me my portion of goods" and his father gave it him. And he, having received his portion, departed and went into a far country, whereupon he wasted all his substance with harlots, living luxuriously. After this there arose a mighty famine in that country, insomuch that the wretched man went to serve a citizen, who set him to feed swine in his property. And while feeding them he assuaged his hunger in company with the swine,[275] eating acorns. But when he came to himself he said: "Oh, how many in my father's house have abundance in feasting, and I perish here with hunger! I will arise, therefore, and will go to my father, and will say unto him? Father, I

---

[275] *in company with the swine.* The reference to the swine in this parable, may be taken to emphasize how low this sinner had sunk before repentance. As both Smith's and Peloubet's Bible dictionaries point out: "Although the Jews did not breed swine during the greater period of their existence as a nation, there can be little doubt that the heathen nations of Palestine used the flesh as food." (art: Swine). The abhorrence which the Israelites held for the swine in accordance with the divine prohibition against it (Lev. 11:7; Deut. 14:8), may be inferred from Isa. 15:4; and II Macc. 6:18-19.

have sinned in heaven against thee; do with me as thou doest unto one of thy servants.''

'The poor man went, whereupon it came to pass that his father saw him coming from afar off, and was moved to compassion over him. So he went forth to meet him, and having come up to him he embraced him and kissed him.

'The son bowed himself down, saying: ''Father, I have sinned in heaven against thee; do unto me as unto one of thy servants, for I am not worthy to be called thy son.''

'The father answered: ''Son, say not so, for thou art my son, and I will not suffer thee to be in the condition of my slave.'' And he called his servants and said: ''Bring hither new robes and clothe this my son, and give him new hosen, give him the ring on his finger, and straightway kill the fatted calf and we will make merry. For this my son was dead[276] and is now come to life again, he was lost and now is found.''

147.

'While they were making merry in the house, behold the elder son came home, and he, hearing that they were making merry within, marvelled, and having called one of the servants, he asked him wherefore they were in such wise making merry.

'The servant answered him: ''Thy brother is come and thy father hath killed the fatted calf, and they are feasting.'' The elder son was greatly angered when he heard this, and would not go into the house. Therefore came his father out to him and said to him: ''Son, thy brother is come, come thou therefore and rejoice with him.''

'The son answered with indignation: ''I have ever served thee with good service, and yet thou never gavest me a lamb to eat with my friends. But as for this worthless fellow that departed from thee, wasting all his portion with harlots, now that he is come thou hast killed the fatted calf.''

'The father answered: ''Son, thou art ever with me and everything is thine; but this one was dead and is alive again, was lost and now is found, therefore we needs must rejoice.''

'The elder son was the more angry, and said: ''Go thou and triumph, for I will not eat at the table of fornicators.'' And he departed from his father without receiving[277] even a piece of money.

---

[276] *For this my son was dead.* Not physically dead, but spiritually dead. In other words, he was a sinner, but has now sincerely repented.

[277] *without receiving.* Such is the attitude of the self-righteous, who lacking in true spirituality and wisdom, can not appreciate the repentance of the repentant.

'As God liveth', said Jesus, 'even so is there rejoicing among the angels of God over one sinner that repenteth'.

And when they had eaten he departed, for that he was fain to go to Judaea. Whereupon the disciples said: 'Master, go not unto Judaea, for we know that the Pharisees have taken counsel with the high priest against thee.'

Jesus answered: 'I knew it before they did it, but I do not fear, for they cannot do anything contrary to the will of God. Wherefore let them do all that they desire: for I fear not them, but fear God.

148.

'Tell me now; the Pharisees of to-day - are they Pharisees? Are they servants of God? Assuredly not. Yea, and I say unto you verily, that there is no worse thing here upon earth than this, that a man cover himself with profession and garb of religion to cover his wickedness. I will tell you one single example of the Pharisees of old time, in order that ye may know the present ones. After the departure of Elijah, by reason of the great persecution by idolaters, that holy congregation of Pharisees was dispersed. For in that same time of Elijah there were slain in one year more than ten thousand prophets[278] that were true Pharisees.

'Two Pharisees went into the mountains to dwell there; and the one abode fifteen years knowing nought of his neighbour, although they were but one hour's journey apart. See, then, if they were inquisitive! It came to pass that there arose a drought on those mountains, and thereupon both set themselves to search for water, and so they found each other. Whereupon the more aged said (for it was their custom that the eldest should speak before every other,[279] and they held it a great sin for a young man to speak before an old one) - the elder, therefore, said: "Where dwellest thou, brother?"

'He answered, pointing out the dwelling with his finger: "Here dwell"; for they were nigh to the dwelling of the younger.

[278] *ten thousand prophets.* See I Kings 18:4, 13; where it is implied that only a hundred of them, over and above the ten thousand slain, escaped the persecution of Jezebel.

[279] *speak before every other.* In the Essene work, known as the Manual of Discipline, we are told: "This is the rule covering public sessions. The priests are to occupy the first place. The elders are to come second; and the rest of the people are to take their places according to their respective ranks." It goes on to say, "no one is to speak in advance of his prescribed rank. Everyone is to speak in turn, as he is called upon. (*The Dead Sea Scriptures*, p. 58). Consider the obvious similarity of custom between the Essenes, and the two Pharisees, who were Pharisees in deeds, but not in name.

'Said the elder: "How long is it, brother, that thou hast dwelt here?"

'The younger answered: "Fifteen years."

'Said the elder: "Perchance thou camest when Ahab slew the servants of God?"

'"Even so," replied the younger.

'Said the elder: "O brother, knowest thou who is now king of Israel?"

'The younger answered: "It is God that is King of Israel, for the idolaters are not kings but persecutors of Israel."

'"It is true," said the elder, "but I meant to say, who is it that now persecuteth Israel?"

'The younger answered: "The sins of Israel persecute Israel, because, if they had not sinned, [God] would not have raised up against Israel the idolatrous princes."

'Then said the elder: "Who is that infidel prince whom God hath sent for the chastisement of Israel?"

'The younger answered: "Now how should I know, seeing these fifteen years I have seen no man save thee, and I know not how to read, wherefore no letters be sent unto me?"

'Said the elder: "Now, how new thy sheepskin be! Who hath given them to thee, if thou hast not seen any man?"

149.

'The younger answered: "He who kept good the raiment of the people of Israel for forty years in the wilderness[280] hath kept my skins even as thou seest."

'Then the elder perceived that the younger was more perfect than he, for he had every year had dealings with men. Whereupon, in order that he might have [the benefit of] his conversation, he said: "Brother, thou knowest not how to read, and I know how to read, and I have in my house the psalms of David. Come, then, that I may each day give thee a reading and make plain to thee what David saith."

'The younger answered: "Let us go now."

'Said the elder: "O brother, it is now two days since I have drunk water; let us therefore seek a little water."

'The younger replied: "O brother, it is now two months since I have drunk water. Let us go, therefore, and see what God saith by his prophet David: the Lord is able to give us water."

'Whereupon they returned to the dwelling of the elder, at the door whereof they found a spring of fresh water.

---

[280] *in the wilderness.* Deut. 8:4.

'Said the elder: "O brother, thou art an holy one of God;[281] for thy sake hath God given this spring."

'The younger answered: "O brother, in humility sayest thou this; but certain it is that if God had done this for my sake he would have made a spring close to my dwelling, that I should not depart in search thereof. For I confess to thee that I sinned against thee. When thou saidst that for two days that thou didst not drink thou soughtest water and I had been for two months without drink, whereupon I felt an exaltation within me, as though I were better than thou."

'Then said the elder: "O brother, thou saidst the truth, therefore thou didst not sin."

'Said the younger: "O brother, thou hast forgotten what our father Elijah said, that he who seeketh God ought to condemn himself alone. Assuredly he wrote it not that we might know it, but rather that we might observe it."

'Said the more aged, perceiving the truth and righteousness of his companion: "It is true; and our God hath pardoned thee.:

'And having said this he took the Psalms, and read that which our father David saith: "I will set a watch over my mouth that my tongue decline not to words of iniquity, excusing with excuse my sin." And here the aged man made a discourse upon the tongue, and the younger departed. Whereupon they were fifteen years more ere they found one another, because the younger changed his dwelling.

'Accordingly, when he had found him again, the elder said: "O brother, wherefore returnedst thou not to my dwelling?"

'The younger answered: "Because I have not yet learned well what thou saidst to me."

'Then said the elder: "How can this be, seeing fifteen years are past?"

'The younger replied: "As for the words, I learned them in a single hour and have never forgotten them; but I have not yet observed them. To what purpose is it, then, to learn too much, and not to observe it? Our God seeketh not that our intellect should be good, but rather our heart. So, on the day of judgment, he will not ask us what we have learned, but what we have done."

---

[281] *an holy one of God.* Here again this Essene title appears in this Gospel account as it has so many times before from the mouth of Jesus. As well as from the lips of others who have identified him by it. Here the Pharisees of old, who were true Pharisees, but did not necessarily so identify themselves, are identified, one by the other, as "holy one(s) of God.

150.

'The elder answered: "O brother, say not so, for thou despisest knowledge, which our God willeth to be prized."

'The younger replied: "Now, how shall I speak now so as not to fall into sin: for thy word is true, and mine also. I say, then, that they who know the commandments of God written in the Law ought to observe those [first] if they would afterwards learn more. And all that a man learneth, let it be to observe it,[282] and not [merely] to know it."

'Said the elder: "O brother, tell me, with whom hast thou spoken, that thou knowest thou hast not learned all that I said?"

'The younger answered: "O brother, I speak with myself. Every day I place myself before the judgment of God, to give account of myself. And ever do I feel within myself one that excuseth my faults."

'Said the elder: "O brother, what faults hast thou, who art perfect?"

'The younger answered: "O brother, say not so, for that I stand between two great faults; the one is that I do not know myself to be the greatest of sinners, the other that I do not desire to do penance for it more than other men."

'The elder answered: "Now, how shouldst thou know thyself to be the greatest of sinners, if thou art the most perfect [of men]?"

'The younger replied: "The first word that my master said to me when I took the habit of a Pharisee was this: that I ought to consider the goodness of others and mine own iniquity for if I should do so I should perceive myself to be the greatest of sinners."

'Said the elder: "O brother, whose goodness or whose faults considerest thou on these mountains, seeing there are no men here?"

'The younger answered: "I ought to consider the obedience of the sun and the planets, for they serve their Creator better than I. But them I condemn, either because they give not light as I desire, or because their heat is too great, or there is too much or too little rain upon the ground."

'Whereupon, hearing this, the elder said: "Brother, where hast thou learned this doctrine, for I am now ninety years old, for seventy-five years whereof I have been a Pharisee?"

'The younger answered: "O brother, thou sayest this in humility, for thou art a holy one of God. Yet I answer thee that God our creator looketh not on time, but looketh on the heart:[283]

---

[282] *let it be to observe it.* That is to say, let it be [to] observe it.
[283] *but looketh on the heart.* I Sam. 16;7.

wherefore David, being fifteen years old, younger than six other his brethren,[284] was chosen king of Israel, and became a prophet of God our Lord.'"

151.

'This man was a true Pharisee,' said Jesus to his disciples: 'and may it please God that we be able on the day of judgment to have him for our friend.

Jesus then embarked on a ship, and the disciples were sorry that they had forgotten to bring bread. Jesus rebuked them, saying: 'Beware of the leaven of the Pharisees of our day, for a little leaven marreth a mass of meal.'

Then said the disciples one to another: 'Now what leaven have we, if we have not even any bread?'

Then said Jesus: 'O men of little faith, have ye then forgotten what God wrought in Nain, where there was no sign of corn? And how many ate and were satisfied with five loaves and two fishes? The leaven of the Pharisee is want of faith in God, and thought of self, which hath corrupted not only the Pharisees of this day, but hath corrupted Israel. For the simple folk, not knowing how to read, do that which they see the Pharisees do, because they hold them for holy ones.

'Know ye what is the true Pharisee? He is the oil of human nature. For even as oil resteth at the top of every liquor, so the goodness of the true Pharisee resteth at the top of all human goodness. He is a living book, which God giveth to the world; for everything that he saith and doeth is according to the law of God. Wherefore, whoso doeth as he doeth observeth the law of God. The true Pharisee is salt that suffereth not human flesh to be putrefied by sin; for every one who seeth him is brought to repentance. He is a light that lighteneth the pilgrims' way, for every one that considereth his poverty with his penitence perceiveth that in this world we ought not to shut up our heart.

'But he that maketh the oil rancid, corrupteth the book, putrefieth the salt, extinguisheth the light - this man is a false Pharisee. If, therefore, ye would not perish, beware that ye do not as do the Pharisee to-day.'

152.

Jesus having come to Jerusalem, and having entered one Sab-

---

[284] *six other his brethren.* Either here, or in I Sam. 16:10, 11; 17:12, 14, there is a scribal or translator's error, for in I Samuel the number given is seven.

bath day into the Temple, the soldiers drew nigh to tempt him and take him, and they said: 'Master, is it lawful to wage war?'

Jesus answered: 'Our faith telleth us that our life is a continual warfare upon the earth.'

Said the soldiers: 'So wouldst thou fain convert us to thy faith, and wouldst that we should forsake the multitude of gods (for Rome alone hath twenty-eight thousand gods that are seen) and should follow thy god who is one only and for that he cannot be seen, it is not known where he is, and perchance he is but vanity.'

Jesus answered: 'If I had created you, as our God hath created you, I would seek to convert you.'

They answered: 'Now how hath thy God created us, seeing it is not known where he is? Show us thy God, and we will become Jews.'

Then said Jesus - 'If ye had eyes to see him I could show him to you, but since ye are blind, I cannot show you him.'

The soldiers answered: 'Of a surety, the honour which this people payeth thee must have taken away thine understanding. For every one of us hath two eyes in his head, and thou sayest we are blind.'

Jesus answered: 'The carnal eyes can only see things gross and external: ye therefore will only be able to see your gods of wood and silver and gold that cannot do anything. But we of Judah have spiritual eyes, which are the fear and the faith of our God, wherefore we can see our God in every place.'

The soldiers answered: 'Beware how thou speakest, for if thou pour contempt on our gods we will give thee into the hand of Herod, who will take vengeance for our gods, who are omnipotent.'

Jesus answered: 'If they are omnipotent as ye say, pardon me, for I will worship them.'

The soldiers rejoiced at hearing this, and began to extol their idols. Then said Jesus: 'Herein is not need of words but of deeds; cause therefore that your Gods create one fly, and I will worship them.'

The soldiers were dismayed at hearing this, and wist not what to say, wherefore Jesus said:

'Assuredly, seeing they make not a single fly afresh, I will not for them forsake that God who hath created everything with a single word; whose name alone affrighteth armies.'

The soldiers answered: 'Now let us see this; for we are fain to take thee,' and they were fain to stretch forth their hands against Jesus.

Then said Jesus: 'Adonai Sabaoth'! Whereupon straight-way the soldiers were rolled out of the Temple as one rolleth casks of wood when they are washed to refill them with wine; insomuch that now their head and now their feet struck the ground, and that without any one touching them.

And they were so affrighted and fled in such wise that they were never more seen in Judaea.

153.

The priests and Pharisees murmured among themselves and said: 'He hath the wisdom of Baal and Ashtaroth, and so in the power of Satan hath he done this.'

Jesus opened his mouth and said: 'Our God commanded that we should not steal our neighbour's goods.[285] But this single precept hath been so violated and abused that it hath filled the world with sin, and such sin as shall never be remitted as other sins are remitted: seeing that for every other sin, if a man bewail it and commit it no more, and fast with prayer and almsgiving, our God, mighty and merciful, forgiveth. But this sin is of such a kind that it shall never be remitted, except that which is wrongly taken be restored.'

Then said a scribe: 'O master, how hath robbery filled all the world with sin? Assuredly now, by the grace of God, there are but few robbers, and they cannot show themselves but they are immediately hanged by the soldiery.'

Jesus answered: 'Whoso knoweth not the goods, they (sic) cannot know the robbers. Nay, I say unto you verily that many rob who know not what they do, and therefore their sin is greater than that of the others, for the disease that is not known is not healed.'

Then the Pharisees drew near to Jesus and said, 'O master, since thou alone in Israel knowest the truth, teach thou us.'

Jesus answered: 'I say not that I alone in Israel know the truth, for this word "alone" appertaineth to God alone and not to others. For he is the truth, who alone knoweth the truth. Wherefore, if I should say so I should be a greater robber, for I should be stealing the honour of God. And in saying that I alone knew God I should be falling into greater ignorance than all. Ye, therefore, committed a grievous sin in saying that I alone know the truth. And I tell you that, if ye said this to tempt me, your sin is greater still.'

Then Jesus, seeing that all held their peace, said again: 'Though I be not alone in Israel knowing the truth, I alone will speak; wherefore hearken to me, since ye have asked me.

'All things created belong to the Creator, in such wise that nothing can lay claim to anything. Thus soul, sense, flesh, time, goods, and honour, all are God's possessions, so that if a man receive

---

[285] *our neighbor's good's.* Ex. 20:15.

them not as God willeth he becometh a robber. And in like manner, if he spend them contrary to that which God willeth, he is likewise a robber. I say, therefore, unto you that, as God liveth in whose presence my soul standeth, when ye take time, saying: "To-morrow I will do thus, I will say such a thing, I will go to such a place," and not saying: "If God will," ye are robbers: And ye are greater robbers when ye spend the better part of your time in pleasing yourselves and not in pleasing God, and spend the worse part in God's service: then are ye robbers indeed.

'Whoso committeth sin, be he of what fashion he will, is a robber; for he stealeth time and the soul and his own life, which ought to serve God, and giveth it to Satan, the enemy of God.'

154.

'The man, therefore, who hath honour, and life, and goods - when his possessions are stolen, the robber shall be hanged; when his life is taken, the murderer shall be beheaded. And this is just, for God hath so commanded. but when a neighbour's honour is taken away, why is not the robber crucified? Are goods, forsooth, better than honour? Hath God, forsooth, commanded that he who taketh goods shall be punished and he that taketh life with goods shall be punished, but he that taketh away honour shall go free? Surely not; for by reason of their murmuring our fathers entered not into the land of promise;[286] but only their children. And for this sin the serpents slew about seventy thousand of our people.[287]

'As God liveth in whose presence my soul standeth, he that stealeth honour is worthy of greater punishment than he that robbeth a man of goods and of life. And he that hearkeneth to the murmurer is likewise guilty, for the one receiveth Satan on his tongue and the other in his ears.

The Pharisees were consumed [with rage] at hearing this, because they were not able to condemn his speech.

Then there drew nigh to Jesus a doctor, and said to him: good master, tell me, wherefore God did not grant corn and fruit to our fathers? Knowing that they must needs fall, surely he should have allowed them corn, or not have suffered men to see it.'

Jesus answered: 'Man, thou callest me good, but thou errest, for God alone is good. And much more dost thou err in asking why God hath not done according to thy brain. Yet I will answer thee all. I tell thee, then, that God our creator in his working conformeth not

---

[286] *land of promise.* Num. 14:29, 30.
[287] *of our people.* Num. 21:5.

himself to us, wherefore it is not lawful for the creature to seek his own way and convenience, but rather the honour of God his creator, in order that the creature may depend on the Creator and not the Creator on the creature. As God liveth in whose presence my soul standeth, if God had granted everything to man, man would not have known himself to be God's servant; and so he would have accounted himself lord of paradise. Wherefore the Creator, who is blessed for evermore, forbade him the food, in order that man might remain subject to him.

And verily I say unto you, that whoso hath the light of his eyes clear seeth everything clear, and draweth light even out of darkness itself; but the blind doeth not so. Wherefore I say that, if man had not sinned, neither I nor thou would have known the mercy of God and his righteousness. And if God had made man incapable of sin he would have been equal to God in that matter; wherefore the blessed God created man good and righteous,[288] but free to do that which he pleaseth in regard to his own life and salvation or damnation.'

The doctor was astounded when he heard this, and departed in confusion.

155.

Then the high-priest called two old priests secretly and sent them to Jesus, who was gone out of the temple, and was sitting in Solomon's porch, waiting to pray the midday prayer. And near him he had his disciples with great multitude of people.

The priests drew near to Jesus and said: 'Master, wherefore did man eat corn and fruit? Did God will that he should eat it, or no?' And this they said tempting him; for if he said: 'God willed it,' they would answer: 'Why did he forbid it?' and if he said: 'God willed it not,' they would say: 'Then man hath more power than God, since he worketh contrary to the will of God.'

Jesus answered: 'Your question is like a road over a mountain, which hath a precipice on the right hand and on the left: but I will walk in the middle.'

When they heard this the priests were confounded, perceiving that he knew their heart.

Then said Jesus: 'Every man, for that he hath need, worketh everything for his own use. But God, who hath no need of anything, wrought according to his good pleasure. Wherefore in creating man

---

[288] *God created man good and righteous*. Not sinful. Thus, man's fall was due to a mistake in judgement, and not the result of a predisposition to sin. Therefore, it is a mistake to think that innocent little babies are born in sin.

he created him free in order that he might know that God had no need of him; Verbi gratia, as doth a King, who to display his riches, and in order that his slaves may love him more, giveth freedom to his slaves.

God, then, created man free in order that he might love his Creator much the more and might know his bounty. For although God is omnipotent, not having need of man, having created him by his omnipotence, he left him free by his bounty, in such wise that he could resist evil and do good. For although God had power to hinder sin, he would not contradict his own bounty (for God hath no contradiction) in order that, his omnipotence and bounty having wrought in man, he should not contradict sin in man, I say, in order that in man might work the mercy of God and his righteousness. And in token that I speak the truth, I tell you that the high-priest hath sent you to tempt me, and this is the fruit of his priesthood.'

The old men departed and recounted all to the high-priest, who said: 'This fellow hath the devil at his back, who recounteth everything to him; for he aspireth to the kingship over Israel; but God will see to that.'

156.

When he had made the midday prayer, Jesus, as he went out of the temple, found one blind from his mother's womb. His disciples asked him saying: 'Master, who sinned in this man, his father or his mother, that he was born blind?'

Jesus answered: 'Neither his father nor his mother sinned in him, but God created him so, for a testimony[289] of the Gospel.' And having called the blind man up to him he spat on the ground and made clay and placed it upon the eyes of the blind man and said to him: 'Go to the pool of Siloam and wash thee!'

The blind man went, and having washed received light; whereupon, as he returned home, many who met him said: 'If this man were blind I should say for certain that it was he who was wont to sit at the beautiful gate of the temple.' Others said: 'It is he, but how hath he received light?' And they accosted him saying: 'Art thou the blind man that was wont to sit at the beautiful gate of the temple?

He answered: 'I am he - and wherefore?'

They said: 'Now how didst thou receive thy sight:'

---

[289] *for a testimony.* What we see as suffering is not always that, in many instances, trials and tribulations serve to enlighten us concerning the strength or weakness of our faith. By the same token they serve to purify our character if we maintain the proper attitude.

He answered: 'A man made clay, spitting on the ground, and this clay he placed upon mine eyes and said to me: "Go and wash thee in the pool of Siloam." I went and washed, and now I see: blessed be the God of Israel!'

When the man born blind was come again to the beautiful gate of the temple, all Jerusalem was filled with the matter. Wherefore he was brought unto the chief of the priests, who was conferring with the priests and the Pharisees against Jesus.

The high-priest asked him, saying: 'Man, wast thou born blind?' 'Yea', he replied.

'Now give glory of God,' said the high-priest, 'and tell us what prophet hath appeared to thee in a dream and given thee light. Was it our father Abraham, or Moses the servant of God, or some other prophet? For others could not do such a thing.

The man born blind replied: 'Neither Abraham nor Moses, nor any prophet have I seen in a dream and been healed by him, but as I sat at the gate of the temple a man made me come near to him and, having made clay of earth with his spittle, put some of that clay upon mine eyes and sent me to the pool of Siloam to wash; whereupon I went, and washed me, and returned with the light of mine eyes.'

The high-priest asked him the name of that man.

The man born blind answered: 'He told me not his name, but a man who saw him called me and said: "Go and wash thee as that man hath said, for he is Jesus the Nazarene, a prophet and an holy one of the God of Israel."'

Then said the high-priest: 'Did he heal thee perchance to-day, that is, the Sabbath?'

The blind man answered: 'To-day he healed me.'

Said the high-priest: 'Behold now, how that this fellow is a sinner, seeing he keepeth not the Sabbath!'

157.

The blind man answered: 'Whether he is a sinner I know not; but this I know, that whereas I was blind, he hath enlightened me.'

The Pharisees did not believe this: so they said to the high priest: 'Send for his father and mother, for they will tell us the truth.' They sent, therefore, for the father and mother of the blind man, and when they were come the high-priest questioned them saying: 'Is this man your son?'

They answered: 'He is verily our son.'

Then said the high-priest: 'He saith that he was born blind, and now he seeth; how hath this thing befallen?'

The father and mother of the man born blind replied 'Verily he was born blind, but how he may have received the light, we know not; he is of age, ask him and he will tell you the truth.'

Thereupon they were dismissed, and the high-priest said again to the man born blind: 'Give glory to God, and speak the truth.'

(Now the father and mother of the blind man were afraid to speak, because a decree had gone forth from the Roman senate that no man might contend for Jesus, the prophet of the Jews, under pain of death: this decree had the governor obtained - wherefore they said: 'He is of age, ask him.')

The high-priest, then said to the man born blind: 'Give glory to God and speak the truth, for we know this man, whom thou sayest to have healed thee, that he is a sinner.'

The man born blind answered: 'Whether he be a sinner, I know not; but this I know, that I saw not and he hath enlightened me. Of a surety, from the beginning of the world to this hour, there hath never yet been enlightened one who was born blind: and God would not hearken to sinners.'[290]

Said the Pharisees: 'Now what did he when he enlightened thee?'

Then the man born blind marvelled at their unbelief, and said: 'I have told you, and wherefore ask ye me again? Would ye also become his disciples?'

The high-priest then reviled him saying: 'Thou wast altogether born in sin, and wouldst thou teach us? Begone, and become thou disciple of such a man! for we are disciples of Moses, and we know that God hath spoken to Moses, but as for this man, we know not whence he is.' And they cast him out of the synagogue and temple, forbidding him to make prayer with the clean among Israel.

158.

The man born blind went to find Jesus, who comforted him saying: 'At no time hast thou been so blessed as thou art now, for thou art blest of our God who spake through David,[291] our father and his prophet, against the friends of the world, saying: "They curse and I bless"; and by Micah[292] the prophet he said: "I curse your blessing" For earth is not so contrary to air, water to fire, light to darkness, cold

---

[290] *God would not hearken to sinners.* If he were not commissioned by God, he would not be able to perform such a miracle. For it is only by the power of God that he has done this thing.

[291] *spake through David.* Ps. 109:28.

[292] *by Micah.* Here we appear to have a translator's error, in which the name Malicah was unintentionally replaced by Micah's name. See Mal. 2:2.

to heat, or love to hate, as is the will that God hath contrary to the will of the world.'

The disciples accordingly asked him, saying: 'Lord, great are thy words; tell us, therefore, the meaning, for as yet we understand not.'

Jesus answered: "When ye shall know the world, ye shall see that I have spoken the truth, and so shall ye know the truth in every prophet.

'Know ye, then, that there be three kinds of worlds comprehended in a single name: the one standeth for the heavens and the earth, with water, air and fire, and all the things that are inferior to man. Now this world in all things followeth the will of God, for, as saith David,[293] prophet of God: "God hath given them a precept which they transgress not."

'The second standeth for all men, even as the "house of such an one" standeth not for the walls, but for the family. Now this world, again, loveth God; because by nature they long after God, forasmuch as according to nature every one longeth after God, even though they err in seeking God. And know ye wherefore all long after God? Because they long everyone after an infinite good without any evil, and this is God alone. Therefore the merciful God hath sent his prophets to this world for its salvation.

'The third world is man's fallen condition of sinning, which hath transformed itself into a law contrary to God, the creator of the world. This maketh man become like unto the demons, God's enemies. And this world our God hateth so sore that if the prophets had loved this world - what think ye? Assuredly God would have taken from them their prophecy. And what shall I say? As God liveth, in whose presence my soul standeth, when the messenger of God shall come to the world, if he should conceive love towards this evil world, assuredly, God would take away from him all that he gave him when he created him, and would make him reprobate: so greatly is God contrary to this world.'

159.

The disciples answered: 'O master, exceeding great are thy words, therefore have mercy upon us, for we understand them not.'

Said Jesus: 'Think ye perchance that God hath created his messenger to be a rival, who should be fain to make himself equal with God? Assuredly not, but rather as his good slave, who should not will that which his Lord willeth not. Ye are not able to understand

---

[293] as saith David. Ps. 148:6.

this because ye know not what a thing is sin. Wherefore hearken unto my words, Verily, verily, I say unto you, sin cannot arise in man save as a contradiction of God, seeing that that only is sin which God willeth not: insomuch that all that God willeth is most alien from sin.[294] Accordingly, if our high-priests and priests, with the Pharisees, persecuted me because the people of Israel hath called me God, they would be doing a thing pleasing to God, and God would reward them; but because they persecute me for a contrary reason, since they will not have me say the truth, how they have contaminated the book of Moses,[295] and that of David, prophets and friends of God, by their traditions, and therefore hate me and desire my death - therefore God hath them in abomination.

'Tell me - Moses slew men[296] and Ahab slew men[297] - is this in each case murder? Assuredly not: for Moses slew the men to destroy idolatry and to preserve the worship of the true God, but Ahab slew the men to destroy the worship of the true God and to preserve idolatry. Wherefore to Moses the slaying of men was converted into sacrifice, while to Ahab it was converted into sacrilege: insomuch that one and the same work produced these two contrary effects.

'As God liveth, in whose presence my soul standeth, if Satan had spoken to the angels in order to see how they loved God, he would not have been rejected of God, but because he sought to turn them away from God, therefore is he reprobate.'

Then answered he who writeth: How, then, is to be understood that which was said in Micaiah the prophet, concerning the lie which God ordained to be spoken by the mouth of false prophets, as is written in the book of the kings of Israel?[298]

Jesus answered: 'O Barnabas, recite briefly all that befell, that we may see the truth clearly.'

160.

Then said he who writeth: 'Daniel the prophet, describing the history of the kings of Israel and their tyrants, writeth thus "the king

[294] *most alien from sin.* That which is unlawful is not willed by God, but merely permitted. For He gave man freewill, and permits man to exercise his freewill to choose between doing good or evil.

[295] *contaminated the book of Moses.* It was the opinion of the Essenes, that the Jews had corrupted the Scriptures. (*The Dead Sea Scriptures*, pp. 5, 6 & 77.

[296] *Moses slew men.* Ex. 32:26-29.

[297] *Ahab slew the men.* Jezebel with her husband Ahab's permission, slew the servants of God (I Ki. 18:13; II Ki. 9:7.), thus the blame is placed by Jesus at Ahab's feet.

[298] *the book of the kings of Israel.* Mic. 2:11; I Ki. 3:31.

of Israel joined himself with the king of Judah to fight against the sons of Belial (that is, reprobates) who were the Ammonites. Now Jehoshaphat, king of Judah, and Ahab, king of Israel, being seated both on a Throne in Samaria, there stood before them four hundred false prophets, who said to the king of Israel: 'Go up against the Ammonites, for God will give them into thy hands, and thou shalt scatter Ammon.'

"'Then said Jehoshaphat: 'Is there here any prophet of the God of our fathers?'

"'Ahab answered: 'There is one only, and he is evil, for he always predicteth evil concerning me; and him I hold in prison.' And this he said, to wit, "There is only one," because as many as were found had been slain by decree of Ahab, so that the prophets, even as thou hast said, O Master, were fled to the mountain tops where men dwelt not.

"'Then said Jehoshaphat: 'Send for him here, and let us see what he saith.'

"'Ahab therefore commanded that Micaiah[299] be sent for thither, who came with fetters on his feet, and his face bewildered like a man that liveth between life and death.

"'Ahab asked him, saying: 'Speak, Micaiah, in the name of God. Shall we go up against the Ammonites? Will God give their cities into our hands?'

"'Micaiah answered: 'Go up, go up, for prosperously shalt thou go up, and still more prosperously come down!'

"'Then the false prophets praised Micaiah as a true prophet of God, and broke off the fetters from his feet.

"'Jehoshaphat, who feared our God, and had never bowed his knees before the idols, asked Micaiah, saying: 'For the love of God of our fathers, speak the truth, as thou hast seen the issue of this war.'

"'Micaiah answered: 'O Jehoshaphat, I fear thy face wherefore I tell thee that I have seen the people of Israel as sheep without a shepherd.'

"'Then Ahab, smiling, said to Jehoshaphat: 'I told thee that this fellow predicteth only evil, but thou didst not believe it.'

"'Then said they both: 'Now how knowest thou this, O Micaiah?'

"'Micaiah answered: 'Methought there assembled a council of the angels in the presence of God, and I heard God say thus: "Who will deceive Ahab that he may go up against Ammon and be slain?"

---

[299] *Micaiah.* This was Micaiah the son of Imlah, and namesake of Micah (Micaiah). Both were prophets, and it is in this account I Ki. 22:3-31; that we find the significance of Mic. 2:11.

Whereupon one said one thing and another said another. Then came an angel and said: "Lord, I will fight against Ahab, and will go to his false prophets and will put the lie into their mouth, and so shall he go up and be slain." And hearing this, God said: "Now go and do so, for thou shalt prevail".'[300]

'"Then were the false prophets enraged, and their chief smote Micaiah's cheek, saying: 'O reprobate of God, when did the angel of truth depart from us and come to thee? Tell us, when came to us the angel that brought the lie?'

'"Micaiah answered: 'Thou shalt know when thou shalt flee from house to house for fear of being slain, having deceived thy king.'

'"Then Ahab was wroth, and said: 'Seize Micaiah, and the fetters which he had upon his feet place on his neck, and keep him on barley bread and water until my return, for now I know not what death I would inflict on him.'

'"They went up, then, and according to the word of Micaiah the matter befell. For the king of the Ammonites said to his servants: 'See that ye fight not against the king of Judah, nor against the princes of Israel, but slay the king of Israel, Ahab, mine enemy'."'

Then said Jesus: 'Stop there, Barnabas: for it is enough for our purpose.'

161.

'Have ye heard all?' said Jesus.

The disciples answered: 'Yea, Lord.'

Whereupon Jesus said: 'Lying is indeed a sin, but murder is a greater, because the lie is a sin that appertaineth to him that speaketh, but the murder, while it appertaineth to him that committeth it, is such that it destroyeth also the dearest thing that God hath here upon earth, that is, man. And lying can be remedied by saying the contrary of that which hath been said; whereas murder hath no remedy, seeing it is not possible to give life again to the dead. Tell me, then, did Moses the servant of God sin in slaying all whom he slew?'

The disciples answered: 'God forbid; God forbid that Moses should have sinned in obeying God who commanded him!'

Then said Jesus: 'And I say, God forbid that that angel should

---

[300] *thou shalt prevail.* The significance here is cause and effect. "He who lives by the sword, shall die by the sword." Which means that he who lives by violence shall die a violent death. So it was with Ahab, who lived by a lie; idolatry; and by violence. For through Jezebel, and by his own hand, and lie, he slew not only the servants of God, but Naboth the vineyard owner and his sons. (II Ki. 9:26.)

have sinned who deceived Ahab's false prophets with the lie; for even as God receiveth the slaughter of men as sacrifice, so received he the lie for praise. Verily, verily, I say unto you, that even as the child erreth which causeth its shoes to be made by the measure of a giant, even so erreth he who would subject God to the law, as he himself as man is subject to the law. When, therefore, ye shall believe that only to be sin which God willeth not, ye will find the truth, even as I have told you. Wherefore, because God is not composite nor changeable, so also is he unable to will and not will a single thing: for so would he have contradiction in himself, and consequently pain, and would not be infinitely blessed.'

Philip answered: 'But how is that saying of the prophet Amos to be understood, that "there is not evil in the city that God hath not done"?'[301]

Jesus answered: 'Now here see, Philip, how great is the danger of resting in the letter, as do the Pharisees, who have invented for themselves the "predestination of God in the elect," in such wise that they come to say in fact that God is unrighteous, a deceiver and a liar and a hater of judgment (which shall fall upon them).

'Wherefore I say that here Amos the prophet of God speaketh of the evil which the world calleth evil: For if he had used the language of the righteous he would not have been understood by the world. For all tribulations are well, either for that they purge the evil that we have done, or are well because they restrain us from doing evil, or are well because they make man to know the condition of this life, in order that we may love and long for life eternal. Accordingly, had the prophet Amos said: "There is no good in the city but what God hath wrought it," he had given occasion for despair to the afflicted, as they beheld themselves in tribulation and sinners living in prosperity. And, what is worse, many, believing Satan to have such sovereignty over man, would have feared Satan and done him service, so as not to suffer tribulation. Amos therefore did as doth the Roman interpreter, who considereth not his words as one speaking in the presence of the high-priest, but considereth the will and the business of the Jew that knoweth not to speak the Hebrew tongue.

162.

'If Amos had said: "There is no good in the city but what God hath done it." as God liveth, in whose presence my soul standeth, he would have made a grievous error, for the world holdeth not for good ought save the iniquities and sins that are done in the way of vanity.

[301] *God hath not done.* Amos 3:6.

Whereupon men would have wrought much more iniquitously, believing that there be not any sin or wickedness "which God hath not done," at hearing whereof the earth trembleth.' And when Jesus had said this, straightway there arose a great earthquake, in so much that every one fell as dead. Jesus raised them up, saying: 'Now see if I have told you the truth. Let this, then, suffice you, that Amos, when he said that "God hath done evil in the city," talking with the world, spake of tribulations, which sinners alone call evil.

'Let us come now to predestination, of which ye desire to know, and whereof I will speak to you near Jordan on the other side, to-morrow, if God will.'

163.

Jesus went into the wilderness beyond Jordan with his disciples, and when the midday prayer was done he sat down near to a palm-tree, and under the shadow of the palm-tree his disciples sat down.

Then said Jesus: 'So secret is predestination, O brethren, that I say unto you, verily, only to one man shall it be clearly known. He it is whom the nations look for,[302] to whom the secrets of God are so clear that, when he cometh into the world, blessed shall they be that shall listen to his words, because God shall overshadow them with his mercy even as this palm-tree overshadoweth us. "Yea, even as this tree protecteth us from the burning heat of the sun, even so the mercy of God will protect from Satan them that believe in that man.'

The disciples answered,[303] O Master, who shall that man be of whom thou speakest, who shall come into the world?'

Jesus answered with joy of heart: 'He is Mohammed, messenger of God, and when he cometh into the world, even as the rain maketh the earth to bear fruit when for a long time it hath not rained, even so shall he be occasion of good works among men, through the abundant mercy which he shall bring. For he is a white cloud full of the mercy of God, which mercy God shall sprinkle upon the faithful like rain.'

164.

'I will accordingly tell you now that little which God hath granted me to know concerning this same predestination.' The

---

[302] *He it is whom the nations look for.* Hag. 2:7.

[303] *the disciples answered.* The implication here, is that the question was asked by some who were new disciples, for the original twelve apostles, and those disciples who joined Jesus' following shortly after, already knew the answer to this question.

Pharisees say that everything hath been so predestined that he who is elect cannot become reprobate, and he who is reprobate cannot by any means become elect; and that, even as God hath predestined well-doing as the road whereby the elect shall walk unto salvation, even so hath he predestined sin as the road by which the reprobate shall walk unto damnation. Cursed be the tongue that said this, with the hand that wrote it, for this is the faith of Satan. Wherefore one may know of what manner are the Pharisees of the present day, for they are faithful servants of Satan.

'What can predestination mean but an absolute will to give an end to a thing whereof one hath the means in hand? For without the means one cannot destine an end. How, then, shall he destine the house who not only lacketh stone and money to spend, but hath not even so much land as to place one foot upon? Assuredly none [could do so]. No more, then, I tell you, is predestination, taking away the free will that God hath given to man of his pure bounty, the law of God. Of a surety it is not predestination but abomination we shall be establishing.

'That man is free the book of Moses showeth, where when our God gave the law upon Mount Sinai, he spake thus:[304] "My commandment is not in the heaven that thou shouldest excuse thyself, saying: Now, who shall go to bring us the commandment of God? And who perchance shall give us strength to observe it? Neither is it beyond the sea, that in like manner thou shouldest excuse thyself. But my commandment is nigh unto thine heart, that when thou wilt thou mayest observe it."

'Tell me, if King Herod should command an old man to become young and a sick man that he should become whole, and when they did it not should cause them to be killed, would this be just?'

The disciples answered: 'If Herod gave this command, he would be most unjust and impious.'

Then Jesus, sighing, said: 'These are the fruits of human traditions, O brethren; for in saying that God hath predestinated the reprobate in such wise that he cannot become elect they blaspheme God as impious and unjust. For he commandeth the sinner not to sin, and when he sinneth to repent; while such predestination taketh away from the sinner the power not to sin, and entirely depriveth him of repentance.'

---

[304] *he spake thus.* Deut. 30:11-14.

165.

'But hear what saith God by Joel the prophet.[305] "As I live, [saith] your God, I will not the death of a sinner, but I seek that he should be converted to penitence." Will God then predestinate that which he willeth not? Consider ye that which God saith, and that which the Pharisees of this present time say.

'Further, God saith by the prophet Isaiah:[306] "I have called, and ye would not hearken unto me." And how much God hath called, hear how he saith by the same prophet:[307] "All the day have I spread out my hands to a people that believe me not, but contradict me." And our Pharisees, when they say that the reprobate cannot become elect, what say they, then, but that God mocketh men even as he would mock a blind man who should show him something white, and as he would mock a deaf man who should speak into his ears? And that the elect can be reprobated, consider what our God saith by Ezekiel the[308] prophet: "As I live, saith God, if the righteous shall forsake his righteousness and shall do abominations, he shall perish, and I will not remember any more any of his righteousness; for trusting therein it shall forsake him before me and it shall not save him."

'And of the calling of the reprobate, what saith God by the prophet Hosea[309] but this: "I will call a people not elect, I will call them elect." God is true, and cannot tell a lie: for God being truth speaketh truth. But the Pharisees of this present time with their doctrine contradict God altogether.'

166.

Andrew replied; 'But how is that to be understood which God said to Moses,[310] that he will have mercy on whom he willeth to have mercy and will harden whom he willeth to harden?'

Jesus answered: 'God saith this in order that man may not believe that he is saved by his own virtue, but may perceive that life and the mercy of God have been granted him by God of his bounty. And he saith it in order that men may shun the opinion that there be other gods than he.

---

[305] *what saith God by Joel the prophet.* In this one sentence, Jesus has defined the contents of chapters one and two of the book of Joel, and explained an aspect of the mercy of God. (See also, Ezek. 18:23).

[306] *Isaiah.* Isa. 65:12.

[307] *by the same prophet.* Isa. 65:2.

[308] *Ezekiel.* Ezek. 18:24.

[309] *Hosea.* Hos. 2:23.

[310] *Moses.* Ex. 33:19; 4:21.

'If, therefore, he hardened Pharaoh he did it because he had afflicted our people and essayed to bring it to nought by destroying all the male children in Israel: whereby Moses was nigh to losing his life.

'Accordingly, I say unto you verily, that predestination hath for its foundation the law of God and human free will. Yea, and even if God could save the whole world so that none should perish he would not will do so lest thus he should deprive man of freedom, which he preserveth to him in order to do despite to Satan, in order that this [lump of] clay scorned of the spirit, even though it shall sin as the spirit did, may have power to repent and go to dwell in that place whence the spirit was cast out. Our God willeth, I say, to pursue with his mercy man's free will, and willeth not to forsake the creature with his omnipotence. And so on the day of judgment none will be able to make any excuse for their sins, seeing that it will then be manifest to them how much God hath done for their conversion, and how often he hath called them to repentance.

167.

'Accordingly, if your mind will not rest content in this, and ye be fain to say again: "Why so?" I will disclose to you a "wherefore." It is this. Tell me wherefore cannot a single stone rest on the top of the water,[311] yet the whole earth resteth on the top of the water? Tell me, why is it that, while water extinguisheth fire, and earth fleeth from air, so that none can unite earth, air, water, and fire in harmony, nevertheless they are united in man and are preserved harmoniously?'[312]

'If, then, ye know not this - nay, all men, as men, cannot know it - how shall they understand that God created the universe out of nothing with a single word? How shall they understand the eternity of God? Assuredly they shall by no means be able to understand this, because, man being finite and composite with the body, which, as

---

[311] *top of the water.* The earth is a sphere engulfed primarily by water, giving the impression to the ancients that the earth rested on water. Since God deals with each generation according to its own level of understanding, this impression is used here by God's prophet, Jesus, to convey a spiritual truth necessary to the salvation of the Israelites. Jesus himself, apparently had no knowledge of the actual structure of the earth. God had not revealed it to him. This was something to be discovered by later generations.

[312] *preserved harmoniously.* The scientific concepts expressed in this whole passage, is traced back to the Egyptians and Babylonians, and the Greeks who borrowed these ideas from these two nations.

saith the prophet Solomon,[313] being corruptible, presseth down the soul, and the works of God being proportionate to God, how shall they be able to comprehend them?

'Isaiah,[314] prophet of God, seeing [it to be] thus, exclaimed, saying: 'Verily thou art a hidden God!" And of the messenger of God, how God hath created him, he saith: "His generation, who shall narrate?[315] And of the working of God he saith: "Who hath been his counsellor?"[316] Wherefore God saith unto human nature: "Even as the heaven is exalted above the earth, so are my ways exalted above your ways and my thoughts above your thoughts."[317]

'Therefore I say unto you, the manner of predestination is not manifest to men, albeit the fact is true, as I have told you.

'Ought man then, because he cannot find out the mode, to deny the fact? Assuredly, I have never yet seen any one refuse health, though the manner of it be not understood. For I know not even now how God by my touch healeth the sick.'

168.

Then said the disciples: 'Verily God speaketh in thee, for never hath man spoken as thou speakest.'

Jesus answered: 'Believe me when God chose me to send me to the house of Israel, he gave me a book like unto a clear mirror which came down into my heart in such wise that all that I speak cometh forth from that book. And when that book shall have finished coming forth from my mouth, I shall be taken up from the world.'

Peter answered: 'O master, is that which thou now speakest written in that book?'

Jesus replied: 'All that I say for the knowledge of God and the service of God, for the knowledge of man and for the salvation of mankind - all this cometh forth from that book, which is my gospel.'

Said Peter: 'Is there written therein the glory of paradise?'

169.

Jesus answered: 'Hearken, and I will tell you of what manner is paradise, and how the holy and the faithful shall abide there without end, for this is one of the greatest blessings of paradise,

---

[313] *Solomon.* Wisdom 9:15.

[314] *I saiah.* Isa. 45:15.

[315] *who shall narrate.* Isa. 53:8.

[316] *his counsellor.* Isa 40:13.

[317] *above your thoughts.* Isa. 55:9.

seeing that everything, however great, if it have an end, becometh small, yea nought.

'Paradise is the home where God storeth his delights, which are so great that the ground which is trodden by the feet of the holy and blessed ones is so precious that one drachm of it is more precious than a thousand worlds.

'These delights were seen by our father, David, prophet of God, for God showed them unto him, seeing he caused him to behold the glories of paradise; whereupon, when he returned to himself, he closed his eyes with both his hands, and weeping said; "Look not any more upon this world, O mine eyes,[318] for all is vain, and there is no good!"

'Of these delights said Isaiah[319] the prophet: "The eyes of man have not seen, his ears have not heard, nor hath the human heart conceived, that which God hath prepared for them that love him." Know ye wherefore they have not seen, heard, conceived such delights? It is because while they live here below they are not worthy to behold such things. Wherefore, albeit our father David verily saw them, I tell you that he saw them not with human eyes, for God took his soul unto himself, and thus, united with God, he saw them with light divine. As God liveth, in whose presence my soul standeth, seeing that the delights of paradise are infinite and man is finite, man cannot contain them;[320] even as a little earthen jar cannot contain the sea.

'Behold, then how beautiful is the world in summer-time, when

---

[318] *O mine eyes.* As a result of a scientific approach to the subject of 'life after death', considerable evidence has emerged demonstrating that death is not the end. Consider the following account: "I 'died' from a cardiac arrest, and as I did, I suddenly found myself in a rolling field. It was beautiful, and everything was an intense green - a color unlike *anything on earth. There was light-beautiful, uplifting light-all around me.* I looked ahead of me, across the field, and I saw a fence. I started moving towards the fence, and I saw a man on the other side of it, moving towards it as if to meet me. I wanted to reach him, but I felt myself being drawn back, irresistibly..." (Life After Life, pp. 73-74.) Consider how this first hand description from our own age, corresponds to the descriptive statement made by David over 2000 years ago concerning the greater beauty of paradise to what we have in this phase of life.

[319] *Isaiah.* Isa. 64:4.

[320] *man cannot contain them.* An indication of what is meant, is further provided once again by modern research. Our general understanding of a language is dependent upon a broad community of common experience in which almost all of us participate. If no such experience exists in another language group, a problem of translation arises. Now the events which those who have experienced death and resuscitation have experienced, is something that generally lies outside of mankind's community of earthly experiences, so that it is not surprising that they have some

all things bear fruit! The very peasant, intoxicated with gladness by reason of the harvest that is come, maketh the valleys and mountains resound with his singing, for that he loveth his labours supremely. Now lift up even so your heart to paradise, where all things are fruitful with fruits proportionate to him who hath cultivated it.

'As God liveth, this is sufficient for the knowledge of paradise, forasmuch as God hath created paradise for the home of his own delights. Now think ye that immeasurable goodness would not have things immeasurably good? Or that immeasurable beauty would not have things immeasurably beautiful? Beware, for ye err greatly if ye think he have them not.

170.

'God saith thus to the man who shall faithfully serve him: "I know thy works, that thou workest for me. As I live eternally, thy love shall not exceed my bounty. Because thou servest me as God thy creator, knowing thyself to be my work, and askest nought of me save grace and mercy to serve me faithfully; because thou settest no end to my service, seeing thou desirest to serve me eternally; even so will I do, for I will reward thee as if thou wert God, mine equal. For not only will I place in thy hands the abundance of paradise, but I will give thee myself as a gift;[321] so that, even as thou art fain to be my servant for ever, even so will I make thy wages for ever."'

linguistic difficulties explaining their experiences to us. As one person put it: "Now there is a real problem for me as I'm trying to tell you this, because all the words I know are three dimensional. As I was going through this [experience], I kept thinking, "Well, when I was taught geometry, they always told me there were only three dimensions, and I always just accepted that. But they were wrong. There are more." And, of course, in our world - the one we're living in now - is three dimensional, but the next one definitely isn't. And that's why its so hard to tell you this. I have to describe it to you in words that are three dimensional. That's as close as I can get to it, but its not really adequate. I can't really give you a complete picture." (Ibid. 25-26).

[321] *Give thee myself as a gift.* "God is the light of the heavens and the earth." (Q:24:35). And his angels are beings of light that He has created. The following encounter with one of his angels commonly experienced by the dying, can perhaps serve to give us a slight indication of the meaning of God's words. As Dr. Moody describes it, what is perhaps the most incredible common element in the accounts he has studied, the one that has had the most profound effect upon the individual, is the encounter with a very bright light. "Typically," he says, "at its first appearance this light is dim, but it rapidly gets brighter until it reaches an unearthly brilliance. Yet, even though this light (usually said to be white or "clear") is of an indescribable brilliance, many make the specific point that it does not in any way hurt their eyes, or dazzle them, or keep them from seeing other things around them (perhaps because at this point they don't have physical "eyes" to be dazzled)." He goes on to explain:

171.

'What think ye,' said Jesus to his disciples, 'of paradise? Is there a mind that could comprehend such riches and delights? Man must needs have a knowledge as great as God's if he would know what God willeth to give to his servants.

'Have ye seen when Herod maketh a present to one of his favourite barons, in what sort he presenteth it?'

John answered: 'I have seen it twice; and assuredly the tenth part of that which he giveth would be sufficient for a poor man.'

Said Jesus: 'But if a poor man shall be presented to Herod what will he give to him?'

John answered: 'One or two mites.'

'Now let this be your book wherein to study the knowledge of paradise,' said Jesus: 'because all that God hath given to man in this present world for his body is as though Herod should give a mite to a poor man; but what God will give to the body and soul in paradise is as though Herod should give all that he hath, yea and his own life, to one of his servants.'

172.

'God saith thus to him that loveth him, and serveth him faithfully: "Go and consider the sands of the sea, O my servant, how many they are. Wherefore, if the sea should give thee one single grain of sand, would it appear small to thee? Assuredly, yea. As I, thy creator, live, all that I have given in this world to all the princes and kings of the earth is less than a grain of sand that the sea would give thee, in comparison of that which I will give thee in my paradise."'

173.

'Consider, then,' said Jesus, 'the abundance of paradise. For if God hath given to man in this world an ounce of well-being, in paradise he will give him ten hundred thousand loads. Consider the quantity of fruits that are in this world, the quantity of food, the quantity of flowers, and the quantity of things that minister to man. As God liveth, in whose presence my soul standeth, as the sea hath

"Despite the light's unusual manifestation, however, not one person has expressed any doubt whatsoever that it was a being, a being of light. Not only that, it is a personal being. It has a very definite personality. *The love and the warmth which emanate from this being to the dying person are utterly beyond words. And he feels completely surrounded by it and taken up in it, completely at ease and accepted in the presence of this being. He senses an irresistible magnetic attraction to this light. he is ineluctably [irresistibly] drawn to it.*" (Life After Life, pp. 58-59).

still sand over and above when one receiveth a grain thereof, even so will the quality and quantity of figs [in paradise] excel the sort of figs we eat here. And in like manner every other thing in paradise.[322] But furthermore, I say unto you that verily, as a mountain of gold and pearls is more precious than the shadow of an ant, even so are the delights of paradise more precious than all the delights of the princes of the world which they have had and shall have even unto the judgment of God when the world shall have an end.'

Peter answered: 'Shall, then, our body which we now have go into paradise?'

Jesus answered: 'Beware, Peter, lest thou become a Sadducee; for the Sadducees say that the flesh shall not rise again, and that there be no angels. Wherefore their body and soul are deprived of entrance into paradise, and they are deprived of all ministry of angels in this world. Hast thou perchance forgotten Job,[323] prophet and friend of God, how he saith: "I know that my God liveth; and in the last day I shall rise again in my flesh, and with mine eyes I shall see God my Saviour"?

'But believe me, this flesh of ours shall be so purified that it shall not possess a single property of those which now it hath; seeing that it shall be purged of every evil desire, and God shall reduce it to such a condition as was Adam's before he sinned.[324]

---

[322] *every other thing in paradise.* Jesus's statement here, that everything in paradise including its figs, is not the same as what we have in this life, is precisely what we are told in the Quran (Q. 2:25), and what modern research has brought to light. Consider the following account: "I had heart failure and clinically died... I remember everything perfectly vividly...Suddenly I felt numb. Sounds began sounding a little distant...All this time I was perfectly conscious of everything that was going on. I heard the heart monitor go off. I saw the nurse come into the room and dial the telephone, and the doctors, nurses, and attendants came in. As things began to fade there was a sound I can't describe; it was like the beat of a snare drum, very rapid, a rushing sound, like a stream rushing through a gorge. And I rose up and I was a few feet up looking down on my body. There I was, with people working on me. I had no fear. No pain. Just peace. After just probably a second or two, I seemed to turn over and go up. It was dark - you could call it a hole or a tunnel - and there was this bright light. It got brighter and brighter. And I seemed to go through it. All of a sudden I was just somewhere else. There was a gold-looking light, everywhere. Beautiful. I couldn't find a source anywhere. There was music. And I seemed to be in a countryside with streams, grass and trees, mountains. But when I looked around - if you want to put it that way - *they were not trees and things like we know them to be.*" (*Reflections on Life After Life*, pp. 15-16.)

[323] *Job.* Job. 19:25-27.

[324] *Adam's before he sinned.* A common experience reported by those who have experienced death, is that they found themselves in another body upon release -through death - from their earthly body. This spiritual body is one of the aspects of

'Two men serve one master in one and the same work. The one
alone seeth the work, and giveth orders to the second, and the second
performeth all that the first commandeth. Seemeth it just to you, I
say, that the master should reward only him who seeth and commandeth, and should cast out of his house him who wearied himself in
the work? Surely not.

'How then shall the justice of God bear this? The soul and the
body with sense of man serve God: the soul only seeth and commandeth the service, because the soul, eating no bread, fasteth not, [the
soul] walketh not, feeleth not cold and heat, falleth not sick, and is
not slain, because the soul is immortal: it suffereth not any of those
corporal pains which the body suffers at the instance of the elements.
Is it, then, just, I say, that the soul alone should go into paradise, and
not the body, which hath wearied itself so much in serving God?'

Peter answered: 'O master, the body, having caused the soul to
sin, ought not to be placed in paradise.'

Jesus answered: 'Now how shall the body sin without the soul?
Assuredly it is impossible. Therefore, in taking away God's mercy
from the body, thou condemnest the soul to hell.'

174.

'As God liveth, in whose presence my soul standeth, our God
promiseth his mercy to the sinner, saying: "In that hour that the
sinner shall lament his sin, by myself, I will not remember his
iniquities for ever."

'Now what should eat the meats of paradise, if the body go not
thither? The soul? Surely not, seeing it is spirit.'[325]

Peter answered: 'So then, the blessed shall eat in paradise; but
how shall the meat be voided without uncleanness?'

Jesus answered: 'Now what blessedness shall the body have if
it eat not nor drink? Assuredly it is fitting to give glory in proportion
to the thing glorified. But thou errest, Peter, in thinking that such
meat should be voided in uncleanness, because this body at the
present time eateth corruptible meats, and thus it is that putrefaction cometh forth; but in paradise the body shall be incorruptible,

the death experience that is hardest to describe in earthly language because there
is nothing in our material world like it. Thus those who try to describe it to us tend
to become frustrated and declare that it can not be described, or words to that effect.
(*Life After Life*, pp. 42-43). This experience is perhaps indicative of what will
happen on the day of Resurrection.

[325] *seeing it is spirit.* Just after release from our earthly body, and just before being
incorporated into our spiritual body, a number of people have the experience of being
pure consciousness. (*Life After Life*, p. 42). In other words, pure spirit.

impassible, and immortal, and free from every misery; and the meats, which are without any defect, shall not generate any putrefaction.

175.

'God saith thus in Isaiah[326] the prophet, pouring contempt on the reprobate: "My servants shall sit at my table in mine house and shall feast joyfully, with gladness and with the sound of harps and organs,[327] and I will not suffer them to have need of anything. But ye that are mine enemies shall be cast away from me, where ye shall die in misery, while every servant of mine despiseth you."

176.

'To what doth it serve to say, "They shall feast"?' said Jesus to his disciples. 'Surely God speaketh plain. But to what purpose are the four rivers of precious liquor in paradise, with so many fruits? Assuredly, God eateth not, the angels eat not, the soul eateth not, the sense eateth not, but rather the flesh, which is our body. Wherefore the glory of paradise is for the body the meats, and for the soul and the sense God and the conversation of Angels and blessed spirits. That glory shall be better revealed by the messenger of God,[328] who (seeing God hath created all things for love of him) knoweth all things better than any other creature.'

---

[326] *God saith thus in Isaiah.* Isa. 65:13.

[327] *sounds of harps and organs.* Indeed, modern research has brought to light that the dying sometimes experience the presence of something in the next life that is perhaps best described in earthly language as music. One young woman who had this experience, described it "as a majestic and really beautiful sort of music." (*Life After Life*, p. 30.) Based on the accumulated evidence, the terms: harps and organs, is metaphorical.

[328] *by the messenger of God.* Concerning that which was revealed to mankind through Prophet Muhammad, the reader is referred to the al-Qur'an. However, let us consider the following passage in connection with those who have died and been resuscitated: "God takes (men's soul at the time of their death, and those that die not, during their sleep. Then He withholds those on whom He has passed the decree of death and sends the others back till an appointed term. Surely there are

signs in this for a people who reflect" (Qur'an 39:42). Indeed, the signs have given us some idea of what the next life is like. And for the unbeliever who is not hardened in his beliefs, evidence of an after life.

Jesus' reference to the four rivers and fruits in paradise is as we have already seen, metaphoric, for nothing in the next life is quite the same as in this phase of life. And this too was revealed to mankind through Prophet Muhammad well over a thousand years ago. Thus we are told in the revelation intrusted to him: "A parable of the Garden which the dutiful are promised: Therein are rivers of water not altering for the worse, the rivers of wine delicious to the drinkers, and rivers of honey clarified; and for them therein are all fruits and protection from their Lord [from ever doing

Said Bartholomew: 'O master, shall the glory of paradise be equal for every man? If it be equal, it shall not be just, and if it be not equal the lesser will envy the greater.'

Jesus answered: 'It will not be equal, for that God is just; and everyone shall be content, because there is no envy there. Tell me, Bartholomew: there is a master who hath many servants, and he clotheth all of those his servants in the same cloth. Do then the boys, who are clothed in the garments of boys, mourn because they have not the apparel of grown men? Surely, on the contrary, if the elders desired to put on them their larger garments they would be wroth, because, the garments not being of their size, they would think themselves mocked.

'Now, Bartholomew, lift thy heart to God in paradise, and thou shalt see that all one glory, although it shall be more to one and less to another, shall not produce ought of envy.'

177.

Then said he who writeth: 'O master, hath paradise light from the sun as this world hath?'

Jesus answered: 'Thus hath God said to me, O Barnabas: "The world wherein ye men that are sinners dwell hath the sun and the moon and the stars that adorn it, for your benefit and your gladness; for this have I created.

'"Think ye, then, that the house where my faithful dwell shall not be better? Assuredly, ye err, so thinking: for I, your God, am the sun of paradise, and my messenger is the moon who from me receiveth all; and the stars are my prophets which have preached to you my will. Wherefore my faithful, even as they received my word from my prophets here, shall in like manner obtain delight and gladness through them in the paradise of my delights."

---

sin again]. (Are these) like those who abide in the Fire and who are made to drink boiling water, so it rends their bowels asunder?" (Qur'an 47:15.) And again in the second surah of the Qur'an it is stated: "And give good news to those who believe and do good deeds, that for them are Gardens in which rivers flow. *Whenever they are given a portion of the fruit thereof, they will say: This is what was given to us before; and they are given the like of it.* And for them therein are pure companions and therein they will abide." (Qur'an 2:25).

As the righteous are given their spiritualized bodies which are purified, so the unrighteous are given spiritualized bodies befitting their misdeeds. Thus we are told: "Those who disbelieve in Our Messages We shall make them enter Fire. As often as their skins are burned, We shall change them for other skins, that they may taste the chastisement. Surely God is ever Mighty, Wise. (Qur'an 4:56).

178.

'And let this suffice you,' said Jesus, 'for the knowledge of paradise.' Whereupon Bartholomew said again: 'O master, have patience with me if I ask thee one word.'

Jesus answered: 'Say that which thou desirest.'

Said Bartholomew: 'Paradise is surely great: for, seeing there be in it such great goods, it needs must be great.'

Jesus answered: "Paradise is so great that no man can measure it. Verily I say unto thee that the heavens are nine, among which are set the planets, that are distant one from another five hundred years' journey for a man: and the earth in like manner is distant from the first heaven five hundred years' journey.

'But stop thou at the measuring of the first heaven, which is by so much greater than the whole earth as the whole earth is greater than a grain of sand. So also the second heaven is greater than the first, and the third than the second, and so on up to the last heaven, each one is likewise greater than the next.[329] And verily I say to thee that paradise is greater than all the earth and all the heavens together, even as all the earth is greater than a grain of sand.'

Then said Peter: 'O master, paradise must needs be greater than God, because God is seen within it.'

Jesus answered: 'Hold thy peace Peter, for thou unwittingly blasphemest.'

179.

Then came the angel Gabriel to Jesus and showed him a mirror shining like the sun, wherein he beheld written these words: 'As I live eternally, even as paradise is greater than all the heavens and the earth, and as the whole earth is greater than a grain of sand, even so am I greater than paradise; and as many times more as the sea hath grains of sand, as there are drops of water upon the sea, as there are [blades of] grass upon the ground, as there are leaves upon the trees, as there are skins upon the beasts; and as many times more as the grains of sand that would go to fill the heavens and paradise and more.'

Then said Jesus: 'Let us do reverence to our God, who is blessed

---

[329]*greater than the next.* As pointed out in the note to chap. 105, this is a Hebraic tradition that was eventually recorded in the Talmud. Since God deals with man according to each individual's level of understanding, the use of such traditions to get across a spiritual truth served a purpose. They served as parables not to be taken literally, but symbolically. For as already pointed out, nothing in the next life is quite the same as it is in this life.

for evermore.' Thereupon they bowed their heads an hundred times and prostrated themselves to earth upon their face in prayer.

When the prayer was done, Jesus called Peter and told him and all the disciples what he had seen. And to Peter he said: 'Thy soul, which is greater than all the earth, through one eye seeth the sun, which is a thousand times greater than all the earth.'

Then said Jesus: 'Even so, through [the eye of] paradise, shalt thou see God our Creator.' And having said this, Jesus gave thanks to God our Lord, praying for the house of Israel and for the holy city. And everyone answered: 'So be it, Lord.'

180.

One day, Jesus being in Solomon's porch, there drew nigh to him a scribe, one of them that made discourse to the people, and said to him: 'O master, I have many times made discourse to this people, and there is in my mind a passage of scripture which I am not able to understand.'

Jesus answered: 'And what is it?'

Said the scribe: 'That which God said to Abraham our father, "I will be thy great reward."[330] Now how could man merit [such reward]?'

Then Jesus rejoiced in spirit, and said: 'Assuredly thou art not far from the kingdom of God! Listen to me, for I will tell thee the meaning of such teaching. God being infinite, and man finite, man cannot merit God - and is this thy doubt, brother?'

The scribe answered, weeping: 'Lord, thou knowest my heart; speak, therefore, for my soul desireth to hear thy voice.'

Then said Jesus: 'As God liveth, man cannot merit a little breath which he receiveth every moment.'

The scribe was beside himself, hearing this, and the disciples likewise marvelled, because they remembered that which Jesus said, that whatsoever they gave for love of God, they should receive an hundredfold.

Then he said: 'If one should lend you an hundred pieces of gold, and ye should spend those pieces, could ye say to that man: "I give thee a decayed vine-leaf; give me therefore thine house, for I merit it"?'

The scribe answered: 'Nay, Lord, for he ought first to pay that which he owed, and then if he wished for anything, he should give him good things, but what booteth a corrupted leaf?'

---

[330] *"I will be thy great reward."* Gen. 15:1.

181.

Jesus answered: 'Well hast thou said, O brother; wherefore tell me, Who created man out of nothing? Assuredly it was God, who also gave him the whole world for his benefit. But man by sinning hath spent it all, for by reason of sin is all the world turned against man, and man in his misery hath naught to give to God but works corrupted by sin. For, sinning every day he maketh his own work corrupt, wherefore Isaiah the prophet[331] saith: Our righteousnesses are "as a menstruous cloth."

'How, then, shall man have merit, seeing he is unable to give satisfaction? Is it, perchance, that man sinneth not? Certain it is that our God saith by his prophet David.[332] Seven times a day falleth the righteous"; how then falleth the unrighteous? And if our righteousnesses are corrupt, how abominable are our unrighteousnesses! As God liveth, there is naught that a man ought to shun more than this saying: "I merit." Let a man know, brother, the works of his hands, and he will straightway see his merit. Every good thing that cometh out of a man, verily man doeth it not, but God worketh it in him; for his being is of God who created him. That which man doeth is to contradict God his creator and to commit sin, whereby he meriteth not reward, but torment.

182.

'Not only hath God created man, as I say, but he created him perfect. He hath given him the whole world; after the departure from paradise he hath given him two angels to guard him, he hath sent him the prophets, he hath granted him the law, he hath granted him the faith, every moment he delivereth him from Satan, he is fain to give him paradise; nay more, God willeth to give himself to man. Consider, then, the debt, if it is great! [a debt] to cancel which ye would need to have created man of yourselves out of nothing, to have created as many prophets as God hath sent, with a world and a paradise, nay, more, with a God great and good as is our God, and to give it all to God. So would the debt be cancelled and there would remain to you only the obligation to give thanks to God. But since ye are not able to create a single fly, and seeing there is but one God who is lord of all things, how shall ye be able to cancel your debt?

---

[331] *Isaiah the prophet.* Isa. 30:22.

[332] *David. The Book of Proverbs* attributed to Solomon, was, as pointed out by C.I. Scofield, a collection of sayings all of which were not those uttered by Solomon. (Intro. to Proverbs, *Scofield Reference Bible*). This particular proverb attributed to David is Prov. 24:16.

Assuredly, if a man should lend you an hundred pieces of gold, ye would be obliged to restore an hundred pieces of gold.

'Accordingly, the sense of this, O brother, is that God, being lord of paradise and of everything, can say that which pleaseth him, and give whatsoever pleaseth him. Wherefore, when he said to Abraham, "I will be thy great reward,"[333] Abraham could not say: "God is my reward," but "God is my gift and my debt." So when thou discoursest to the people, O brother, thou oughtest thus to explain this passage: that God will give to man such and such things if man worketh well.

'When God shall speak to thee, O man, and shall say: "O my servant, thou hast wrought well for love of me; what reward seekest thou from me, thy God?" answer thou: "Lord, seeing I am the work of thy hands, it is not fitting that there should be in me sin, which Satan loveth. Therefore, Lord, for thine own glory, have mercy upon the works of thy hands.

'And if God say: "I have pardoned thee, and now I would fain reward thee"; answer thou: "Lord, I merit punishment for what I have done, and for what thou hast done thou meritest to be glorified. Punish, Lord, in me what I have done, and save that which thou hast wrought."

'And if God say: "What punishment seemeth to thee fitting for thy sin?" do thou answer: "As much, O Lord, as all the reprobate shall suffer."

'And if God say: "Wherefore seekest thou so great punishment, O my faithful servant?" answer thou: "Because every one of them, if they had received from thee as much as I have received, would have served thee more faithfully than I have done."

'And if God say: "When wilt thou receive this punishment, and for how long a time?" answer thou: "Now, and without end."

'As God liveth, in whose presence my soul standeth, such a man would be more pleasing to God than all his holy angels. For God loveth true humility, and hateth pride.'

Then the scribe gave thanks to Jesus, and said to him, 'Lord, let us go to the house of thy servant, for thy servant will give meat to thee and to thy disciples.'

Jesus answered: 'I will come thither when thou wilt promise to call me "Brother," and not "Lord," and shalt say thou art my brother, and not my servant.'

The man promised, and Jesus went to his house.

---

[333] *when he said to Abraham.* Gen. 15:1.

183.

While they sat at meat the scribe said: 'O master, thou saidst that God loveth true humility. Tell us therefore what is humility, and how it can be true and false.'

[Jesus replied:] 'Verily I say unto you that he who becometh not as a little child shall not enter into the kingdom of heaven.'

Every one was amazed at hearing this, and they said one to another: 'Now how shall he become a little child who is thirty or forty years old? Surely, this is a hard saying.'

Jesus answered: 'As God liveth in whose presence my soul standeth, my words are true. I said unto you that [a man] hath need to become as a little child: for this is true humility. For if ye ask a little child: "Who hath made thy garments?" he will answer: "My father." If ye ask him whose is the house where he liveth, he will say: "My father's." If ye shall say: "Who giveth thee to eat?" he will reply: "My father." If ye shall say: "Who hath taught thee to walk and to speak?" he will answer: "My father." But if ye shall say: "Who hath broken thy forehead, for that thou hast thy forehead so bound up?" he will answer: "I fell down, and so did I break my head." If ye shall say: "Now why didst thou fall down?" he will answer: "See ye not that I am little, so that I have not the strength to walk and run like a grown man? so my father must needs take me by the hand if I would walk firmly. But in order that I might learn to walk well, my father left me for a little space, and I, wishing to run, fell down." If ye shall say: "And what said thy father?" he will answer: "Now why didst thou not walk quite slowly? See that in future thou leave not my side."

184.

'Tell me, is this true?' said Jesus.

The disciples and the scribe answered: 'It is most true.'

Then said Jesus: 'He who in truth of heart recognizeth God as the author of all good, and himself as the author of sin, shall be truly humble. But whoso shall speak with the tongue as the child speaketh, and shall contradict [the same] in act, assuredly he hath false humility and true pride.

'For pride is then at its height when it maketh use of humble things, that it be not reprehended and spurned of men.

'True humility is a lowliness of the soul whereby man knoweth himself in truth; but false humility is a mist from hell which so darkeneth the understanding of the soul that what a man ought to ascribe to himself, he ascribeth to God, and what he ought to ascribe to God, he ascribeth to himself. Thus, the man of false humility will say that he is a grievous sinner, but when one telleth him that he is a sinner he will wax wroth against him, and will persecute him.

'The man of false humility will say that God hath given him all that he hath, but that he on his part hath not slumbered, but done good works.

'And these Pharisees of this present time, brethren, tell me how they walk.'

The scribe answered, weeping: 'O master, the Pharisees of the present time have the garments and the name of Pharisees, but in their heart and their works they are Canaanites. And would to God they usurped not such a name, for then would they not deceive the simple? O ancient time, how cruelly hast thou dealt with us, that hast taken away from us the true Pharisees and left us the false!'

185.

Jesus answered: 'Brother, it is not time that hath done this, but rather the wicked world. For in every time it is possible to serve God in truth, but by companying with the world, that is with the evil manners in each time, men become bad.

'Now knowest thou not that Gehazi,[334] servant of Elisha the prophet, lying, and shaming his master, took the money and the raiment of Naaman the Syrian? And yet Elisha had a great number of Pharisees[335] to whom God made him to prophesy.

'Verily I say unto thee, that men are so inclined to evil working, and so much doth the world excite them thereto, and Satan entice them to evil, that the Pharisees of the present day avoid every good work and every holy example: and the example of Gehazi is sufficient for them to be reprobated of God.'

The scribe answered: 'It is most true': whereupon Jesus said: 'I would that thou wouldst narrate to me the example of Haggai and Hosea both prophets of God, in order that we may behold the true Pharisee.';

The scribe answered: 'O master what shall I say? Of a surety many believe it not, although it is written by Daniel the prophet; but in obedience to thee I will narrate the truth.

'Haggai was fifteen years old when, having sold his patrimony and given it to the poor, he went forth from Anathoth to serve

---

[334] *Gehazi.* II Kings, 5.

[335] *number of Pharisees.* They were not called Pharisees in name at this time, but are referred to here by that name because in deeds they were righteous as the true Pharisees, not unrighteous as the false Pharisees. See chapters 157-158; 162, 166.

Obadiah the prophet. Now the aged Obadiah, who knew the humility of Haggai, used him as a book wherewith to teach his disciples. Wherefore he oftentimes presented him raiment and delicate food, but Haggai ever sent back the messenger, saying: "Go, return to the house, for thou hast made a mistake. Shall Obadaih send me such things? Surely not: for he knoweth that I am good for naught, and only commit sins."

'And Obadiah, when he had anything bad used to give it to the one next to Haggai in order that he might see it. Whereupon Haggai, when he saw it, would say to himself: "Now, behold, Obadiah hath certainly forgotten thee, for this thing is suited to me alone, because I am worse than all. And there is nothing so vile but that, receiving it from Obadiah, by whose hands God granteth it to me, it were a treasure."

186.

'When Obadiah desired to teach any one how to pray, he would call Haggai and say: "Recite here thy prayer so that every one may hear thy words." Then Haggai would say: "Lord God of Israel, with mercy look upon thy servant, who calleth upon thee, for that thou hast created him. Righteous Lord God, remember thy righteousness and punish the sins of thy servant in order that I may not pollute thy work. Lord my God, I cannot ask thee for the delights that thou grantest to thy faithful servants, because I do nought but sins. Wherefore, Lord, when thou wouldst give an infirmity to one of thy servants, remember me thy servant, for thine own glory."

'And when Haggai did so,' said the scribe, 'God so loved him that to every one who in his time stood by him God gave the gift of prophecy. And nothing did Haggai ask in prayer that God withheld.'

187.

The good scribe wept as he said this, as the sailor weepeth when he seeth his ship broken up.

And he said: 'Hosea, when he went to serve God, was prince over the tribe of Naphtali, and aged fourteen years. And so, having sold his patrimony and given it to the poor, he went to be disciple of Haggai.

'Hosea was so inflamed with charity that concerning all that was asked of him he would say: "This hath God given me for thee, O brother; accept it, therefore!"

'For which cause he was soon left with two garments only, namely, a tunic of sackcloth and a mantle of skins. He sold, I say, his patrimony and gave it to the poor, because otherwise no one would be suffered to be called a Pharisee.

'Hosea had the book of Moses, which he read with greatest earnestness. Now one day Haggai said to him: "Hosea, who hath taken away from thee all that thou hadst?"

'He answered: "The book of Moses.

'It happened that a disciple of a neighbouring prophet was fain to go to Jerusalem, but had not a mantle. Wherefore, having heard of the charity of Hosea, he went to find him and said to him: "Brother, I would fain go to Jerusalem to perform a sacrifice to our God, but I have not a mantel wherefore I know not what to do."

'When he heard this, Hosea said: "Pardon me, brother, for I have committed a great sin against thee: because God hath given me a mantle in order that I might give it to thee and I had forgotten. Now therefore accept it, and pray to God for me." The man, believing this, accepted Hosea's mantle and departed. And when Hosea went to the house of Haggai, Haggai said: "Who hath taken away thy mantle?"

'Hosea replied: "The book of Moses."

'Haggai was much pleased at hearing this, because he perceived the goodness of Hosea.

'It happened that a poor man was stripped by robbers and left naked. Whereupon Hosea, seeing him, stripped off his own tunic and gave it to him that was naked; himself being left with a little piece of goat-skin over the privy parts. Wherefore, as he came not to see Haggai, the good Haggai thought that Hosea was sick. So he sent with two disciples to find him: and they found him wrapped in palm-leaves. Then said Haggai: "Tell me now, wherefore hast thou not been to visit me?"

'Hosea answered: "The book of Moses hath taken away my tunic, and I feared to come thither without a tunic." Whereupon Haggai gave him another tunic.

'It happened that a young man, seeing Hosea read the book of Moses, wept, and said: "I also would learn to read if I had a book." Hearing which, Hosea gave him the book, saying: 'Brother, this book is thine; for God gave it me in order that I should give it to one who, weeping, should desire a book."

'The man believed him, and accepted the book.

188.

'There was a disciple of Haggai nigh to Hosea: and he, wishing to see if his own book was well written, went to visit Hosea and said to him: "Brother, take thy book and let us see if it is even as mine."

'Hosea answered: "It hath been taken away from me."

'"Who hath taken it from thee?" said the disciple.

'Hosea answered: "The book of Moses." Hearing which, the other went to Haggai and said to him: "Hosea hath gone mad, for he saith the book of Moses hath taken away from him the book of Moses."

'Haggai answered: "Would to God, O brother, that I were mad in like manner, and that all mad folk were like unto Hosea!"

'Now the Syrian robbers,[336] having raided the land of Judaea, seized the son of a poor widow, who dwelt hard by Mount Carmel, where the prophets and Pharisees abode. It chanced, accordingly, that Hosea having gone to cut wood met the woman, who was weeping. Thereupon he straightway began to weep for whenever he saw any one laugh he laughed, and whenever he saw any one weep he wept. Hosea then asked the woman touching the reason of her weeping, and she told him all.

'Then said Hosea: "Come, sister, for God willeth to give thee thy son."

'And they went both of them to Hebron, where Hosea sold himself, and gave the money to the widow, who, not knowing how he had gotten that money, accepted it, and redeemed her son.

'He who had bought Hosea took him to Jerusalem, where he had an abode, not knowing Hosea.

'Haggai, seeing that Hosea was not to be found, remained afflicted thereat. Whereupon the angel of God told him how he had been taken as a slave to Jerusalem.

'The good Haggai, when he heard this, wept for the absence of Hosea as a mother weepeth for the absence of her son. And having called two disciples he went to Jerusalem. And by the will of God, in the entrance of the city he met Hosea, who was laden with bread to carry it to the labourers in his master's vineyard.

'Having recognized him, Haggai said: "Son, how is it that thou hast forsaken thine old father, who seeketh thee mourning?"

'Hosea answered: "Father, I have been sold."

'Then said Haggai in wrath: "Who is that bad fellow who hath sold thee?"

'Hosea answered: "God forgive thee, O my father; for he who hath sold me is so good that if he were not in the world no one would become holy."[337]

---

[336] *the Syrian robbers.* II Kings 5:2.

[337] *become holy.* In accordance with Essene thought, the meaning being conveyed here in this parable-like story, is that the "holy ones of God," are those who diligently follow the Book of Moses.

"'Who, then, is he?" said Haggai.

'Hosea answered: "O my father, it was the book of Moses."

'Then the good Haggai remained as it were beside himself, and said: "Would to God, my son, that the book of Moses would sell me also with all my children, even as it hath sold thee!"

'And Haggai went with Hosea to the house of his master, who when he saw Haggai said: "Blessed be our God, who hath sent his prophet unto my house"; and he ran to kiss his hand. Then said Haggai: "Brother, kiss the hand of thy slave whom thou hast bought, for he is better than I." And he narrated to him all that had passed; whereupon the master gave Hosea his freedom.

And that is all that thou desiredst, O Master,' said the scribe.

189.

Then said Jesus: 'This is true, because I am assured thereof by God. Wherefore, that every one may know that this is the truth, in the name of God let the sun stand still, and not move for twelve hours!' And so it came to pass, to the great terror of all Jerusalem and Judaea.

And Jesus said to the scribe: 'O brother, what seekest thou to learn from me, seeing thou hast such knowledge? As God liveth, this is sufficient for man's salvation, inasmuch as the humility of Haggai, with the charity of Hosea, fulfilleth all the law and all the prophets. 'Tell me, brother, when thou camest to question me in the temple, didst thou think, perchance, that God had sent me to destroy the law and the prophets?

'Certain it is that God will not do this, seeing he is unchangeable, and therefore that which God ordained as man's way of salvation, this hath he caused all the prophets to say. As God liveth, in whose presence my soul standeth, if the book of Moses with the book of our father David had not been corrupted by the human traditions of false Pharisees and doctors, God would not have given his word to me. And why speak I of the book of Moses and the book of David? Every prophecy have they corrupted,[338] in so much that do-day a thing is not sought because God hath commanded it, but men look whether the doctors say it, and the Pharisees observe it, as though God were in error, and men could not err.

'Woe, therefore, to this faithless generation, for upon them shall come the blood of every prophet and righteous man, with the blood

---

[338] *every prophecy have they corrupted.* This position characterizes the attitude of the Essenes, for they maintained that the Torah (Book of Moses) had successively been garbled and perverted.

of Zechariah son of Berachiah, whom they slew between the temple and the altar!

'What prophet have they not persecuted? What righteous man have they suffered to die a natural death? Scarcely one! And they seek now to slay me. They boast themselves to be children of Abraham, and to possess the beautiful temple. As God liveth, they are children of Satan, and therefore they do his will: Therefore the temple, with the holy city, shall go to ruin, in so much that there shall not remain of the temple one stone upon another.'

190.

'Tell me, brother, thou that art a doctor learned in the law - in whom was the promise of the Messiah made to our father Abraham? In Isaac or in Ishmael?'

The scribe answered: 'O master, I fear to tell thee this, because of the penalty of death.'

Then said Jesus: 'Brother, I am grieved that I came to eat bread in thy house, since thou lovest this present life more than God thy creator; and for this cause thou fearest to lose thy life, but fearest not to lose the faith and the life eternal, which is lost when the tongue speaketh contrary to that which the heart knoweth of the law of God.'

Then the good scribe wept, and said: 'O master, if I had known how to bear fruit, I should have preached many things which I have left unsaid lest sedition should be roused among the people.'

Jesus answered: 'Thou shouldst respect neither the people, nor all the world, nor all the holy ones, nor all the angels, when it should cause offence to God. Wherefore let the whole [world] perish rather than offend God thy creator, and preserve it not with sin. For sin destroyeth and preserveth not, and God is mighty to create as many worlds as there are sands in the sea, and more.'

191.

The scribe then said: 'Pardon me, O master, for I have sinned.'

Said Jesus: 'God pardon thee; for against him hast thou sinned.'

Whereupon said the scribe: 'I have seen an old book written by the hand of Moses and Joshua (he who made the sun stand still as thou hast done), servants and prophets of God, which book is the true book of Moses. Therein is written that Ishmael is the father of Messiah,[339] and Isaac the father of the messenger of the Messiah. And thus saith the book, that Moses said: "Lord God of Israel, mighty and

---

[339] *Ishmael is the father of the Messiah.* See notes to chapters 13 & 43.

merciful manifest to thy servant the splendour of thy glory.[340]
Whereupon God showed him his messenger in the arms of Ishmael,
and Ishmael in the arms of Abraham. Nigh to Ishmael stood Isaac,
in whose arms was a child, who with finger pointed to the messenger
of God, saying: "This is he for whom God hath created all things."

'Whereupon Moses cried out with joy: "O Ishmael, thou hast in
thine arms all the world, and paradise! Be mindful of me, God's
servant, that I may find grace in God's sight by means of thy son, for
whom God hath made all."

192.

'In that book it is not found that God eateth the flesh of cattle
or sheep; in that book it is not found that God hath locked up his
mercy in Israel alone, but rather that God hath mercy on every man
that seeketh God his creator in truth.

'All of this book I was not able to read, because the high priest,
in whose library I was, forbade me, saying that an Ishmaelite had
written it.'

Then said Jesus: 'See that thou never again keep back the truth,
because in the faith of the Messiah God shall give salvation to men,
and without it shall none be saved.[341]

And there did Jesus end his discourse. Whereupon, as they sat
at meat, lo! Mary, who wept at the feet of Jesus, entered into the house
of Nicodemus (for that was the name of the scribe), and weeping
placed herself at the feet of Jesus, saying: 'Lord, thy servant, who
through thee hath found mercy with God, hath a sister, and a brother
who now lieth sick in peril of death.'

Jesus answered: 'Where is thy house? Tell me, for I will come to
pray God for his health.'

Mary answered: 'Bethany is the home of my brother and my
sister, for my own house is Magdala: my brother, therefore, is in
Bethany.'

Said Jesus to the woman: 'Go thou straightway to thy brother's

[340] *of thy glory.* Ex. 33:18.

[341] *non be saved.* In the Qur'an we are told to rejoice when we see men entering the
religion prescribed by God for man's salvation, in multitudes. (Q. 110). The reason is
given to the Israelites by Jesus, himself, who proclaimed: "in the faith of the Messiah
[Muhammad] God shall give salvation to men, and without it shall none be saved."
The basis of the teachings of all the Biblical prophets was monotheism and submission
to God through obedience to His Holy Laws. Of this religion prescribed by God and
preached by all of the prophets, Professor Philip K. Hitti, states in effect that Islam
as contained in the Holy Quran and the Hadis, is the logical perfection of that religion.
(History Of The Arabs, p. 8).

house, and there await me, for I will come to heal him. And fear thou not, for he shall not die.'

The woman departed, and having gone to Bethany found that her brother had died that day, wherefore they laid him in the sepulchre of their fathers.

193.

Jesus abode two days in the house of Nicodemus, and the third day he departed for Bethany; and when he was nigh to the town he sent two of his disciples before him, to announce to Mary his coming. She ran out of the town, and when she had found Jesus, said, weeping: 'Lord, thou saidst that my brother would not die; and now he hath been buried four days. Would to God thou hadst come before I called thee, for then he had not died!'

Jesus answered: 'Thy brother is not dead, but sleepeth,[342] therefore I come to awake him.'

Mary answered, weeping: 'Lord, from such a sleep he shall be awakened on the day of judgment by the angel of God sounding his trumpet.'

Jesus answered: 'Mary, believe me that he shall rise before [that day], because God hath given me power over his sleep; and verily I say to thee he is not dead, for he alone is dead who dieth without finding mercy with God.[343]

Mary returned quickly to announce to her sister Martha the coming of Jesus.

Now there were assembled at the death of Lazarus a great number of Jews from Jerusalem, and many scribes and Pharisees. Martha, having heard from her sister Mary of the coming of Jesus, arose in haste and ran outside, whereupon the multitude of Jews, scribes, and Pharisees followed her to comfort her, because they supposed she was going to the sepulchre to weep over her brother. When therefore she arrived at the place where Jesus had spoken to

---

[342]*but sleepeth.* This should be understood in light of what is stated in the Qur'an: "God takes (men's) souls at the time of death, and those that die not during their sleep. Then he withholds those on whom He has passed the decree of death and sends the others back till an appointed term. Surely there are signs in this for a people who reflect. (Q. 39:42) The miracle was in God giving Jesus the power to awaken him.

[343]*without finding mercy with God.* The truly dead are those who have condemned their own souls to Hell by their own rebelliousness against God. Having died in such a state they have forfeited the mercy God would grant them in response to sincere repentance.

Mary, Martha weeping said: 'Lord, would to God thou hadst been here, for then my brother had not died!'

Mary then came up weeping; whereupon Jesus shed tears, and sighing said: 'Where have ye laid him?' They answered: 'Come and see.'

The Pharisees said among themselves: 'Now this man, who raised the son of the widow at Nain, why did he suffer this man to die, having said that he should not die?'

Jesus having come to the sepulchre, where every one was weeping, said: 'Weep not, for Lazarus sleepeth, and I am come to awake him.'

The Pharisees said among themselves: 'Would to God that thou didst so sleep!' Then said Jesus: 'Mine hour is not yet come; but when it shall come I shall sleep in like manner, and shall be speedily awakened.' Then said Jesus again: 'Take away the stone from the sepulchre.'

Said Martha: 'Lord, he stinketh, for he hath been dead four days.'

Said Jesus: 'Why then am I come hither, Martha? Believest thou not in me, that I shall awaken him?'

Martha answered: 'I know that thou art the holy one of God, who hath sent thee into this world.'

Then Jesus lifted up his hands to heaven, and said: 'Lord God of Abraham, God of Ishmael and Isaac, God of our fathers, have mercy upon the affliction of these women, and give glory to thy holy name.' And when every one had answered 'Amen,' Jesus said with a loud voice:

'Lazarus, come forth!'

Whereupon he that was dead arose; and Jesus said to his disciples: 'Loose him.' For he was bound in the grave-clothes with the napkin over his face, even as our fathers were accustomed to bury [their dead].

A great multitude of the Jews and some of the Pharisees believed in Jesus, because the miracle was great. Those that remained in their unbelief departed and went to Jerusalem and announced to the chief of the priests the resurrection of Lazarus, and how that many were become Nazarenes;[344] for so they called them

---

[344] *become Nazarenes.* Nazarenes, not Christians. Jesus' true followers were always properly called Nazarenes. While those who to this day follow the spurious doctrines of the Nicolaitans expounded by Paul of Tarsus, are called Christians.

who were brought to penitence through the word of God[345] which Jesus preached.

194.

The scribes and Pharisees took counsel with the high priest to slay Lazarus; for many renounced their traditions and believed in the word of Jesus, because the miracle of Lazarus was a great one, seeing that Lazarus had conversation with men, and ate and drank. But because he was powerful, having a following in Jerusalem, and possessing with his sister Magdala and Bethany, they knew not what to do.

Jesus entered into Bethany, into the house of Lazarus, and Martha, with Mary, ministered unto him.

Mary, sitting one day at the feet of Jesus, was listening to his words, whereupon Martha said to Jesus: 'Lord, seest thou not that my sister taketh no care for thee, and provideth not that which thou must eat and thy disciples?'

Jesus answered: 'Martha, Martha, do thou take thought for that which thou shouldst do; for Mary hath chosen a part which shall not be taken away from her for ever.

Jesus, sitting at a table with a great multitude that believed in him, spake, saying: 'Brethren, I have but little time to remain with you, for the time is at hand that I must depart from the world. Wherefore I bring to your mind the words of God spoken to Ezekiel

---

[345] *the word of God.* Here too, as in the Acts of Barnabas, we have reference to the Gospel, the divine revelation revealed to Jesus, by God, to preach to the Israelite people. In its entirety the Gospel is lost, but here in the Gospel of Barnabas, more properly rendered: the Gospel History of Jesus according to Barnabas, we have reliable excerpts from the Gospel incorporated with many of the sayings and deeds of Jesus as the Israelite Messiah. From Matthew's and Barnabas' narratives of Jesus' "narratives and miracles written in Hebrew, and not Greek, we get the manner in which Jesus taught the Israelites of his age incorporating in the Essene manner the natural philosophy of that age to convey certain moral truths. By the same token, it is from these sources that we are made aware of his miracles. From these three sources was derived what we still have today - in translated form - as the Gospel of Barnabas. Which is essentially an introductory teaching document, a synthesis of all three documents designed to be easily transportable. The words that Jesus repeated from The Gospel (The Word of God) intrusted to him by God, is that which is in agreement with revelation preached by all the prophets of God, culminating in the final revelation propagated by Prophet Muhammad. This is how one can tell the difference between revelation and what Prophet Jesus said as a man of his time. Indeed, in the Gospel of Barnabas, we have the most accurate detailed portrayal of Jesus' life and ministry in existence today.

the prophet,[346] saying: 'As I, your God, live eternally, the soul that sinneth, it shall die, but if the sinner shall repent he shall not die but live."

'Wherefore the present death is not death, but rather the end of a long death: even as the body when separated from the sense in a swoon, though it have the soul within it, hath no other advantage over the dead and buried save this, that the buried [body] awaiteth God to raise it again, but the unconscious waiteth for the sense to return.

'Behold, then, the present life that it is death, through having no perception of God.[347]

195.

'They that shall believe in me shall not die eternally, for through my word they shall perceive God within them,[348] and therefore shall work out their salvation.

'What is death but an act which nature doth by commandment of God? As it would be if one held a bird tied, and held the cord in his hand; when the head willeth the bird to fly away, what doeth it? Assuredly it commandeth naturally the hand to open; and so straightway the bird flieth away. 'Our soul," as saith the prophet David,[349] "is as a sparrow freed from the snare of the fowler," when man abideth under the protection of God. And our life is like a cord whereby nature holdeth the soul bound to the body and the sense of man. When therefore God willeth, and commandeth nature to open, the life is broken and the soul escapeth in the hands of the angels whom God hath ordained to receive souls.

'Let not, then, friends weep when their friend is dead; for our God hath so willed. But let him weep without ceasing when he sinneth, for [so] the soul dieth, seeing it separateth itself from God, the true Life.

'If the body is horrible without its union with the soul, much more frightful is the soul without union with God, who with his grace and mercy beautifieth and quickeneth it.'

And having said this Jesus gave thanks to God; whereupon Lazarus said: 'Lord, this house belongeth to God my creator, with all

---

[346] *Ezekiel the prophet.* Ezek. 18:20-32.

[347] *no perception of God.* For real life that is to say, life on a high spiritual level, is to be aware of God, who is in fact The Ever-Living source of life. To have Him in your thoughts every day.

[348] *perceive God within them.* The positive side of human nature, which on a lower level bears a resemblance to the attributes of God.

[349] *the prophet David.* Ps. 124:7.

that he hath given into my keeping, for the service of the poor. Wherefore, since thou art poor, and hast a great number of disciples, come thou to dwell here when thou pleasest, and as much as thou pleasest, for the servant of God will minister to thee as much as shall be needful, for love of God.'

196.

Jesus rejoiced when he heard this, and said: 'See now how good a thing it is to die! Lazarus hath died once only, and hath learned such doctrine as is not known to the wisest men in the world that have grown old among books! Would to God that every man might die once only and return to the world, like Lazarus, in order that men might learn to live.[350]

John answered: 'O master, is it permitted to me to speak a word?'

'Speak a thousand,' answered Jesus, 'for just as a man is bound to dispense his goods in the service of God, so also is he bound to dispense doctrine: and so much the more is he bound so to do inasmuch as the word hath power to raise up a soul to penitence, whereas goods cannot bring back life to the dead. Wherefore he is a murderer who hath power to help a poor man and when he helpeth him not the poor man dieth of hunger; but a more grievous murderer is he who could by the word of God convert the sinner to penitence, and converteth him not, but standeth, as saith God, "like a dumb dog.[351] Against such saith God: "The soul of the sinner that shall perish because thou hast hidden my word, I will require it at thy hands, o unfaithful servant."[352]

---

[350]*men might learn to live.* Many who have died and been resuscitated, and given a glimpse of the next phase of life during that experience, have come back with a different attitude toward life. As one young man put it: "At this time - it was before I had gone off to college— I had grown up in a very small town, with very small-minded people, the people I was associated with, anyway. I was a typical high school fraternity brat. You just weren't "it" unless you belonged to my fraternity. But after this thing happened to me, I wanted to know more. At the time, though, I didn't think there was a person who would know anything about this, because I had never been out of this little world that I was in. I didn't know anything about psychology, or anything like that. All I knew was that I felt like I had aged overnight after this happened, because it opened up a whole new world for me that I never knew could possibly exist. I kept thinking, "There's so much that I've got to find out." In other words, there's more to life than Friday night movies and the football game. And there's more to me that I don't even know about." (*Life After Life*, pp. 77 & 89).

[351]*"like a dumb dog."* Isa. 56:10.

[352]*unfaithful servant.* Ezek. 33:4, 6.

'In what condition, then, are now the scribes and Pharisees who have the key and will not enter, nay hinder them who would fain enter, into eternal life?

'Thou askest me, O John, permission to speak one word, having listened to an hundred thousands words of mine. Verily I say unto thee, I am bound to listen to thee ten times for every one that thou hast listened to me. And he who will not listen to another, every time that he shall speak he shall sin; seeing that we ought to do to others that which we desire for ourselves, and not do to others that which we do not desire to receive.'

Then said John: 'O master, why hath not God granted this to men, that they should die once and return as Lazarus hath done, in order that they might learn to know themselves and their creator?'

197.

Jesus answered: 'Tell me, John: there was an householder who gave a perfect axe to one of his servants in order that he might cut down the wood which obstructed the view of his house.

'But the labourer forgot the axe, and said: "If the master would give me an old axe I should easily cut down the wood." Tell me, John, what said the master? Assuredly he was wroth, and took the old axe and struck him on the head, saying: "Fool and knave! I gave thee an axe wherewith thou mightest cut down the wood without toil, and seekest thou this axe, wherewith one must work with great toil, and all that is cut is wasted and good for nought? I desire thee to cut down the wood in such wise that thy work shall be good." Is this true?'

John answered: 'It is most true.' Then said Jesus: 'As I live eternally,' saith God, 'I have given a good axe to every man, which is the sight of the burial of one dead. Whoso wield well this axe remove the wood of sin from their heart without pain; wherefore they receive my grace and mercy; giving them merit of eternal life for their good works. But he who forgetteth that he is mortal, though time after time he see others die, and saith. 'If I should see the other life, I would do good works" my fury shall be upon him, and I will so smite him with death that he shall never more receive any good.' 'O John,' said Jesus, 'how great is the advantage of him who from the fall of others learneth to stand on his feet!'

198.

Then said Lazarus: 'Master, verily I say unto thee, I cannot conceive the penalty of which he is worthy who time after time seeth the dead borne to the tomb and feareth not God our creator. Such an one ... ... offendeth his creator who hath given him all.'

Then said Jesus to his disciples: 'Ye call me Master, and ye do well, seeing that God teacheth you by my mouth. But how will ye call Lazarus? Verily he is here master of all the masters that teach doctrine in this world. I indeed have taught you how ye ought to live well, but Lazarus will teach you how to die well. As God liveth, he hath received the gift of prophecy; listen therefore to his words, which are truth. And so much the more ought ye to listen to him, as good living is vain if one die badly.'

Said Lazarus: 'O master, I thank thee that thou makest the truth to be prized; therefore will God give thee great merit.'

Then said he who writeth this: 'O master, how speaketh Lazarus the truth in saying to thee "Thou shalt have merit,' whereas thou saidst to Nicodemus that man meriteth nought but punishment? Shalt thou accordingly be punished of God?'

Jesus answered: 'May it please God that I receive punishment of God in this world, because I have not served him so faithfully as I was bound to do.

'But God hath so loved me, by his mercy, that every punishment is withdrawn from me, in so much that I shall only be tormented in another person. For punishment was fitting for me, for that men have called me God; but since I have confessed, not only that I am not God, as is the truth, but have confessed also that I am not the Messiah, therefore God hath taken away the punishment from me, and will cause a wicked one to suffer it in my name, so that the shame alone shall be mine. Wherefore I say to thee, my Barnabas, that when a man speaketh of what God shall give to his neighbour let him say that his neighbour meriteth it: but let him look to it that, when he speaketh of what God shall give to himself, he say: "God will give me." And let him look to it that he say not, 'I have merit," because God is pleased to grant his mercy to his servants when they confess that they merit hell for their sins.

199.

'God is so rich in mercy that, albeit the water of a thousand seas, if so many were to be found, could not quench a spark of the flames of hell, yet a single tear of one who mourneth at having offended God quencheth the whole of hell, by the great mercy wherewith God succoureth him. God, therefore, to confound Satan and to display his own bounty, willeth to call merit in the presence of his mercy every good work of his faithful servant, and willeth him so to speak of his neighbor. But of himself a man must beware of saying: "I have merit"; for he would be condemned.'

200.

Jesus then turned to Lazarus, and said: 'Brother, I must needs for a short time abide in the world, wherefore when I shall be near to thine house I will not ever go elsewhere, because thou wilt minister unto me, not for love of me, but for love of God.'

It was nigh unto the Passover of the Jews, wherefore Jesus said to his disciples: 'Let us go to Jerusalem to eat the paschal lamb.' And he sent Peter and John to the city, saying: 'Ye shall find an ass near the gate of the city with a colt, loose her and bring her hither: for I needs must ride thereon into Jerusalem. And if any one ask you saying, "Wherefore loose ye her?" say unto them: "The Master hath need thereof," and they will suffer thee to bring her.'

The disciples went, and found all that Jesus had told them and accordingly they brought the ass and the colt.[353] The disciples accordingly placed their mantles upon the colt, and Jesus rode thereon. And it came to pass that, when the men of Jerusalem heard that Jesus of Nazareth was coming, the men went forth with their children eager to see Jesus, bearing in their hands branches of palm and olive,[354] singing: 'Blessed be he that cometh to us in the name of God. Hosanna, son of David!'

Jesus having come into the city, the men spread out their garments[355] under the feet of the ass, singing: 'Blessed be he that cometh to us in the name of the Lord God; hosanna, son of David!'[356]

The Pharisees rebuked Jesus, saying: 'Seest thou not what these say? Cause them to hold their peace!'

Then said Jesus: 'As God liveth in whose presence my soul standeth, if men should hold their peace, the stones would cry out against the unbelief of malignant sinners.' And when Jesus had said

[353] *the ass and the colt.* Only the colt was needed, the ass followed by natural instinct.

[354] *branches of palm and olive.* The palm was taken by the Israelites as a symbol of the righteous man (Ps. 92:12). While the olive was taken as a symbol of spiritual beauty and strength. (Jer. 11:16; Hos. 14:7).

[355] *spread out their garments.* The spreading of garments in this manner, was a custom observed in token of honor and welcome to important personages such as kings. (II Ki. 9:13).

[356] *hosanna son of David.* The Psalm from which the term: Hosanna (save, we pray) was derived is the 118th, which they were familiar with since they recited the 25th and 26th verses at their Feast of Tabernacles. It is part of that petition to God to send prosperity, and therefore blessings (Ps 118:25).

this all the stones of Jerusalem cried out with a great noise: 'Blessed be he who cometh to us in the name of the Lord God!'

Nevertheless the Pharisees remained still in their unbelief, and, having assembled themselves together, took counsel to catch him in his talk.

201.

Jesus having entered into the temple, the scribes and Pharisees brought unto him a woman taken in adultery. They said among themselves: 'If he saves her, it is contrary to the law of Moses, and so we have him as guilty, and if he condemn her it is contrary to his own doctrine, for he preacheth mercy.' Wherefore they came to Jesus and said: 'Master, we have found this woman in adultery. Moses commanded that [such] should be stoned: what then sayest thou?'

Thereupon Jesus stooped down and with his finger made a mirror on the ground wherein every one saw his own iniquities. As they still pressed for the answer, Jesus lifted up himself and, pointing to the mirror with his finger, said: 'He that is without sin among you, let him be first to stone her.' And again he stooped down, shaping the mirror.

The men, seeing this, went out one by one, beginning from the eldest, for they were ashamed to see their abominations.

Jesus having lifted up himself, and seeing no one but the woman, said: 'Woman, where are they that condemned thee?'

The woman answered, weeping: 'Lord, they are departed; and if thou wilt pardon me, as God liveth, I will sin no more.'

Then said Jesus: 'Blessed be God! Go thy way in peace and sin no more, for God hath not sent me to condemn thee.'

Then, the scribes and Pharisees being assembled, Jesus said to them: 'Tell me: if one of you had an hundred sheep, and should lose one of them, would ye not go to seek it, leaving the ninety and nine? And when ye found it, would ye not lay it upon your shoulders and, having called together your neighbours, say unto them: "Rejoice with me, for I have found the sheep which I had lost?" Assuredly ye would do so.

'Now tell me, shall our God love less man, for whom he hath made the world? As God liveth, even so there is joy in the presence of the angels of God over one sinner that repenteth; because sinners make known God's mercy.'

202.

'Tell me, by whom is the physician more loved: by them that

have never had any sickness, or by them whom the physician hath
healed of grievous sickness?'

Said the Pharisees to him: 'And how shall he that is whole love
the physician? assuredly he will love him only for that he is not sick;
and not having knowledge of sickness he will love the physician but
little.'

Then with vehemence of spirit Jesus spake, saying: 'As God
liveth, your own tongues condemn your pride, inasmuch as our God
is loved more by the sinner that repenteth, knowing the great mercy
of God upon him, than by the righteous. For the righteous hath not
knowledge of the mercy of God. Wherefore there is more rejoicing in
the presence of the angels of God over one sinner that repenteth than
over ninety and nine righteous persons.

'Where are the righteous in our time? As God liveth in whose
presence my soul standeth, great is the number of the righteous
unrighteous; their condition being like to that of Satan.'

The scribes and Pharisees answered: 'We are sinners, wherefore
God will have mercy on us.' And this they said tempting him; for the
scribes and Pharisees count it the greatest insult to be called sinners.

Then said Jesus: 'I fear that ye be righteous unrighteous. For if
ye have sinned and deny your sin, calling yourselves righteous, ye
are unrighteous; and if in your heart ye hold yourselves righteous,
and with your tongue ye say that ye are sinners, then are ye doubly
righteous unrighteous.'

Accordingly the scribes and Pharisees hearing this were confounded and departed, leaving Jesus with his disciples in peace, and
they went into the house of Simon the leper, whose leprosy he [had]
cleansed. The citizens had gathered together the sick unto the house
of Simon and prayed Jesus for the healing of the sick.

Then Jesus, knowing that his hour was near, said: 'Call the sick,
as many as there be, because God is mighty and merciful to heal
them.

They answered: 'We know not that there be any other sick folk
here in Jerusalem.'

Jesus weeping answered: 'O Jerusalem, O Israel, I weep over
thee, for thou knowest not thy visitation; because I would fain have
gathered thee to the love of God thy creator, as a hen gathereth her
chickens under her wings, and thou wouldst not.'[357] Wherefore God
saith thus unto thee -

---

[357] *wouldst not.* The Passover was instituted as a commemoration of the Israelites having been raised by God, through Moses, from the condition of servitude

203.

'"O city, hard-hearted and perverse of mind, I have sent to thee my servant, to the end that he may convert thee to thine heart, and thou mayest repent; but thou, O city of confusion,[358] hast forgotten all that I did upon Egypt and upon Pharaoh for love of thee, O Israel. Many times weepest thou that my servant may heal thy body of sickness: and thou seekest to slay my servant because he seeketh to heal thy soul of sin.

'"Shalt thou, then, alone remain unpunished by me? Shalt thou, then, live eternally? And shall thy pride deliver thee from my hands? Assuredly not. For I will bring princes with an army against thee, and they shall surround thee with might, and in such wise will I give thee over into their hands[359] that thy pride shall fall down into hell.

'"I will not pardon the old men or the widows, I will not pardon the children, but I will give you all to famine, the sword, and derision, and the temple whereon I have looked with mercy, I will make desolate with the city, insomuch that ye shall be for a fable, a derision, and a proverb among the nations. So is my wrath abiding upon thee, and mine indignation sleepeth not."'

204.

Having said this, Jesus said again: 'Know ye not that there be other sick folk? As God liveth, they be fewer in Jerusalem that have their soul sound than they that be sick in body. And in order that ye may know the truth, I say unto you, O sick folk, in the name of God, let your sickness depart from you!

And when he had said this, immediately they were healed.

The men wept when they heard of the wrath of God upon Jerusalem, and prayed for mercy: when Jesus said: '"If Jerusalem shall weep for her sins and do penance, walking in my ways." saith God, "I will not remember her iniquities any more, and I will not do

---

under a foreign idolatrous tyrant to that of a free people owing allegiance only to God. Now once again they were being ruled over by foreign idolatrous tyrants, only this time they were Romans. And although the people in general either supported Jesus' cause or totally submitted themselves to God by adhering to his Gospel, the Jewish leadership rejected him and sealed their own doom. And the doom of the Holy City in their charge, by continually leading the multitudes over the decades into perdition.

[358] *city of confusion.* Isa. 24:10.

[359] *into their hands.* here we have a reference to the prophecy contained in Ezekiel 38 and 39, concerning Gog and Magog.

unto her any of the evil which I have said.'[360] But Jerusalem weepeth for her ruin and not for her dishonouring of me, wherewith she hath blasphemed my name among the nations. Therefore is my fury kindled much more. As I live eternally, if Job, Abraham, Samuel, David, and Daniel my servants, with Moses, should pray for this people, my wrath upon Jerusalem will not be appeased.'[361] And having said this, Jesus retired into the house, while every one remained in fear.

205.

While Jesus was supping with his disciples in the house of Simon the leper, behold Mary the sister of Lazarus entered into the house, and, having broken a vessel, poured ointment over the head and garment of Jesus. Seeing this, Judas the traitor was fain to hinder Mary from doing such a work, saying: 'Go and sell the ointment and bring the money that I may give it to the poor.'

Said Jesus: 'Why hinderest thou her? Let her be, for the poor ye shall have always with you, but me ye shall not have always.

Judas answered: 'O master, this ointment might be sold for three hundred pieces of money: now see how many poor folk would be helped.'

Jesus answered: 'O Judas, I know thine heart: have patience, therefore, and I will give thee all.'

Every one ate with fear, and the disciples were sorrowful, because they knew that Jesus must soon depart from them. But Judas was indignant, because he knew that he was losing thirty pieces of money for the ointment not sold, seeing he stole the tenth part of all that was given to Jesus.

He went to find the high priest, who assembled in council of priests, scribes, and Pharisees; to whom Judas spake saying: 'What will ye give me, and I will betray into your hands Jesus, who would fain make himself king of Israel?'

They answered: 'Now how wilt thou give him into our hand?'

Said Judas: 'When I shall know that he goeth outside the city to pray I will tell you, and will conduct you to the place where he shall be found; for to seize him in the city will be impossible without a sedition.'

The high priest answered: 'If thou wilt give him into our hand

---

[360] *which I have said.* Jer. 18:8.
[361] *will not be appeased.* Ezek. 14:14.

we will give thee thirty pieces of gold[362] and thou shalt see how well
I will treat thee.'

206.

When day was come, Jesus went up to the temple with a great
multitude of people. Whereupon the high priest drew near, saying:
'Tell me, O Jesus, hast thou forgotten all that thou didst confess, that
thou art not God, nor son of God, nor even the Messiah?'

Jesus answered: 'No, of a surety, I have not forgotten; for this is
my confession which I shall bear before the judgment-seat of God on
the day of judgment. For all that is written in the book of Moses is
most true, inasmuch as God our creator is God alone, and I am God's
servant and desire to serve God's messenger whom ye call Messiah.'

Said the high priest: 'Then what booteth it to come to the temple
with so great a multitude of people? Seekest thou, perchance, to make
thyself king of Israel? Beware lest some danger befall thee!'

Jesus answered: 'If I sought mine own glory and desired my
portion in this world, I had not fled when the people of Nain would
fain have made me king. Believe me, verily, that I seek not anything
in this world.'

Then said the high priest: 'We want to know a thing concerning
the Messiah.' And then the priests, scribes, and Pharisees made a
circle round about Jesus.

Jesus answered: 'What is that thing which thou seekest to know
about the Messiah? Perchance it is the lie? Assuredly I will not tell
thee the lie. For if I had said the lie I had been adored by thee, and
by the scribes [and] Pharisees with all Israel: but because I tell you
the truth ye hate me and seek to kill me.'

Said the high priest: 'Now we know that thou hast the devil at
thy back; for thou art a Samaritan, and hast not respect unto the
priest of God.'

207.

Jesus answered: 'As God liveth, I have not the devil at my back,
but I seek to cast out the devil. Wherefore, for this cause the devil
stirreth up the world against me, because I am not of this world, but
I seek that God may be glorified, who hath sent me into the world.
Hearken therefore to me, and I will tell you who hath the devil at his
back. As God liveth, in whose presence my soul standeth, he who
worketh after the will of the devil, he hath the devil at his back, who

---

[362]*thirty piece of gold.* Gold, not silver.

hath put on him the bridle of his will and ruleth him at his pleasure, making him to run into every iniquity.

'Even as a garment changeth its name when it changeth its owner, although it is all the same cloth: so also men, albeit they are all of one material, are different by reason of the works of him who worketh in the man.

'If I (as I know) have sinned, wherefore do ye not rebuke me as a brother, instead of hating me as an enemy? Verily the members of a body succour one another when they are united with the head, and they that are cut off from the head give it no succour. For the hands of one body do not feel the pain of another body's feet, but that of the body in which they are united. As God liveth, in whose presence my soul standeth, he who feareth and loveth God his Creator hath the feeling of mercy over them [over] whom God his head hath mercy: and seeing that God willeth not the death of the sinner, but waiteth for each one to repent, if ye were of that body wherein I am incorporate, as God liveth, ye would help me to work according to mine head.

208.

'If I work iniquity, reprove me, and God will love you because ye shall be doing his will, but if none can reprove me of sin it is a sign that ye are not sons of Abraham as ye call yourselves, nor are ye incorporate with that head wherein Abraham was incorporate. As God liveth, so greatly did Abraham love God, that he not only brake in pieces the false idols and forsook his father and mother, but was willing to slay his own son in obedience to God.

The high priest answered: 'This I ask of thee, and I do not seek to slay thee, wherefore tell us: Who was this son of Abraham?

Jesus answered: 'The zeal of thine honour, O God, enflameth me, and I cannot hold my peace. Verily I say, the son of Abraham was Ishmael, from whom must be descended the Messiah promised to Abraham, that in him should all the tribes of the earth be blessed.'[363]

Then was the high priest wroth, hearing this, and cried out: 'Let us stone this impious fellow, for he is an Ishmaelite, and hath spoken blasphemy against Moses and against the law of God.'

Whereupon every scribe and Pharisee, with the elders of the people, took up stones to stone Jesus, who vanished from their eyes and went out of the temple. And then, through the great desire that they had to slay Jesus, blinded with fury and hatred, they struck one another in such wise that there died a thousand men; and they

---

[363] *tribes of the earth be blessed.* Gen. 22:18.

polluted the holy temple. The disciples and believers, who saw Jesus go out of the temple (for from them he was not hidden), followed him to the house of Simon.

Thereupon Nicodemus came thither and counselled Jesus to go out of Jerusalem beyond the brook Cedron, saying: 'Lord, I have a garden with a house beyond the brook Cedron, I pray thee, therefore, go thither with some of thy disciples, to tarry there until this hatred of our priests be past; for I will minister to you what is necessary. And the multitude of disciples leave thou here in the house of Simon and in my house, for God will provide for all.'

And this Jesus did, desiring only to have with him the twelve first called apostles.

209.

At this time, while the Virgin Mary, mother of Jesus, was standing in prayer, the angel Gabriel visited her and narrated to her the persecution of her son, saying: 'Fear not, Mary, for God will protect him from the world. Wherefore Mary, weeping, departed from Nazareth, and came to Jerusalem to the house of Mary Salome, her sister, seeking her son.

But since he had secretly retired beyond the brook Cedron she was not able to see him any more in this world; save after the deed of shame, for that the angel Gabriel, with the angels Michael, Rafael, and Uriel, by command of God brought him to her.

210.

When the confusion in the temple ceased by the departure of Jesus, the high priest ascended on high, and having beckoned for silence with his hands he said: 'Brethren, what do we? See ye not that he hath deceived the whole world with his diabolical art? Now, how did he vanish, if he be not a magician? Assuredly, if he were an holy one and a prophet, he would not blaspheme against God and against Moses [his] servant, and against the messiah, who is the hope of Israel. And what shall I say? He hath blasphemed all our priesthood, wherefore verily I say unto you, if he be not removed from the world Israel will be polluted, and our God will give us to the nations. Behold now, how by reason of him this holy temple hath been polluted.'

And in such wise did the high priest speak that many forsook Jesus, wherefore the secret persecution was converted into an open one, insomuch that the high priest went in person to Herod, and to the Roman governor, accusing Jesus that he desired to make himself king of Israel, and of this they had false witnesses.

Thereupon was held a general council against Jesus, forasmuch as the decree of the Romans made them afraid. For so it was that twice the Roman Senate had sent a decree concerning Jesus: in one decree it was forbidden, on pain of death, that any one should call Jesus of Nazareth, the prophet of the Jews, either God or Son of God; in the other it forbade, under capital sentence, that any one should contend concerning Jesus of Nazareth, prophet of the Jews. Wherefore, for this cause, there was a great division among them. Some desired that they should write again to Rome against Jesus; others said that they should leave Jesus alone, regardless of what he said, as of a fool: others adduced the great miracles that he wrought.

The high priest therefore spake that under pain of anathema none should speak a word in defence of Jesus; and he spake to Herod, and to the governor, saying: 'In any case we have an ill venture in our hands, for if we slay this sinner we have acted contrary to the decree of Caesar, and, if we suffer him to live and he make himself king, how will the matter?' Then Herod arose and threatened the governor, saying: 'Beware lest through thy favouring of that man this country be rebellious: for I will accuse thee before Caesar as a rebel.' Then the governor feared the Senate and made friends with Herod (for before this they had hated one another unto death), and they joined together for the death of Jesus, and said to the high priest: Whenever thou shalt know where the malefactor is, send to us, for we will give thee soldiers.' This was done to fulfil the prophecy of David[364] who had foretold of Jesus, prophet of Israel, saying: 'The princes and kings of the earth are united against the holy one of Israel, because he announceth the salvation of the world.'

Thereupon, on that day, there was a general search for Jesus throughout Jerusalem.

211.

Jesus, being in the house of Nicodemus beyond the brook Cedron, comforted his disciples, saying: 'The hour is near that I must depart from the world; console yourselves and be not sad, seeing that where I go I shall not feel any tribulation.

---

[364] *prophecy of David.* What is given here, is an abbreviation of the following statement: "The Kings of the earth set themselves, and the rulers take counsel together, against the Lord [God], and against his anointed [Messiah]." (Ps.2:2). The rest of this Psalm in its present state appears to be corrupted by way of the introduction of Canaanite paganistic influences referred to by Professor Albright in his work entitled: From The Stone Age To Christianity, pp.261-262.

'Now, shall ye be my friends if ye be sad at my welfare? Nay, assuredly, but rather enemies. When the world shall rejoice, be ye sad, because the rejoicing of the world is turned into weeping; but your sadness shall be turned into joy and your joy shall no one take from you; for the rejoicing that the heart feeleth in God its creator not the whole world can take away. See that ye forget not the words which God hath spoken to you by my mouth. Be ye my witnesses against every one that shall corrupt the witness that I have witnessed with my gospel against the world, and against the lovers of the world.

212.

Then lifting up his hands to the Lord, he prayed, saying: 'Lord our God, God of Abraham, God of Ishmael and Isaac. God of our fathers have mercy upon them that thou hast given me, and save them from the world. I say not, take them from the world, because it is necessary that they shall bear witness against them that shall corrupt my gospel. But I pray thee to keep them from evil, that on the day of thy judgment they may come with me to bear witness against the world and against the house of Israel that hath corrupted thy testament, Lord God, mighty and jealous, that takest vengeance upon idolatry against the sons of idolatrous fathers even unto the fourth generation, do thou curse eternally every one that shall corrupt my gospel that thou gavest me, when they write that I am thy son. For I, clay and dust, am servant of thy servants, and never have I thought my self to be thy good servant; for I cannot give thee aught in return for that which thou hast given me, for all things are thine. Lord God, the merciful, that shewest mercy unto a thousand generations upon them that fear thee, have mercy upon them which believe my words that thou hast given me. For even as thou art true God, so thy word which I have spoken is true; for it is thine, seeing I have ever spoken as one that readeth, who cannot read save that which is written in the book that he readeth: even so have I spoken that which thou hast given me.

'Lord God the Saviour,[365] save them whom thou hast given me, in order that Satan may not be able to do aught against them, and save not only them, but every one that shall believe in them.

'Lord, bountiful and rich in mercy, grant to thy servant to be in the congregation of thy Messenger on the day of judgment; and not me only, but every one whom thou hast given me, with all them that

---

[365] *Lord God the Saviour.* Isa. 45:21-23.

shall believe on me through their preaching. And this do, Lord, for thine own sake, that Satan boast not himself against thee, Lord.

'Lord God, who by thy providence providest all things necessary for thy people Israel, be mindful of all the tribes of the earth, which thou didst create the world. Have mercy on the world and send speedily thy Messenger, that Satan thine enemy may lose his empire.' And having said this, Jesus said three times: 'so be it, Lord, great and merciful!'

And they answered, weeping: 'So be it,' all save Judas, for he believed nothing.

213.

The day having come for eating the lamb, Nicodemus sent the lamb secretly to the garden for Jesus and his disciples, announcing all that had been decreed by Herod with the governor and the high priest.

Whereupon Jesus rejoiced in spirit, saying: 'Blessed be thy holy name, O Lord, because thou hast not separated me from the number of thy servants that have been persecuted by the world and slain. I thank thee, my God, because I have fulfilled thy work.' And turning to Judas, he said to him: 'Friend, wherefore tarriest thou? My time is nigh, wherefore go and do that which thou must do.'

The disciples thought that Jesus was sending Judas to buy something for the day of the Passover: but Jesus knew that Judas was betraying him, wherefore, desiring to depart from the world, he so spake.

Judas answered: 'Lord, suffer me to eat, and I will go.'

'Let us eat,' said Jesus, for I have greatly desired to eat this lamb before I am parted from you.' And having arisen, he took a towel and girded his loins, and having put water in a basin, he set himself to wash his disciples' feet. Beginning from Judas, Jesus came to Peter. Said Peter: 'Lord, wouldst thou wash my feet?'

Jesus answered: 'That which I do thou knowest not now, but thou shalt know hereafter.

Peter answered: 'Thou shalt never wash my feet.'

Then Jesus rose up, and said: 'Neither shalt thou come in my company on the day of judgment.'

Peter answered: 'Wash not only my feet, Lord, but my hands and my head.'

When the disciples were washed and were seated at table to eat, Jesus said: 'I have washed you, yet are ye not all clean, forasmuch as all the water of the sea will not wash him that believeth me not.' This said Jesus, because he knew who was betraying him. The disciples were sad at these words, when Jesus said again? 'Verily I say unto you, that one of you shall betray me, insomuch that I shall be sold like a sheep; but woe unto him, for he shall fulfil all that our father David[366] said of such an one, that "he shall fall into the pit which he had prepared for others."'

Whereupon the disciples looked one upon another, saying with sorrow: 'Who shall be the traitor?'

Judas then said: 'Shall it be I, O Master?'

Jesus answered: 'Thou hast told me who it shall be that shall betray me.' And the eleven apostles heard it not.

When the lamb was eaten, the devil came upon the back of Judas, and he went forth from the house, Jesus saying to him again: 'Do quickly that which thou must do.'

214.

Having gone forth from the house, Jesus retired into the garden to pray, according as his custom was to pray, bowing his knees an hundred times and prostrating himself upon his face. Judas, accordingly, knowing the place where Jesus was with his disciples, went to the high priest, and said: 'If ye will give me what was promised, this night will I give into your hand Jesus whom ye seek: for he is alone with eleven companions.'

The high priest answered: 'How much seekest thou?'

Said Judas, 'Thirty pieces of gold.'

Then straightway the high priest counted unto him the money, and sent a Pharisee to the governor to fetch soldiers, and to Herod, and they gave a legion of them, because they feared the people; wherefore they took their arms, and with torches and lanterns upon staves went out of Jerusalem.

215.

When the soldiers with Judas drew near to the place where Jesus was, Jesus heard the approach of many people, wherefore in fear he withdrew into the house. And the eleven were sleeping.

Then God, seeing the danger of his servant, commanded Gabriel, Michael, Rafael, and Uriel, his ministers, to take Jesus out of the world.

The holy angels came and took Jesus out by the window that looketh toward the South. They bare him and placed him in the third heaven in the company of angels[367] blessing God for evermore.

---

[366] *our father David.* Psa.7:15.

[367] *in the company of angels.* Herein lies the mystery comparable to the Miraj of the

216.

Judas entered impetuously before all into the chamber whence Jesus had been taken up. And the disciples were sleeping. Whereupon the wonderful God acted wonderfully, insomuch that Judas was so changed in speech and in face to be like Jesus that we believed him to be Jesus. And he, having awakened us, was seeking where the Master was. Whereupon we marvelled, and answered: 'Thou, Lord, art our master; hast thou now forgotten us?'

And he, smiling, said: 'Now are ye foolish, that know not me to be Judas Iscariot!'

And as he was saying this the soldiery entered, and laid their hands upon Judas, because he was in every way like to Jesus.[368]

We having heard Judas' saying, and seeing the multitude of soldiers; fled as beside ourselves.

And John, who was wrapped in a linen cloth, awoke and fled, and when a soldier seized him by the linen cloth he left the linen cloth and fled naked. For God heard the prayer of Jesus, and saved the eleven from evil.

Prophet Muhammad (SAWS). It is reported that the Prophet Muhammad (SAWS) was resting one night within the enclosures of the Ka'ba at Mecca when suddenly the angel Gabriel came and took the Prophet from Mecca to the site of the Temple of the Lord at Jerusalem, where the Prophet ascended with Gabriel into the seven heavens. His wife Ayesha, held that the experience was spiritual, while the majority of his disciples held that he was in his body when he had this experience. Yusuf Ali, in his commentary on Quran (17:1) says: "Even on the supposition of a miraculous bodily journey, it is conceded that the body was almost transformed into a spiritual fineness." The accumulated testimony of a multitude of persons God has provided a glimpse of paradise to, through the near death experience, informs us that after leaving our physical body as pure consciousness, we are given a spiritualized body for our sojourn in the next life. The evidence indicates that in a sense, both Ayesha, the prophet's wife, and the majority of the Prophet's disciples were right in their understanding of the nature of the Prophet's ascent. Which also sheds light on Jesus' ascent.

In the Quran we are told that: "God takes (men's) souls at the time of their death, and those that die not during their sleep. Then he withholds those on whom He has passed the decree of death and sends the others back till an appointed term." (Q.39:42). The key to understanding Jesus' ascent is in God's statement that "He withholds [permanently] those on whom He has passed the decree of death," while He "sends the others back till an appointed term." No matter how long a human soul is with Him, it is not dead until God passes the decree that it is not to return to its physical body for an appointed term. In Jesus' case, although his stay has been quite lengthy by our understanding of time, it is temporary and not permanent, since God has ordained that he will return to the earth for an appointed term. The body may not be the same, but the consciousness will be.

Thus we are told by God, in the Quran: "And because of their saying: We slew the Messiah Jesus son of Mary, God's messenger - They slew him not nor crucified him,

217.

The soldiers took Judas and bound him, not without derision. For he truthfully denied that he was Jesus; and the soldiers, mocking him, said; 'Sir, fear not, for we are come to make thee king of Israel, and we have bound thee because we know that thou dost refuse the kingdom.'

Judas answered: 'Now have ye lost your senses! Ye are come to take Jesus of Nazareth, with arms and lanterns as [against] a robber; and ye have bound me that have guided you, to make me king!'

Then the soldiers lost their patience, and with blows and kicks they began to flout Judas, and they led him with fury into Jerusalem.

John and Peter followed the soldiers afar off; and they affirmed to him who writeth that they saw all the examination that was made of Judas by the high priest, and by the council of the Pharisees, who were assembled to put Jesus to death. Whereupon Judas spake many words of madness, insomuch that every one was filled with laughter, believing that he was really Jesus, and that for fear of death he was feigning madness. Whereupon the scribes bound his eyes with a bandage, and mocking him said: 'Jesus, prophet of the Nazarenes; (for so they called them who believed in Jesus), 'tell us, who was it that smote thee?' And they buffeted him and spat in his face.

When it was morning there assembled the great council of scribes and elders of the people; and the high priest with the Pharisees sought false witness against Judas, believing him to be Jesus: and they found not that which they sought.' And why say I that the chief priests believed Judas to be Jesus? Nay, all the disciples, with him who writeth, believed it; and more, the poor virgin mother of Jesus, with his kinsfolk and friends, believed it, insomuch that the sorrow of every one was incredible. As God liveth, he who writeth forgot all that Jesus had said: how that he should be taken up from the world, and that he should suffer in a third person, and

---

but it appeared so unto them; and lo! Those who disagree concerning it are in doubt thereof; they have no knowledge thereof save pursuit of a conjecture; they slew him not for certain. But God took him up unto Himself. God is ever Mighty, Wise. *There is not one of the People of the Scripture but will believe in him before his death,* and on the Day of Resurrection he will be a witness against them." (Q. 4:157-159.)

[368] *in every way like to Jesus.* God had created an illusion in the minds of all concerned, soldiers, disciples, etc. that Judas was Jesus. Thus the statement in the Qur'an: "They slew him not, nor crucified him, *but it appeared so unto them.*" (Q. 4:157). Throughout the whole crucifixion incident they were under this divinely inspired illusion. and in this manner the malefactor fell into his own snare he engineered at the instigation of Satan against Jesus.

that he should not die until near the end of the world. Wherefore he went with the mother of Jesus and with John to the cross.

The high priest cause Judas to be brought before him bound, and asked him of his disciples and his doctrine.

Whereupon Judas, as though beside himself, answered nothing to the point. The high priest then adjured him by the living God of Israel that he would tell him the truth.

Judas answered: 'I have told you that I am Judas Iscariot, who promised to give into your hands Jesus the Nazarene; and ye, by what art I know not, are beside yourselves, for ye will have it by every means that I am Jesus.'

The high priest answered: 'O perverse seducer, thou hast deceived all Israel, beginning from Galilee even unto Jerusalem here, with thy doctrine and false miracles: and now thinkest thou to flee the merited punishment that befitteth thee by feigning to be mad? As God liveth, thou shalt not escape it!' And having said this he commanded his servants to smite him with buffetings and kicks, so that his understanding might come back into his head. The derision which he then suffered at the hands of the high priest's servants is past belief. For they zealously devised new inventions to give pleasure to the council. So they attired him as a juggler, and so treated him with hands and feet that it would have moved the very Canaanites to compassion if they had beheld that sight.

But the chief priests and Pharisees and elders of the people had their hearts so exasperated against Jesus that, believing Judas to be really Jesus, they took delight in seeing him so treated.

Afterwards they led him bound to the governor, who secretly loved Jesus. Whereupon he, thinking that Judas was Jesus, made him enter into his chamber, and spake to him, asking him for what cause the chief priests and the people had given him into his hands.

Judas answered: 'If I tell thee the truth, thou wilt not believe me; for perchance thou art deceived as the (chief) priests and the Pharisees are deceived.'

The governor answered (thinking that he wished to speak concerning the Law): 'Now knowest thou not that I am not a Jew? But the (chief) priests and the elders of thy people have given thee into my hand; wherefore tell us the truth, that I may do what is just. For I have power to set thee free and to put thee to death.'

Judas answered: 'Sir, believe me, if thou put me to death, thou shalt do a great wrong, for thou shalt slay an innocent person; seeing that I am Judas Iscariot, and not Jesus, who is a magician, and by his art hath so transformed me.'

When he heard this the governor marvelled greatly, so that he sought to set him at liberty. The governor therefore went out, and smiling said: 'In the one case, at least, this man is not worthy of death, but rather of compassion.' 'This man saith,' said the governor, 'that he is not Jesus, but a certain Judas who guided the soldiery to take Jesus, and he saith that Jesus the Galilean hath by his art magic so transformed him. Wherefore, if this be true, it were a great wrong to kill him, seeing that he were innocent. But if he is Jesus and denieth that he is, assuredly he hath lost his understanding, and it were impious to slay a madman.'

Then the chief priests and elders of the people, with the scribes and Pharisees, cried out with shouts, saying: 'He is Jesus of Nazareth, for we know him; for if he were not the malefactor we would not have given him into thy hands. Nor is he mad; but rather malignant, for with this device he seeketh to escape from our hands, and the sedition that he would stir up if he should escape would be worse than the former.'

Pilate (for such was the governor's name), in order to rid himself of such a case, said: 'He is a Galilean, and Herod is King of Galilee: wherefore it pertaineth not to me to judge such a case, so take ye him to Herod.'

Accordingly they led Judas to Herod, who of a long time had desired that Jesus should go to his house. But Jesus had never been willing to go to his house, because Herod was a Gentile, and adored the false and lying gods, living after the manner of unclean Gentiles. Now when Judas had been led thither, Herod asked him of many things, to which Judas gave answers not to the purpose, denying that he was Jesus.

Then Herod mocked him, with all his court, and caused him to be clad in white as the fools are clad, and sent him back to Pilate, saying to him, 'Do not fail in justice to the people of Israel!

And this Herod wrote, because the chief priests and scribes and the Pharisees had given him a good quantity of money. The governor having heard that this was so from a servant of Herod, in order that he also might gain some money, feigned that he desired to set Judas at liberty. Whereupon he caused him to be scourged by his slaves, who were paid by the scribes to slay him under the scourges. But God, who had decreed the issue, reserved Judas for the cross, in order that he might suffer that horrible death to which he had sold another. He did not suffer Judas to die under the scourges, notwithstanding that the soldiers scourged him so grievously that his body rained blood. Thereupon, in mockery they clad him in an old purple garment, saying: 'It is fitting to our new king to clothe him and crown him': so they gathered thorns and made a crown, like those of gold and precious stones which kings wear on their heads. And this crown of thorns they placed upon Judas' head, putting in his hand a reed for scepter, and they made him sit in a high place. And the soldiers came before him, bowing down in mockery, saluting him as King of the Jews. And they held out their hands to receive gifts, such as new kings are accustomed to give; and receiving nothing they smote Judas, saying: 'Now, how art thou crowned, foolish king, if thou wilt not pay thy soldiers and servants?'

The chief priests with the scribes and Pharisees, seeing that Judas died not by the scourges, and fearing lest Pilate should set him at liberty, made a gift of money to the governor, who having received it gave Judas to the scribes and Pharisees as guilty unto death. Whereupon they condemned two robbers with him to the death of the cross.

So they led him to Mount Calvary, where they used to hang malefactors, and there they crucified him naked, for the greater ignominy.

Judas truly did nothing else but cry out: 'God, why hast thou forsaken me, seeing the malefactor hath escaped and I die unjustly?'

Verily I say that the voice, the face, and the person of Judas were so like to Jesus, that his disciples and believers entirely believed that he was Jesus; wherefore some departed from the doctrine of Jesus, believing that Jesus had been a false prophet, and that by art magic he had done the miracles which he did: for Jesus had said that he should not die till near the end of the world; for that at that time he should be taken away from the world.

But they that stood firm in the doctrine of Jesus were so encompassed with sorrow, seeing him die[369] who was entirely like to Jesus, that they remembered not what Jesus had said. And so in company with the mother of Jesus they went to Mount Calvary, and were not only present at the death of Judas, weeping continually, but by means of Nicodemus and Joseph of Abarimathia they obtained

---

[369] *seeing him die.* By the evil he had done all along, and for the betrayal of a Prophet of God whom he pretended to befriend, Judas condemned his own soul to this fate. And having died upon the cross (the cross being the symbol of a tree in ancient thought), the statement in Deuteronomy was applicable to him; which caused some having little conviction in the revelation intrusted to Jesus, to abandon it in the belief that Judas was Jesus, and therefore a false prophet. For in Deuteronomy we are told: "And if a man have committed a sin worthy of death, and he be put to death, and thou hang him on a tree, his body shall not remain all night upon the tree, but thou shalt surely bury him that same day; *for he who is hanged [on a tree] is accursed* by God [for being worthy of such a death], that thy land be not defiled, which the Lord thy God giveth thee for an inheritance." (Deut.21:22-23).

from the governor the body of Judas to bury it. Whereupon, they took him down from the cross with such weeping as assuredly no one would believe, and buried him in the new sepulchre of Joseph; having wrapped him up in an hundred pounds of precious ointments.

218.

Then returned each man to his house. He who writeth, with John and James his brother, went with the mother of Jesus to Nazareth.'

Those disciples who did not fear God went by night [and] stole the body of Judas and hid it, spreading a report that Jesus was risen again; whence great confusion arose. The high priest then commanded, under pain of Anathema, that no one should talk of Jesus of Nazareth. And so there arose a great persecution, and many were stoned and many beaten, and many banished from the land, because they could not hold their peace on such a matter.

The news reached Nazareth how that Jesus, their fellow-citizen, having died on the cross was risen again. Whereupon, he that writeth prayed the mother of Jesus that she would be pleased to leave off weeping, because her son was risen again. Hearing this, the Virgin Mary, weeping, said: 'Let us go to Jerusalem to find my son. I shall die content when I have seen him.'

219.

The Virgin returned to Jerusalem with him who writeth, and James and John, on that day on which the decree of the high priest went forth.

Whereupon, the Virgin, who feared God, albeit she knew the decree of the high priest to be unjust, commanded those who dwelt with her to forget her son. Then how each one was affected? - God who discerneth the heart of men knoweth that between grief at the death of Judas whom we believed to be Jesus our master, and the desire to see him risen again, we, with the mother of Jesus, were consumed.

So the angels that were guardians of Mary ascended to the third heaven, where Jesus was in the company of angels and recounted all to him.

Wherefore Jesus prayed God that he would give him power to see his mother and his disciples. Then the merciful God commanded his four favorite angels, who are Gabriel, Michael, Rafael, and Uriel, to bear Jesus into his mother's house, and there keep watch over him for three days continually, suffering him only to be seen by them that believed in his doctrine.

Jesus came, surrounded with splendour, to the room where abode Mary the Virgin with her two sisters, and Martha and Mary Magdalen and Lazarus, and him who writeth, and John and James and Peter. Whereupon, through fear they fell as dead. And Jesus lifted up his mother and the others from the ground, saying: 'Fear not, for I am Jesus; and weep not for I am alive and not dead.' They remained every one for a long time beside himself at the presence of Jesus, for they altogether believed that Jesus was dead. Then the Virgin, weeping, said: 'Tell me, my son, wherefore God, having given thee power to raise the dead, suffered thee to die, to the shame of thy kinsfolk and friends, and to the shame of thy doctrine?[370] For every one that loveth thee hath been as dead.'

220.

Jesus replied, embracing his mother: 'Believe me, mother, for verily I say to thee that I have not been dead at all; for God hath reserved me till near the end of the world.' And having said this he prayed the four angels that they would manifest themselves, and give testimony how the matter had passed.

Thereupon the angels manifested themselves like four shining suns,[371] insomuch that through fear every one again fell down as dead.

Then Jesus gave four linen cloths to the angels that they might cover themselves, in order that they might be seen and heard to speak by his mother and her companions. And having lifted up each one, he comforted them, saying: 'These are the ministers of God: Gabriel, who announceth God's secrets; Michael, who fighteth against God's enemies; Rafael, who receiveth the souls of them that die; and Uriel, who will call every one to the judgment of God at the last day.'

Then the four angels narrated to the Virgin how God had sent for Jesus, and had transformed Judas, that he might suffer the punishment to which he had sold another.

Then said he who writeth: 'O Master, is it lawful for me to question thee now, as it was lawful for me when thou dwelledst with us?'

---

[370] *to the shame of thy doctrine.* The reference made here by Jesus' mother, is influenced by Deut. 21:22-23. See previous note.

[371] *like four shining suns.* The meaning is clear, the angels being beings of light, their brilliance can only be compared to the sun. But as we already know, no earthly language can truly describe them.

Jesus answered: 'Ask what thou pleasest, Barnabas, and I will answer thee.'

Then said he who writeth: 'O Master, seeing that God is merciful, wherefore hath he so tormented us, making us to believe that thou wert dead? And thy mother hath so wept for thee that she hath been nigh to death: and thou, who art an holy one of God, on thee hath God suffered to fall the calumny that thou wert slain amongst robbers on the Mount Calvary?'

Jesus answered: 'Believe me, Barnabas, that every sin, however small it be, God punisheth with great punishment, seeing that God is offended at sin. Wherefore, since my mother and my faithful disciples that were with me loved me a little with earthly love, the righteous God hath willed to punish this love with the present grief, in order that it may not be punished in the flames of Hell. And though I have been innocent in the world, since men have called me "God," and "Son of God," God, in order that I be not mocked of the demons on the day of judgment, hath willed that I be mocked of men in this world by the death of Judas, making all men to believe that I died upon the cross. And this mocking shall continue until the advent of Mohammed, the messenger of God, who, when he shall come, shall reveal this deception to those who believe in God's law.'

Having thus spoken, Jesus said: 'Thou art just, O Lord our God, because to thee only belongeth honour and glory without end.'

221.

And Jesus turned himself to him who writeth, and said: 'See, Barnabas, that by all means thou write my gospel concerning all that hath happened through my dwelling in the world. And write in like manner that which hath befallen Judas, in order that the faithful may be undeceived, and every one may believe the truth.'

Then answered he who writeth: 'All will I do, if God will, O Master; but how it happened unto Judas, I know not, for I saw not all.'

Jesus answered: 'Here are John and Peter who have seen all, and they will tell you all that has passed.'

And then Jesus commanded us to call his faithful disciples that they might see him. Then did James and John call together the seven disciples with Nicodemus and Joseph, and many other of the seventy-two, and they ate with Jesus.

The third day Jesus said: 'Go to the Mount of Olives with my mother, for there will I ascend again unto heaven, and ye will see who shall bear me up.'

So there went all, saving twenty-five of the seventy-two dis-

The Gospel of Barnabas   229

ciples, who for fear had fled to Damascus.[372] And as they all stood in prayer, at mid-day came Jesus with a great multitude of angels who were praising God: and the splendour of his face made them sore afraid, and they fell with their faces to the ground. But Jesus lifted them up, comforting them, and saying: 'Be not afraid, I am your master.'

And he reproved many who believed him to have died and risen again, saying: 'Do ye then hold me and God for liars? For God hath granted to me to live almost unto the end of the world, even as I said unto you. Verily I say unto you, I died not, but Judas the traitor. Beware, for Satan will make every effort to deceive you, but be ye my witnesses in all Israel, and throughout the world,[373] of all things that ye have heard and seen.'

And having thus spoken, he prayed God for the salvation of the faithful, and the conversion of sinners. And, his prayer ended, he embraced his mother, saying: 'Peace be unto thee, my mother, rest thou in God who created thee and me.' And having thus spoken, he turned to his disciples, saying: 'May God's grace and mercy be with you.'

Then before their eyes the four angels carried him up into heaven.

222.

After Jesus had departed, the disciples scattered through the different parts of Israel and of the world, and the truth, hated, of Satan, was persecuted, as it always is, by falsehood. For certain evil men, pretending to be disciples, preached that Jesus died and rose not again. Others preached that he really died, but rose again. Others preached, and yet preach, that Jesus is the Son of God, among whom is Paul deceived.[374] But we, as much as I have written, that preach we to those who fear God, that they may be saved in the last day of God's Judgment. Amen.

---

[372] *fled to Damascus.* Once again, as in other Essene writings, Damascus figures prominently as a place of refuge.

[373] *throughout the world.* For the Israelites were scattered throughout the known world of that day, and his ministry was unto the Israelites.

[374] *among whom is Paul deceived.* See *The Dead Sea Scrolls, The Gospel of Barnabas, and The New Testament,* pp. 35-97.